"Global cooperation is today more needed than ever. If you think that current levels of global interdependence cannot be reversed, you need to read Nicolás Albertoni's work. Using statistical and qualitative research he convincingly and elegantly argues that the same vehicles that help spread global integration, such as preferential trade agreements and global value chains, are now being used to introduce new and murkier forms of protectionism. This excellent study is a must read for any scholar interested in the political economy of trade policy, and policymakers trying to kick-start global cooperation in the area of international trade."

Marcelo Olarreaga, *Professor of Economics,*
University of Geneva, Switzerland

"This study is an extraordinary balance between the contribution to the literature and the practice of trade policy. It gathers new evidence on a key issue: the risk of protectionism through non-tariff measures in an inevitably interdependent world. It is a bold investigation that persists in the urgency of continuing to deepen trade integration based on pillars that promote transparency and encourage those responsible and scholars of trade policy to advance in this regard."

Andrés Rebolledo, *Former Minister of Energy of Chile (2016–2018);*
President of Chile's National Oil Company; Vice Minister
of International Economic Relations of Chile

"Since the Treaty of Westphalia, States are entities that, as Lord Palmerston said, have no friends, but permanent interests. Therefore, integration has been and is a response to the global geopolitics that modernity poses. The contribution of Nicolás Albertoni (colleague from USC) is realistic and courageous. He shows that protectionist regulations are aimed at neutralizing the trade openness that the fall in tariffs deepens. A book that, in my opinion, takes into account without saying so the four demons that coexist with integration: ideology, asymmetry, autarky and hypocrisy. For this reason, his proposal is challenging and opportune, not only for the academy, but for politicians, diplomats, businessmen, workers and especially students. An excellent synthesis of professional seriousness and political maturity."

Sergio Abreu, *Secretary General of the Latin American*
Integration Association; Former Minister of Foreign
Relations of Uruguay (1993–1995)

Trade Protectionism in an Uncertain and Interconnected Global Economy

Trade Protectionism in an Uncertain and Interconnected Global Economy presents the results of almost five years of research on the political economy of trade policy. It argues that in a global context dominated by economic uncertainty and interdependencies, the mechanisms that have fueled the diffusion of trade liberalization under the World Trade Organization (preferential trade agreements and global value chains) can also become channels for protectionism (based on less observable non-tariff or murkier measures).

Countries have changed the way they respond to protectionism, which impacts bilateral relations. The author explores why and how increased global trade interconnectivity has also become a channel for new forms of trade protectionism, and especially how this impacts the developing world. These counterintuitive dynamics constitute the newest wave in the literature on trade interdependence. Previous research on trade policy has often concentrated on just one aspect of the effects of an interconnected global economy: the more political and economic linkages countries build among themselves, the fewer tensions they will generate across borders. From a trade policy perspective, this causal claim has held steady for many decades. This book bridges academic analysis with trade policymaking and offers a road map for the kinds of commercial policy reforms that will be essential for the successful revival of world markets after global economic crises as it was the COVID-19 pandemic.

This book will appeal to postgraduates, researchers, and academics interested in international political economy, comparative political economy, development, business, and all those with a particular interest in Latin American trade policy dynamics. It will also be of interest to trade policy scholars, practitioners, and readers with an interest in how governments, firms, and regions around the developing world transition into more knowledge-intensive activities.

Nicolás Albertoni is Fulbright-Laspau Scholar and Professor at the Universidad Católica del Uruguay. He is an active researcher at the Uruguayan National System for Researchers (SNI-ANII) and non-resident associate researcher at the University of Southern California's Security and Political Economy (SPEC) Laboratory, USA. He is currently Uruguay's deputy minister of foreign affairs. He holds a

PhD in political science and international relations from the University of Southern California (USC), where he received the Order of Arethe, the highest honor accorded to graduate students. He received a master's degree from Georgetown University's School of Foreign Service in Latin American Studies, and a master's degree in Economics, and a master's degree in Politics and International Relations from USC.

Trade Protectionism in an Uncertain and Interconnected Global Economy

Nicolás Albertoni

LONDON AND NEW YORK

First published 2024
by Routledge
4 Park Square, Milton Park, Abingdon, Oxon OX14 4RN

and by Routledge
605 Third Avenue, New York, NY 10158

Routledge is an imprint of the Taylor & Francis Group, an informa business

© 2024 Nicolás Albertoni

The right of Nicolás Albertoni to be identified as author of this work has been asserted in accordance with sections 77 and 78 of the Copyright, Designs and Patents Act 1988.

All rights reserved. No part of this book may be reprinted or reproduced or utilised in any form or by any electronic, mechanical, or other means, now known or hereafter invented, including photocopying and recording, or in any information storage or retrieval system, without permission in writing from the publishers.

Trademark notice: Product or corporate names may be trademarks or registered trademarks, and are used only for identification and explanation without intent to infringe.

British Library Cataloguing-in-Publication Data
A catalogue record for this book is available from the British Library

Library of Congress Cataloging-in-Publication Data
Names: Albertoni, Nicolás, author.
Title: Trade protectionism in an uncertain and interconnected global economy / Nicolás Albertoni.
Description: Abingdon, Oxon ; New York, NY : Routledge, 2024. |
Includes bibliographical references and index.
Identifiers: LCCN 2023018451 (print) | LCCN 2023018452 (ebook) |
ISBN 9781032374789 (hardback) | ISBN 9781032374796 (paperback) |
ISBN 9781003340393 (ebook)
Subjects: LCSH: Commercial policy. | Protectionism. | Free trade. | International trade.
Classification: LCC HF1411 .A397 2024 (print) | LCC HF1411 (ebook) |
DDC 382/.3–dc23/eng/20230706
LC record available at https://lccn.loc.gov/2023018451
LC ebook record available at https://lccn.loc.gov/2023018452

ISBN: 978-1-032-37478-9 (hbk)
ISBN: 978-1-032-37479-6 (pbk)
ISBN: 978-1-003-34039-3 (ebk)

DOI: 10.4324/9781003340393

Typeset in Times New Roman
by Newgen Publishing UK

Contents

Acknowledgments   x

1   Trade protectionism in an uncertain global economy and the necessity for a new framework of analysis   1
    1.1 Definition and conceptualization 8
         1.1.1 Trade policy and the different ways of measuring it 8
    1.2 Theoretical approaches in the literature and initial hypotheses 18
         1.2.1 State-level dynamics in trade protectionism 18
         1.2.2 Contribution of this book to the trade policy literature 21
    1.3 A two-step research design 22
         1.3.1 Large-N analysis 22
         1.3.2 Small-n analysis and case studies 23
    1.4 Historical context and significance of this research 24
    1.5 Outline of the book 25

2   A historical overview of twenty-first-century protectionism: How did we arrive at this point?   30
    2.1 Introduction 30
    2.2 The winding road of the world trade system since World War II 30
    2.3 China's accession to the World Trade Organization in 2001 33
    2.4 Global trade after the 2008–09 global financial crisis 36
    2.5 Bilateral tensions between the United States and China in the present and the past 36
         2.5.1 US–China trade tensions step by step 39
    2.6 Final comments on twenty-first-century protectionism from a historical perspective 40

3   Understanding trade protectionism piece by piece: Evidence from the data   44
    3.1 Introduction 44

viii Contents

    3.2 A descriptive analysis at the state level of trade policy dynamics 44
        3.2.1 Twenty-first-century protectionism piece by piece: states, sectors, and measures 45
    3.3 A descriptive analysis of preferential trade agreements and global value chains 51
        3.3.1 Preferential trade agreements 52
        3.3.2 Global value chains 52
    3.4 Final thoughts on rising protectionism vis-à-vis the COVID-19 pandemic 53

4 Protectionism and trade policy responses: A quantitative approach 58
    4.1 Introduction 58
    4.2 The models 59
    4.3 The data 60
        4.3.1 Measurement of the dependent variables 61
        4.3.2 Measurement of regressors of interest 61
        4.3.3 Control variables 62
    4.4 State-level analysis results 62
    4.5 Political and economic magnitude of findings at the state-level analysis 68

5 A comparative approach: Protectionism and trade policy responses in Latin America 73
    5.1 Introduction 73
    5.2 Case selection: why Latin America and why these three countries? 74
    5.3 Fieldwork: interviews with key trade policy actors in Latin America 83
        5.3.1 Interview design and methodology 84
    5.4 A brief background of Latin America's trade policy evolution 85
        5.4.1 Latin America regional integration 91
    5.5 Trade protectionism from a regional perspective 94
    5.6 Country case studies 98
        5.6.1 The case of Mexico 99
        5.6.2 Mercosur and a brief contextualization of trade policy in Argentina and Brazil 114
        5.6.3 The case of Argentina 116
        5.6.4 The case of Brazil 127
    5.7 Conclusions and country case summary 143

6 Conclusions and final thoughts 152
    6.1 This book's main contribution and why it is relevant to the field 152

6.2 Implications for international political economy theory and
    practice 153
6.3 Implications for policy 160
6.4 Insights for further research 162

References   166
Appendix: Detailed analysis of the data sources used in
this book   178
   Global Trade Alert (GTA) 178
   BACI-CEPII trade data 181
   The IPE Data Resource 181
   Data sources for other variables of interest: PTAs and GVCs 182
      Measuring preferential trade agreements (PTAs) 182
      Measuring global value chains (GVCs) 182
Index   184

Acknowledgments

Over the last decade, while writing this book, I have benefited from the advice and support of many mentors, friends, colleagues, and students. I cannot imagine having written this book without their enormous support. First, in the Department of Political Science and International Relations at the University of Southern California (USC) as a doctoral student, then teaching at my alma matter, the Catholic University of Uruguay, and now just taking functions as a deputy minister of foreign affairs of Uruguay, I have been lucky to work closely with so many scholars and practitioners who were crucial to the conclusion of this book. From all of them I received excellent comments and suggestions that constituted an important part of the ideas and arguments I am presenting in this book.

Personally, I would like to start by thanking my family: Josefina, Jacinta, Carlos, Sylvia, Florencia, and Alfonsina. They are my biggest supporters and I owe all of my successes to them. I also owe many thanks to my great mentors and friends: Professor Carol Wise, and Professors Jeff Nugent and Joshua Aizenman. They not only taught me how to improve my research and better contribute to the discipline; they also taught me how to become a better scholar and practitioner.

I would especially like to thank Carol for her immense support during these past years that I have been working in this book. As a graduate student at Georgetown University, I read and followed her academic work, and I would never have imagined at that time that I would work with her as one of her doctoral students at USC. Now, I can say that I am extremely grateful for her having invited me, for her guidance, patience, encouragement, and intellectual and personal support: sometimes a teacher; sometimes like a mother; sometimes a senior scholar who supported my research. Always a mentor. Her many suggestions and careful reading improved every aspect of my academic work. In thanking her, I would also like to extend my thanks to Roger, as he and Carol always let Josefina, my wife, and me feel like we had a family in Los Angeles.

I would also like to thank Joshua Aizenman for his continuous encouragement to pursue new ideas. His support allowed me to reshape my research project. From Joshua, I learned that our scholarly research has to be oriented toward a better interpretation of the world. To Jeff Nugent, whom I would especially like to thank for his enormous generosity. Having him as a professor for my economics classes was a gift. He was always attentive to my research progress and supportive throughout my graduate studies. From Jeff, I learned that the details are worth exploring.

I would also like to thank Hannah Rich and Leigh Westerfield from Routledge, Taylor & Francis, editor and copy editor of this book, for their immense support during this long journey. I am also extremely grateful to Ben Graham for his generous support over the last years. Ben gave me invaluable advice and comments on earlier drafts of my research project. It was due to his enthusiasm that I entered to USC's Security and Political Economy (SPEC) Lab where I created the Trade Policy Project. There, I was given the opportunity to create a fabulous team of students to work on my research projects. In that regard, I wish to thank the many students who have been part of the Trade Policy Project and from whom I received excellent research assistance: Madeline Zheng, Emily Heuring, John *Jack* Schwartz, Shir Attias, Sonum Patel, Amanda Joseph, and Kartik Mathur. I would also like to thank the USC Center for International Studies that awarded me the student research fund in 2020 and allowed me to work with Claire Schreder and Claire Post, from whom I received very helpful comments and edits of this book.

Several faculty members at USC have been tremendously generous with their time and support: Gerardo Munck, Wayne Sandholtz, Saori Katada, Pablo Barberá, Patrick James, Iva Bozovic, and James Lo from my Department of Political Science and International Relations. Ratika Narag, Geert Ridder, and Hyungsik Roger Moon from the Department of Economics. Lastly, George Gerald Vega Yon, Kayla de la Haye, and Tom Valente from USC's Center for Applied Network Analysis (CANA) for their suggestions on earlier versions of this book. George specifically has been a source of immense support in this journey. I will always be extremely grateful for his support with the data analysis and the dataset on which we worked together that improved the quantitative analysis of this book.

Many scholars around the world contributed with insightful comments on different steps of this research project, including Marcelo Olarreaga (University of Geneva), Barbara Kotschwar (Georgetown University), Ricardo Ernst (Georgetown University), Diana Kapiszewski (Georgetown University), Andrew Bennett (Georgetown University), Andrés Rebolledo (Universidad SEK, Chile), Roberto Horta (Universidad Católica del Uruguay), Bryn Rosenfeld (Cornell University), and Dorotea Lopez (University of Chile). I also thank the more than 20 individuals from various backgrounds and professions around Latin America who accepted to be interviewed for this book.

For their invaluable advice and comments on earlier drafts, I am grateful to many colleagues: Victoria Chonn Ching, Timo Dahler, Paul Orner, Miriam Barnum, Gabrielle Cheung, Kyle Rapp, Eboni Nola Haynes, Kelebogile Zvobgo, Brian Knafou, Joey Huddleston, Daniela Maag, and Manuel Martinez. I am also grateful for the constant support of Veri Chavarin and the entire staff of the Department of Political Science and International Relations. I would also like to thank the Global Trade Alert Dataset team, especially Piotr Lukaszuk, for his generosity in explaining to me many key details about the dataset.

This book has benefited from many grants and scholarships that allowed me to improve my research. I thank the National Science Foundation (NSF) for the

Fellowship (1558713) I received to support my participation in the 11th Annual Political Networks Conference, where I received very useful comments on this project; the National Council on International Trade and Development (NCITD) for the 2018–2019 Award for this research project, which provided important support; and the USC Center for International Studies (CIS) fund for graduate research (2020) and the USC Korean Studies Institute Grad Student Affiliates' grant, which also helped me in my fieldwork.

Thanks to this book project, I also obtained the American Political Science Association's 2020 Fund for Latino Scholarship, and I was also recognized as the New Public Intellectuals in Latin America in 2018 by the *Global American Journal*. Additionally, I was awarded a USC research enhancement grant to participate at the Institute for Qualitative and Multi-Method Research, where I received many comments and suggestions that positively impacted my work.

Naturally, any errors that remain are my own responsibility.

1 Trade protectionism in an uncertain global economy and the necessity for a new framework of analysis*

> We live in a difficult world. If everyone is becoming more protectionist, then we have to protect ourselves too. We know, though, that we have to be careful with our close trading partners, as not to escalate the problem. That's why our union asked the government to work "in silence" and implement policies that could help us become more competitive without being as obvious to the rest of the world. We are not trying to hurt our partners; we are just asking the government to help us be more competitive in this difficult international context.
>
> (Industrial Union Leader in Mexico)[1]

It has been more than a decade since the 2008–09 global financial crisis (GFC) and the accompanying collapse of trade (Baldwin, 2009).[2] In the last decade, many countries have erected new trade barriers that contrast sharply with the thrust of global trends over the past 70 years, which saw a sustained opening of national markets under the Bretton Woods system.[3] The World Trade Organization (WTO) has been urging its members "to resist protectionism and get trade moving again" (WTO, 2016b).[4] However, the recent literature on trade policy suggests this is not occurring as research has focused on bilateral trade tensions that are occurring around the world, such as the "US–China trade war," which formally began in March 2018 when the United States imposed safeguard tariffs on a long list of Chinese products (Bown & Kolb, 2019). Most of the academic work on trade protectionism has concentrated on bilateral trade conflicts such as the current "trade war" between the United States and China, rather than on understanding what has really happened in the decade since the 2008–09 GFC. My main departure point concerns the rise of trade protectionism between the outbreak of the 2008–09 GFC and the current US–China trade war. Figure 1.1 shows unilateral measures implemented by 170 countries of different regions across the world, representing 98% of global trade flows.

This book analyzes the rise of a new pattern of trade protectionism beginning with the GFC up to the present. How have countries in the developing world responded to rising protectionism in a context of high trade interdependence and economic uncertainty? This question is vital to theoretical and policy

DOI: 10.4324/9781003340393-1

2 Trade protectionism in an uncertain global economy

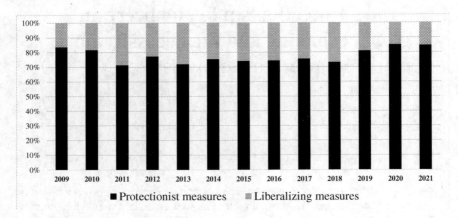

Figure 1.1 Comparing protectionist and liberalizing measures between 2009 and 2021.

Source: Author's creation based on Global Trade Alert, www.globaltradealert.org/

debates about international political economies and trade. Currently, major trade policy tensions are erupting faster than the generation of theories to explain them. This study of trade policy trends from the GFC to the present promises to put the Sino-American tariff war in perspective and situate it as part of a deeper and longer pattern of twenty-first-century protectionism (Evenett, 2019).

One distinctive aspect of this rising protectionism is that it is occurring against a backdrop of intense globalization. Paradoxically, through preferential trade agreements (PTAs) and global value chains (GVCs), countries around the globe are becoming more interconnected even as they erect new trade barriers. This trend starkly contrasts with past patterns of protectionist escalation, which receive near sole attention in the current literature on trade interdependence; the literature argues that the more interconnected countries are, the less protectionist they are likely to become (Baldwin, 2012; Gawande et al., 2015; Jensen et al., 2015; Lamy, 2013). However, it has barely spoken to this newer contradictory phenomenon where trade protectionism occurs under conditions of high interdependence (Farrell & Newman, 2019) and economic uncertainty (Ahir et al., 2018).

This book is motivated by this contradiction. I hypothesize that protectionist trends over the last decade reveal a possible downside of PTAs and GVCs. That is, protectionism is rising in the form of less observable, non-tariff measures (NTMs) despite more open trade and production schemes. In other words, economic interdependence in the context of high trade uncertainty is devolving into a spiral of protectionism because "many governments simultaneously face pressure to reflate national economies and defend national commercial interests" (Evenett, 2019, p. 26).

This research project offers preliminary evidence that institutional mechanisms like PTAs, which for decades have fueled the diffusion of trade liberalization, can also become channels for the spread of protectionism in the context of high economic uncertainty.[5]

Regarding GVCs, the goal of this book is to introduce a preliminary analysis of their potential effects in bilateral protectionism dynamics, given the challenges of measuring them (Gaulier et al., 2019). As I will explain later, they refer to international production sharing, a phenomenon where production is broken into activities and tasks carried out in different countries. Hence, given its complex structure, there is considerable debate about how to properly measure GVCs (Gaulier et al., 2019; Hummels et al., 2001). The share of intermediate goods traded between two countries is normally used as a proxy measure for the GVC between them. As Gaulier et al. (2019) show, in the last decade, "the share of intermediate goods in world trade in nominal terms is fairly well correlated to various Global Value Chain (GVC) indicators based on international input-output matrices" (p. 1).Thus, I use the exchange of intermediate goods as the best approximation to measure the potential "GVC interconnection" between two countries (Escaith et al., 2010; De Backer & Miroudot, 2014). In further chapters, I uncover the potential biases in econometric work presented in Chapter 4.

At its heart, this book is an analysis of how countries' bilateral protectionist dynamics have evolved over the last decade. My focus will be on: (1) the role of PTAs, GVCs, and NTMs in the escalation of trade protectionism, and (2) how emerging economies (with a focus on Latin America) have been affected by and responded to rising protectionist trends. In sum, my research highlights the risk of protectionism in an interconnected world. As China's President Xi Jinping remarked, "in a world of deepening economic globalization, practices of the law of the jungle and winner-takes-all only represent a dead end" (Xi Jinping, p. 14).[6]

As the COVID-19 pandemic has stopped globalization in its tracks, these extraordinary circumstances make for a natural experiment on the effects of drastically slowed trade on the global economy and developing countries in particular.[7] Keeping this in mind, I compile a novel dataset that captures how global trade has been hampered by the rise of protectionist policy interventions over the past decade. The significance of this book is the empirical documentation of the damage that closed markets and trade nationalism can inflict on developing countries. In essence, this book is a cautionary tale about economic nationalism in an era of trade interdependence and high levels of uncertainty. It also contributes to the debate among trade policy scholars on whether or not the rise of protectionism following the GFC is on par with other major trade collapses in history, such as that which occurred during the Great Depression of the 1930s. Some scholars have prematurely argued that there was a limited increase in protectionism after the GFC (Rodrik, 2009; Boffa & Olarreaga, 2012; Bems, Johnson, & Yi, 2013, Kee, Neagu, & Nicita 2013; Bems, Johnson, & Yi, 2013) and stated that this "should be seen as a victory for the political consensus and economic institutions that underpin the global economy" (Bems et al., 2013, p. 376). However, hindsight now shows that increases in protectionism were much larger and more pervasive than these scholars originally thought.

In this book, I argue that there is a need for improved measurement and careful analysis of the various types of protectionism that have evolved since the GFC. As Evenett (2019, p. 10) has highlighted, trade policy theories and practices are now in a state of flux:

> The global financial crisis and its aftermath is an excellent laboratory to test the robustness of key research findings in extreme circumstances. Abrupt shifts in government preferences may result in big shifts in public policy (such as attitudes towards more interventionist industrial policy) opening the door for fresh testing of theories of the impact of business–government relations on policy choice.

I contend that the standing research on post-GFC protectionism has not caught up with the array of responses (especially in the global south) in the form of less observable NTMs. This rise of less visible protectionist measures has important policy implications. First, by showing that the developing world has indeed responded to protectionism by relying on NTMs and less transparent tools, I can capture a pattern of backsliding on trade policy reform in many countries. As Baldwin (1970) argued long ago, a decrease in tariff measures over the last decades is most likely offset by NTMs; this practice has accelerated at an alarming pace since the GFC.

Additionally, I will show that, although the proliferation of PTAs may have changed the way that countries trade among themselves (Baldwin, 2012; Gawande, Hoekman, & Cui, 2015), these institutions have not been deterred from an increased reliance on NTMs. I also study whether the same mechanisms happen where there exist potential GVC linkages. In other words, greater trade interconnectivity between countries through PTAs has not limited the escalation of protectionism (Baldwin, 2012; Boffa & Olarreaga, 2012; Gawande et al., 2015; Rodrik, 2009; Jensen et al., 2015; Lamy, 2013). In short, the current context of international trade requires a broader conception of what constitutes trade restrictions. As Evenett (2019, p. 6) states, "an up-to-date definition of protectionism would refer to all government acts that actually discriminate in favor of local commercial interests over one or more foreign rivals whatever the form of international commerce or the form of policy instrument used." Following Evenett's (2019) approach, this book is based on a broader conceptualization of trade protectionism and requires a new method of measurement (which will be explained below).

As the literature and the real world have shown, in a context of crisis and uncertainty, governments face social and business pressures to cushion their economies from harsh external blows. Under such circumstances, "the likelihood of 'copycat' behavior arises, especially with respect to discriminatory measures that go against the spirit, if maybe not the law, of international trade norms" (Evenett, 2019, p. 13). My theoretical intuition is that PTAs—and to some extent GVCs too—create trade dependencies, which under conditions of high economic uncertainty, can increase defensive trade mechanisms between partner countries.

GVCs in particular—which require further analysis in the future once data become more accessible—have eroded the influence of large firms over national-level trade policymaking.[8] Of course, shifting employment abroad leaves less support for domestic workers, which affects the "political influence" that large firms have to combat trade protectionism (Gereffi, 2014). Hence, the effect of GVCs can go either way (Ghodsi & Stehrer, 2016): they can have an important effect on trade liberalization, but also give rise to protectionism (Gereffi, 2018). In my interview with a research economist with the WTO,[9] they stated:

> The network of trade agreements and the rise of global value chains have undoubtedly impacted the way in which countries design trade policy since they have changed the underlying parameters of trade policy in numerous ways. Most of the effects have been in favor of a more liberal trading system but not all. Trade agreements [the most important one in this context being the WTO] have limited countries' policy space. In order to obtain greater market access abroad, countries have committed to keep their tariffs below certain bound levels, move away from quantitative restrictions, improve transparency on non-tariff barriers [...] This, by default, implies that countries' responses to events like the financial crisis, that traditionally would have led to higher policy-related trade costs, are more muted since they operate in a more confined environment. [...] The more countries have constrained their tariffs, the more likely it is that they switch to alternative measures that can reach the same objectives.

As true as this may be, the types of protectionism now occurring in an increasingly interconnected world are less transparent. New, evasive NTMs can make it difficult for policymakers to quickly identify when and how their country is being adversely affected by a trading partner (Grundke & Moser, 2019; Baldwin & Evenett, 2009).

In sum, this book takes the rise of protectionism following the GFC as a fait accompli. My focus is not to prove the existence of this phenomenon, but to identify those factors that drive and perpetuate it. In 2017 (before the start of the US–China trade war), the WTO (2017, p. 6) secretariat lamented that

> G20 economies may have opted in favor of implementing less traditional and transparent measures to curtail trade, the secretariat may have had more difficulties in gaining access to the relevant information and/or G20 economies implemented fewer such measures during this particular review period.

My methodological approach is geared toward theory expansion. It is both deductive and inductive. It is deductive in that I revisit previous theories in the

6 *Trade protectionism in an uncertain global economy*

Table 1.1 General and specific research questions of this book

General research question	Specific research questions	Research design
How do countries respond to trade protectionism in a context of high economic uncertainty and trade interconnectivity?	**STATE-LEVEL DYNAMICS** - How does economic interconnectivity (PTAs and GVCs) affect **countries' propensity to engage in protectionist retaliation?** - How does economic interconnectivity (PTAs and GVCs) affect **the type of measures countries deploy to respond to protectionism?**	Large-N quantitative analysis using primary data
	REGIONAL DYNAMICS - How have **Latin American emerging economies** been affected by and responded to protectionism in the decade since the GFC?	Qualitative analysis. Case studies: Mexico, Brazil, and Argentina; secondary sources and process-tracing interviews.

Source: Author's creation

trade policy literature, first identifying a pattern and then testing whether data fit within a new international context. It is inductive in that I analyze data to identify a pattern that can contribute to theory building. Table 1.1 summarizes the connection between research questions and research design.

Why is this topic relevant from a global development perspective? As I will show in the following chapters, sectors, workers, and consumers are all hurt by protectionist measures like opaque NTMs. For example, over the past ten years, G20 members[10] have implemented around 1,200 protectionist measures that have affected the trade flows of the 47 nations constituting the less developed countries (LDC)[11] group (Evenett & Fritz, 2018). The United Nations estimates that three-quarters of this 880 million population residing in the LDC group are living in poverty. As Evenett & Fritz (2018, p. 49) highlight:

> Without suggesting that they have specifically targeted the LDCs, three G20 members have put in place over 100 policy interventions since November 2008 that harm exporters, their employees, and migrant workers from the LDCs. The three G20 countries and the number of times they have hit LDC commercial interests are, respectively, China (101 times), India (235 times), and the United States (344 times).

When we disaggregate those protectionist instruments that G20 countries have used most often against the LDCs, as I have done in Figure 1.2, we see

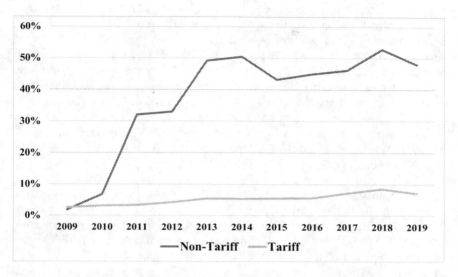

Figure 1.2 Between 2009 and 2018, the effect of G20 protectionism on LDCs has been concentrated in non-tariff measures.

Source: Author's creation based on Global Trade Alert, www.globaltradealert.org/

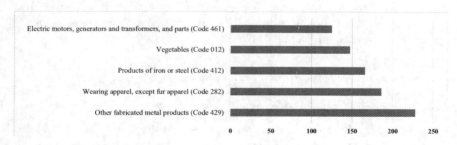

Figure 1.3 Sectors within LDCs that have been most affected by G20 protectionism.

Source: Author's creation based on Global Trade Alert, www.globaltradealert.org/

that a majority of them are NTMs (e.g., non-automatic licensing, quotas, price-control measures, subsidies).[12] The figure shows the differences between tariff and NTMs in terms of their impact on exports from LDCs to G20 countries. While in 2018 the G20's tariff measures only affected 9% of LDC exports to G20 countries, its NTMs affected 53% of LDC exports to G20 countries. This figure offers just one insight into how protectionism in general and NTMs in particular are having an impact on the developing world.

Figure 1.3 shows the five sectors within the LDCs that were most adversely affected by G20 protectionism (both tariff and NTMs) between 2009 and 2018.[13]

Metal products (Central Product Classification or CPC 429)[14] have been the target of 228 protectionist interventions; Wearing apparel, except fur apparel (CPC 282) were hit by 186 interventions; Products of iron or steel (CPC 412) by 166 interventions; Vegetables (CPC 012) by 147 interventions; and Electric motors, generators & transformers and parts (CPC 461) by 125 protectionist interventions.

When we expand the analysis globally, we can see that there are important variations in the impact of and responses to protectionism according to region. Table 1.2 summarizes key information about trade protectionism in sub-Saharan Africa, South Asia, North America, the Middle East and North Africa, Latin America and the Caribbean, the European Union (EU), and the East Asia Pacific. For each region, the table shows:

1) the number of protectionist and liberalizing measures the region implemented (2009–2019);
2) the percentage of exports in a region affected by protectionism emanating from the rest of world (RoW) and vice versa (percentage of RoW exports to the region affected by a given region´s protectionism);
3) which sectors have been most affected by RoW protectionism and vice versa (which sectors have been more protected by each region).

1.1 Definition and conceptualization

There are at least four key concepts related to the main variables of interest in this book: 1) trade policy and the different types of measures used, 2) trade policy retaliation, 3) PTAs, and 4) GVCs.

1.1.1 Trade policy and the different ways of measuring it

1.1.1.1 What does trade policy really mean?

Trade policy can be defined as that which regulates the flow of goods and services across borders and has a direct or indirect impact on the domestic prices of those imports and exports (Rodrik, 1995; Milner, 1999).[15] For example, the implementation of an import tariff on a specific product or group of products constitutes trade policy.

The key conceptual element of trade policy measurement is that it concerns a specific measure implemented by a given country. This measure could affect one specific country or a group of countries. Protectionist trade policy refers to defensive measures implemented by one country that affect market access and commercial interests of other countries. This includes both tariffs and NTMs (e.g., quotas), which limit market access to foreign commercial interests. Moreover, trade policy covers the flows of goods, services, and capital (portfolio and foreign direct investment (FDI)) (Evenett, 2019). Trade policymaking involves the dynamics of supply and demand, both of which are embedded in politics (Milner, 1999). The demand side of trade policy is shaped by domestic

Table 1.2 Mapping trade policy dynamics by region

TRADE POLICY INFORMATION	Sub-Saharan Africa	North America	Middle East & North Africa	Latin Am. & the Caribbean	European Union	East Asia Pacific
Number of protectionist measures implemented (2009–18)	613	2,619	1,015	2,151	2,701	4,842
Number of liberalizing measures implemented (2009–18)	398	348	494	1,366	423	2,657
Share of protectionist interventions that use nontransparent ("murky") instruments	40%	77%	51%	44%	87%	83%
Region's percentage of exports affected by RoW's protectionism (average 2009–18)	29%	30%	27%	36%	22%	39%
RoW's exports to the region affected by the region's protectionism (average 2009–18)	25%	40%	10%	19%	23%	21%
Region's most-used protectionist measures affecting RoW's exports	Finance measures that affect trade	Subsidies	Tariff measures	Tariff measures and Non-automatic licensing	Subsidies	Subsidies and Non-automatic licensing

(*Continued*)

Trade protectionism in an uncertain global economy 9

Table 1.2 (Continued)

TRADE POLICY INFORMATION	Sub-Saharan Africa	North America	Middle East & North Africa	Latin Am. & the Caribbean	European Union	East Asia Pacific
Region's most affected sector by RoW's protectionism	- Motor vehicles, trailers .. (CPC 491) - Machinery for mining (CPC 444)	- Products of iron or steel (CPC 412) - Fabricated metal products (CPC 429)	- Products of iron or steel (CPC 412) - Basic organic chemicals (CPC 341)	- Products of iron or steel (CPC 412) - Fabricated metal products (CPC 429)	- Motor vehicles, trailers (CPC 491) - Products of iron or steel (CPC 412)	- Products of iron or steel (CPC 412) - Basic organic chemicals (CPC 341)

Source: Author's creation based on Global Trade Alert, 2019.

Notes: RoW (Rest of the World), sub-Saharan Africa consists of 47 countries, North America by 3 countries, the Middle East and North Africa by 20 countries, Latin Am. and the Caribbean 39 countries (Mexico included), the EU 28 countries (China included), and East Asia Pacific 37 countries (China included).

interest groups (e.g., unions) and individuals, who in turn will be affected by trade policy outcomes. These actors demand that political institutions implement a specific type of trade policy. The supply side is shaped by government (i.e., the executive, congress, and administrative courts), all of which guide the implementation of trade policy decisions (Rodrik, 1995). These two dimensions will be relevant for further discussions.

1.1.1.2 Tariffs, non-tariff measures, and "murky" protectionism

Again, trade policy outcomes are the result of various countries' specific trade measures, which can be divided into tariff (taxes on trade) and non-tariff instruments. Import tariff measures are taxes imposed, in percentage terms, on the value of a good. For example, a 10% tariff means that importers must pay 10% of the appraised value of a good to the importing government before selling their product in that government's domain.[16] While tariff measures are easy to identify and define, NTMs are just the opposite. NTMs require more detailed definition and differentiation. The United Nations Conference on Trade and Development (UNTAD) Multi-Agency Support Team (MAST)[17] says,

> NTMs are policy measures other than ordinary customs tariffs that can potentially have an economic effect on international trade in goods, changing quantities traded, or prices or both. A detailed classification is therefore critical in order to clearly identify and distinguish among the various forms of NTMs.[18]

This taxonomical definition will be used throughout the book. I will further complement this definition of NTMs with details found in the Global Trade Alert (GTA) dataset, as measures such as import tariff increases, factors affecting the flow of workers across borders, and factors affecting capital flows are not included in the MAST classification. The International Monetary Fund (IMF) has noted that the GTA database "has the most comprehensive coverage of all types of trade-discriminatory and trade-liberalizing measures, although it begins only in 2008" (IMF, 2016, p. 76). Unlike tariff measures, NTMs are categorized into many different types. All of these in some way affect trade flows from one country to another.

Overall, NTMs are less transparent than tariffs, which are more objective and explicit at the moment countries implement them. As the Transparency in Trade (TNT) initiative states:

> As tariffs have been gradually reduced, increasingly prevailing trade restrictions take the form of so-called non-tariff measures (NTMs). These are inherently less visible and transparent than simple tariffs. [...] The situation is particularly murky for firms when it comes to trade in services, where it is often necessary for companies to hire specialists to help decipher which policies determine whether they will be able to provide their services to buyers in a foreign market.[19]

To define these new measures that go beyond the traditional import tariff, Baldwin and Evenett (2009, p. 4) clarify "murky protectionism" as policies that

> are not direct violations of WTO obligations; they are abuses of legitimate discretion which are used to discriminate against foreign goods, companies, workers and investors. Examples include abuses of health and safety regulations, and clauses in stimulus packages that confine spending to domestic producers.

Considering these definitions of tariffs and NTMs, the GTA database, a freely available dataset that I use for quantitative analysis, includes the following measures that "discriminate against foreign commercial interests"[20] in their list of trade interventions and categorizes them as transparent (non-murky) or nontransparent.[21] Table 1.3 shows the list of all intervention types considered by the GTA database and their level of transparency. As mentioned, this list is based on the UN MAST classification of NTMs and supplemented by additional categories not found in MAST (such as import tariff increases, and measures affecting the flow of FDI).[22]

1.1.1.3 The complex task of defining policy responses

It is not an easy task to define a "trade policy response."[23] First, many of the policies a country implements constitute unilateral protectionist dynamics rather than retaliatory measures. Second, countries do not necessarily convey that their policy is a direct response to another country's policy.

In some cases, the term "policy response" is used in a more general way throughout the literature (e.g., Aizenman & Marion, 1996; Gawande et al., 2011, 2015; Bussière et al., 2011; Aizenman & Jinjarak, 2010; Wise & Quiliconi, 2007). These types of studies analyze what happens before and after a given political and/or economic event to see how countries, companies, or people "responded" to it (e.g., the China shock, an international crisis, etc.). For instance, Bussière et al. (2011) studied how countries responded overall to the GFC and found that until 2011, there was no significant increase in protectionist measures. Aizenman and Jinjarak (2010) study the role of fiscal policy in response to the financial crisis.

Other trade policy studies use the term "response" in a more specific way in the context of examining trade policymaking at the bilateral level. For instance, Boffa and Olarreaga (2012) investigated instances of bilateral retaliation after the GFC and found that up until 2012, there was little evidence of retaliation. Their definition of a protectionist response is the following (p. 746):

> Arguably, a share of the overall protectionist response may be associated with retaliation, and anecdotal evidence suggests that this was the case during the recent global crisis. For example, China's response to the 35% tariff on imports of Chinese tires imposed by the US, was to impose

Table 1.3 Interventions and their level of transparency

Transparent	Nontransparent
Import tariff	Consumption subsidy
Sanitary and phytosanitary measure	Capital injection and equity stakes
Technical barrier to trade	Financial assistance in foreign market
Anti-circumvention	Financial grant
Antidumping	Import incentive
Anti-subsidy	In-kind grant
Import monitoring	Interest payment subsidy
Safeguard	Loan guarantee
Special safeguard	Price stabilization
Import quota	Production subsidy
Import tariff quota	State aid
Instrument unclear	State loan
Export quota	Tax or social insurance relief
Export tariff quota	Import ban and licensing requirement
Export tax	Internal taxation of imports
	Local labor, operations, and sourcing
	Localization incentive
	Trade balancing measure
	Intellectual property protection
	Control on personal and commercial transactions, and investments
	Controls on credit operations
	Repatriation & surrender requirements
	Entry and ownership rule
	Financial incentive
	Treatment and operations
	Competitive devaluation
	Trade payment measure
	Import-related non-tariff measure
	Public procurement access
	Public procurement localization and preference margin
	Public procurement
	Labor market access
	Post-migration treatment
	Export ban, licensing requirement, subsidy
	Export-related non-tariff measure
	Foreign customer limit
	Tax-based export incentive
	Trade finance

Source: Author's creation based on Global Trade Alert, www.globaltradealert.org/

countervailing duties of 31% on imports of chicken from the United States, later increased to 105%. Another example is the response by some Canadian towns to the "Buy America" provisions in the U.S. fiscal package. In May 2009 some Canadian towns adopted legislation that barred U.S. companies from municipal contracts [...] To move beyond anecdotic evidence we [...] examine whether countries that have been affected by a protectionist measure adopted by a trading partner, systematically retaliate by adopting measures that hurt exports of that trading partner.

The conceptual framework of retaliation suggested by Boffa and Olarreaga (2012) considers a potential retaliation policy as any protectionist measure that country A implements against country B at time *t*, after country B implemented an original protectionist measure against country A at time *t-1*. We can see this depicted in Figure 1.4. It is important to highlight the idea of a systematic pattern of protectionism. If we consider the notion of policy response within a window of just two years, we may only observe a bilateral measure implemented by coincidence between two countries. However, if this pattern occurs in a systematic and consistent way over an extended period of time, and we include controls for other bilateral factors and countries' fixed effects, we can then argue that this mechanism is more than just anecdotal. That is why my window of time for the quantitative analysis extends from 2009 to 2018.

For the quantitative analysis that undergirds this book, I used a linear model with lagged variables of analysis to avoid making erroneous assumptions. The independent variable is lagged so that the influence a trading partner has on a focal country (and vice versa) can be more carefully studied. The lagged influence model accounts for the time that the country of interest may take before it decides to retaliate. I will discuss this model in more detail in Chapter 4.

1.1.1.4 Preferential trade agreements (PTAs)

PTAs are probably one of the most important transformative changes in international trade policy since the early 1990s. They have expanded in number and diversity. In the 1990s, there were 50 PTAs; as of January 2020, there were 303.[24] The World Bank's definition provides a general description of international trade agreements as "all the agreements that have the potential to liberalize trade" (Dür et al. 2014, p. 1).[25] I use this definition because it is the one most used in the literature (Hofmann et al., 2019; Ruta, 2017). Hence, when I refer to a PTA, I am including free trade agreements (FTAs), customs unions (CUs), and partial FTAs, which can take bilateral (e.g., two countries),

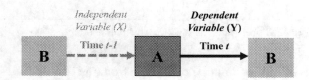

Figure 1.4 A retaliatory dynamic.

Source: Author's creation.

plurilateral (e.g., many countries), plurilateral with a third country (e.g., EU–Australia Trade Agreement), or region-region (e.g., EU-Mercosur Trade Agreement) forms.

These distinctions are important since the WTO categorizes PTAs as non-reciprocal preferential schemes. Examples include the Generalized System of Preferences (GSP), under which developed countries grant other developed countries preferential tariffs on their imports. RTAs, on the other hand, are reciprocal preferential trade agreements between two or more partners. Hence, under the WTO's framework, these two terms are distinct. Thus, the WTO keeps two separate databases for PTAs and RTAs.[26] RTAs are allowed under WTO rules as exemptions and are subject to the rules stated in the General Agreement on Trade and Tariffs (GATT) Article XXIV, Article V, and the Enabling Clause.[27]

The main function of the WTO—which succeeded the GATT in 1995—is to ensure that international trade is conducted as smoothly, predictably, and freely as possible.[28] In seeking to fulfill this key objective, the WTO created the idea of the "most favored nation" (MFN) treatment, a central norm within the global trading system, which holds that any benefit one member country grants to another must also be granted to each other member of the organization.[29] Specifically, MFN states that

> any advantage, favor, privilege or immunity granted by a contracting party to a product originating in or destined for another country, shall be granted immediately and unconditionally to any similar product originating in the territories of all other contracting parties or destined to them.[30]

It is valid to imagine that no country would prefer to open up, as it would then be obligated to grant the same benefits to all WTO members. That is why Article XXIV of the GATT establishes exceptions to MFN treatment. It stipulates that when a free trade zone or a customs union is created, signatory countries are not required to extend the same benefits to all WTO member countries. In other words, a given country is not in violation of the MFN rule when it enters into an FTA or a CU.

As for FTAs, the WTO states, "the trade within the group is duty free but members set their own tariffs on imports from nonmembers (e.g., NAFTA)."[31] Article XXIV of the GATT is more specific and says,

> A free-trade area shall be understood to mean a group of two or more customs territories in which the duties and other restrictive regulations of commerce are eliminated on substantially all the trade between the constituent territories in products originating in such territories.[32]

The clause "substantially all trade" is not clearly defined, but is usually understood to mean 80% of the volume of trade between the countries entering into the agreement.[33]

When two or more countries decide to deepen their trade integration, they can go from an FTA to a CU, which is another type of PTA. The WTO defines a CU as an integration scheme in which the members apply a "common external tariff," or CET (e.g., the African Union). Hence, in a CU, members not only remove regulations "on substantially all" bilateral trade, but also create a common external tariff. The CET is meant to prevent tariff-jumping, or the ability of outsiders to enter the integration scheme through lower tariff member countries. In the absence of a CET, most PTAs (and RTAs) set rules of origin or content requirements.

Finally, when countries decide to further advance the depth of integration within a PTA, they create a common market (CM). A CM establishes not only a common external tariff, but also the free movement of factors of production among the signatory countries. For example, any citizen within the CM can work freely in any of the countries that are part of the agreement (e.g., the EU) without restrictions. All of the agreement types mentioned above are normally referred to as preferential (or regional) trade agreements (PTAs). Of the 303 PTAs currently in force, approximately 90% of these agreements are free trade areas, while the remaining 10% represent deeper integration projects, such as a CU.[34] The number of PTAs has been growing consistently since the 1990s, a trend defined in the literature as the "New Wave of Regionalism" (Mansfield & Milner, 1999, p. 589).[35] As I will explain in greater detail later, to measure PTAs between countries, I will rely on data from the Design of Trade Agreements (DESTA) project, which "systematically collects data on various types of preferential trade agreements (PTAs). These may be customs unions or free trade agreements."[36] DESTA is today "the most comprehensive [dataset] in terms of both items coded and number of agreements included" (Dür et al., 2014, p. 353).

1.1.1.5 Global value chains (GVCs)

GVCs are also among the most important transformative changes in international trade policy in the last decade. However, they are very complex to measure and to fully understand in terms of their real impact on the world economy. As Ruta (2017, p. 175) states, the "GVC has changed international trade, with trade in parts and components increasing almost six times between 1990 and 2015, faster than the 4.5 times for other forms of trade." A recent report from the World Bank (2020a) entitled *Trading for Development in the Age of Global Value Chains* defines GVCs as follows: "a global value chain breaks up the production process across countries. Firms specialize in a specific task and do not produce the whole product" (p. 5).

Given the complex structure of GVCs, there is considerable debate about how to properly measure them (Gaulier et al., 2019; Hummels et al., 2001). The share of intermediate goods traded between two countries is normally used as a proxy measure for the GVC between them. Gaulier et al. (2019) shows that in the last decade, "the share of intermediate goods in world trade

Table 1.4 Capital, intermediate, and consumption goods (in BEC Classification)

Capital goods	Intermediate goods	Consumption goods
41—Capital goods (except transport equipment) 521—Transport equipment, industrial	111—Food and beverages, primary, mainly for industry 121—Food and beverages, processed, mainly for industry 21—Industrial supplies not elsewhere specified, primary 22—Industrial supplies not elsewhere specified, processed 31—Fuels and lubricants, primary 322—Fuels and lubricants, processed (other than motor spirit) 42—Parts and accessories of capital goods (except transport equipment) 53—Parts and accessories of transport equipment	112—Food and beverages, primary, mainly for household consumption 122—Food and beverages, processed, mainly for household consumption 321—Fuels and lubricants, processed (motor spirit) 522—Transport equipment, non-industrial 61—Consumer goods not elsewhere specified, durable 62—Consumer goods not elsewhere specified, semi-durable 63—Consumer goods not elsewhere specified, non-durable

Source: Author's creation based on UN Trade Statistics, *Intermediate Goods in Trade Statistics*, https://unstats.un.org/unsd/tradekb/Knowledgebase/50090/Intermediate-Goods-in-Trade-Statistics

in nominal terms is fairly well correlated to various Global Value Chain (GVC) indicators based on international input-output matrices" (p. 1). Hence, I use the exchange of intermediate goods as the best approximation to measure the potential "GVC interconnection" between two countries (Escaith et al., 2010; De Backer & Miroudot, 2014).

To specifically measure the share of trade, I rely on the classification groups created by Broad Economic Categories (BEC), which provide "a means for international trade statistics to be analyzed by broad economic categories such as food, industrial supplies, capital equipment, consumer durables and consumer non-durables." Table 1.4 shows the three basic classes of goods categorized in the BEC. Intermediate goods are those in the middle of the table.[37] When speaking about the intermediate goods' linkages with trade protectionism, Bems et al. (2009) state that:

> Intermediates have distinct implications for the response of trade to changes in final demand. These effects operate independently of, and in addition to, standard trade transmission channels that work through the endogenous response of final demand to shocks. First, imported intermediate goods

linkages imply that a country's exports and imports tend to move in the same direction in response to changes in either domestic or foreign demand. For example, a decline in U.S. demand for cars will typically imply decreased demand for cars imported from Canada. Since Canadian cars are produced using imported inputs from the US, a decline in the production of Canadian cars will mean fewer U.S. exports of car parts to Canada, both U.S. imports and exports fall. This does not happen if the imported intermediates channel is absent. Second, imported intermediate goods linkages influence each country's exposure to foreign shocks.[38]

Thus, GVCs are another example of countries' interconnectedness, not only through their trade relations (something that PTAs mostly show), but also through their trade production. This is why GVCs are another relevant variable for understanding trade interconnectivity in the current international political economy.

1.2 Theoretical approaches in the literature and initial hypotheses

How systemic dynamics shape international trade policymaking processes remains an open question in the literature on international trade. As Lake (2009, p. 237) stresses, if international institutions "really matter, they will alter the interest and possibly institutions within states as well." With this in mind, I aim to provide preliminary evidence that reciprocity can also have a negative face. That is, when trading partners apply protectionist measures, locally affected industries can lobby for domestic tariff increases as a defensive mechanism. This could press a partner into removing tariff or non-tariff barriers that they implemented previously, or it could spiral into higher trade barriers.

1.2.1 State-level dynamics in trade protectionism

Broadly, the characteristics of a given state can affect the likelihood that policymakers will resort to retaliatory protectionism (Gould & Woodbridge, 1998; Miyagiwa et al., 2016). In particular, the degree of bilateral trade integration (Kono, 2007), GVCs (Gereffi, 2018; Gawande et al., 2015; Tanaka, 2009; Yi, 2009), and the relative economic size of a country (Miyagiwa et al., 2016; Evenett, 2019) can shape its trade policy dynamics. Concerning relative economic size, Evenett (2019, pp. 24—5) argues that:

> Larger economies tend to resort less to traditional trade restrictions. Perhaps governments in larger economies feel they are under more scrutiny and so resort to less transparent forms of discrimination. However, economic size might matter in different ways. For instance, nations with larger domestic markets may be more inclined to implement industrial policies that seek to nurture domestic firms, doing so not with tariffs but with state largesse that a larger tax base may support. Rather than attribute agency to government,

MNEs [multinational enterprises] may lobby for different types of assistance in economies of different sizes, again the size of a nation's tax base may influence how deep its government's pockets are or the scale of lending by state-controlled development banks.

Governments invariably pursue policies that maximize their support from influential political groups. Studies have shown that uncertainty about an economic outcome will lead one country in a group of two or more to impose a gradually rising tariff on the others (Baldwin & Evenett, 2009). Eventually, this added cost on imported goods induces retaliation from the other nations. This retaliation can encourage either liberalization or a protectionist war, with market characteristics acting as the deciding factor. At the same time, the very threat of retaliation may play a key role in triggering trade liberalization (Gould & Woodbridge, 1998).

The extent of protectionism triggered by the GFC remains open to debate. As mentioned, early studies conducted in the wake of the GFC found no evidence of trade retaliation between 2008 and 2010; rather, this research found just the opposite. This was the case for Boffa and Olarreaga (2012), who analyzed protectionist measures from November 2009 to December 2010. Similarly, in their study on the use of antidumping duties and tariffs post-GFC, Kee et al. (2013) showed that bilateral responses along these lines were minimal. In this book, I extend this analysis through 2018 and include the effects of GVCs and PTAs on trade dynamics., finding that with a longer timeline and additional variables, a more protectionist scenario takes shape.

Most studies on the role of GVCs and PTAs suggest that trade interdependence fosters more trade liberalization. This argument goes back to the IPE and peace research agenda, which state that increased economic and political interdependence reduces the likelihood of conflict between countries (Copeland, 1996). However, realist authors, mostly after the Cold War, contested this argument and questioned the relationship between economic interdependence and international peace (Barbieri, 1996). In fact, Waltz (2000, p. 14) highlights that interdependence "multiplies the occasions for conflicts":

> Close interdependence is a condition in which one party can scarcely move without jostling others, a small push ripples through society. The closer the social bonds, the more extreme the effect becomes, and one cannot sensibly pursue an interest without taking others' interests into account. One country is then inclined to treat another country's acts as events within its own polity and to attempt to control them.

The literature on the political economy of PTAs has been concentrated mostly on why countries negotiate and sign PTAs (Baccini & Dür, 2012; R. Baldwin, 1993; Chase, 2003; Manger, 2009) and, more recently, on the effect PTAs have in signatories' countries in terms of trade flows (Baier & Bergstrand, 2007) and other areas of political concern, such as their ability to reduce bilateral conflict between PTA members (Hafner-Burton, 2005; Mansfield et al., 2008; Mansfield & Reinhardt, 2008).

Overall, academic studies have focused on the positives of interdependence (through PTAs or GVCs) and have not sufficiently considered how interdependence can create and encourage channels of protectionism. Only a few authors to date have probed interdependence protectionism (Blanchard et al., 2016; Bems et al., 2009; Yi, 2009; Manger, 2009), with Yi (2009) arguing that "massive reorientation of trade flows towards multiple-step supply chains" has played an important role in current protectionist dynamics (p. 2). In my interview with an employee of the University of Chile, they said that "the effects of free trade agreements, probably in the deformation of economists, are rather more a legal instrument than an instrument of real economic connection. Sometimes I think free trade agreements have been overvalued, in terms of what they generate."[39]

The main goal of this book is to increase our understanding of this interdependence protectionism. Here, I present my hypotheses concerning state-level dynamics in trade protectionism. The first set of hypotheses concerns a general perspective on how countries respond to protectionism and the effects of PTAs and GVCs in those responses.

First, I hypothesize that when a country is adversely affected by another country's protectionist measures, it will systematically respond to that country with retaliatory protectionist measures. Hence, in Hypothesis 1, I suggest that an increase in import restrictions by country B on country A at time $t-1$ has a positive effect on import restrictions by A on B at time t. However, the existence of PTAs between two countries reduces the possibility of protectionist escalation. In other words, a PTA, ceteris paribus, lowers the probability/severity of bilateral protectionist dynamics. In line with the literature on trade interdependence, we would expect that the more interconnected countries are, the less protectionist they are likely to become (e.g., Baldwin, 2012; Gawande et al., 2015; Rodrik, 2009; Jensen et al., 2015; Lamy, 2013). Hence, in Hypothesis 2, I suggest that PTAs and GVCs are negatively correlated with protectionist responses. In Hypothesis 3, I also test to what extent GVCs decrease the likelihood of protectionist responses.

A second group of hypotheses concerning state-level dynamics in trade protectionism test how responses vary when they are divided between tariff and NTMs. In Hypotheses 4 and 5, I suggest that countries with high trade interdependence (PTAs and GVCs) will retaliate more with NTMs (less transparent) than they will with tariff measures. Hence, PTAs and GVCs are negatively correlated with protectionist tariff responses (Hypothesis 4) but positively correlated with non-tariff responses (Hypothesis 5).

General Hypotheses (Hypotheses 1, 2, and 3)

RESEARCH PROPOSITION A: In general terms, when a country is adversely affected by a protectionist measure adopted by another country, it will systematically respond to that country by adopting protectionist measures in return.

However, the existence of PTAs and GVCs decreases the likelihood of a protectionist response.

HYPOTHESIS 1: Countries will retaliate against those nations that initially target them with a protectionist measure (***Direct Retaliation***).

HYPOTHESIS 2: Preferential trade agreements (PTAs) are negatively correlated with protectionist responses (***Conditional Effect of PTAs***).

HYPOTHESIS 3: Global value chains (GVCs) are negatively correlated with protectionist responses (***Conditional Effect of GVCs***).

The Relationship between Tariffs and NTMs with PTAs and GVCs (Hypotheses 4 and 5)

RESEARCH PROPOSITION B: Countries with high trade interdependence (PTAs and GVCs) will retaliate more with NTMs (less transparent) than with tariff measures.

HYPOTHESIS 4: Preferential trade agreements (PTAs) are positively correlated with protectionist non-tariff responses and negatively correlated with tariff responses (***Conditional Effect of PTAs***).

HYPOTHESIS 5: Global value chains (GVCs) are positively correlated with protectionist non-tariff responses and negatively correlated with tariff responses (***Conditional Effect of GVCs***).

1.2.2 Contribution of this book to the trade policy literature

There are three major challenges presented by the current literature on protectionism and policy responses in the context of high trade interdependence. The first is related to the data used in current research on protectionist responses. To date, the literature has focused on the magnitude of retaliation with regard to protectionist responses and calculates this magnitude by counting the total number of measures trading partners adopted, not the share of domestic trade affected (Boffa & Olarreaga, 2012; Evenett, 2019). In this book, I go a step further and also analyze how these policy interventions affect the actual share of trade in bilateral goods. By so doing, I can better specify how countries harm one another when implementing protectionist measures. The new measures presented in this study have important implications for global trade moving forward, as will become evident in the case study chapters of this book.[40]

Additionally, most of the current literature is still centered on the developed economies (Evenett & Fritz, 2018). Those scholars who investigate developing countries focus primarily on tariffs, to the exclusion of other types of discriminatory measures (Gawande et al., 2011). Most of the work to date has been large-N cross-country analyses. Few scholars have focused on analyses of developing economies to assess how different sectors have been more impacted than others (Gawande et al., 2011; Evenett & Fritz, 2018).

Finally, the broader research agenda on post-GFC trade policies is still limited due to the emergence of new types and forms of trade protectionism that have yet to be measured. This book contributes to the debate on trade policy substitution between NTMs and tariffs, a topic that has been under-researched (Beverelli et al., 2019; Niu et al., 2018). We know the more tariffs are lowered via bindings created by WTO rules, the more countries rely on NTMs, but this raises bigger questions about the relationship between trade policy and transparency. Of this relationship, Kono (2006, p. 369) writes that

> democracy has contradictory effects on different types of trade policies because electoral competition generates more information about some than about others. It generates considerable information about policies whose effects on consumer welfare are easy to explain to voters, but less information about policies whose effects are more complex.

In the same vein, Garrett (2000) argues that democracies are relatively more protectionist because they are more responsive to the demands of citizens than autocracies. More specifically, he indicates that "democracy makes leaders more accountable to their citizens, promoting trade liberalization to the extent that this is good for society as a whole" (p. 973).

The research agenda to which this book seeks to contribute is still limited due to the limited ways countries know to enact protectionist measures, but new types and forms of trade protectionism are still being discovered and yet to be measured. Evenett (2019) talks about the consequences of limited data in measuring twenty-first-century projectionism. This creates an "inadequate scrutiny bias," which means that once an idea has been established, it becomes unquestionable, such as the argument that the GFC has not substantially increased protectionism (p. 12). Data limitations also create a pattern of "omitted variable bias" in regression studies, which is "particularly important when analyzing the impact of commercial policy, as governments can substitute between transparent and murkier forms of protectionism" (p.13). Still, as mentioned before, Evenett (2019, p. 13) highlights that the GFC and its aftermath can be "an excellent laboratory to test the robustness of key research findings in extreme circumstances." Taking all of this into account, I leverage the empirical findings in the literature since the GFC and glean new insights to gain a better understanding of the sheer volume and nature of twenty-first-century protectionism. I present a unified database that expands and combines data from multiple datasets to draw a clearer picture of the unfavorable impacts of protectionism.[41]

1.3 A two-step research design

1.3.1 Large-N analysis

The first portion of this book is based on a large-N quantitative analysis constructed using directed dyad-year data at the state and industry levels.

Ultimately, two datasets will be created by generating new data and merging it with existing data. To test the state- and industry-level hypotheses, I use a lagged model, as it does not assume contemporaneous influence; rather, influence is lagged so that a focal country is influenced by its trading partners' networks after those trading partners have implemented protectionist policies that affect the focal country. Hence, what the lagged influence model considers is the time that the focal country may take (e.g., quarters within one year) before it decides to retaliate.

1.3.2 Small-n analysis and case studies

A central chapter of this book focuses on a more in-depth analysis of three emerging economies in Latin America, specifically Mexico, Brazil, and Argentina. For each, I will compile a country narrative of trade policy performance amid current protectionist trends. Complementing the large-N quantitative analysis, this case study section offers robust examinations of these country cases.

The three cases that I investigate offer rich theoretical insights. First, all three states are G20 members, and the G20 represents 80% of gross world product (GWP) and three-quarters of global trade.[42] Second, considering all of the G20's protectionist measures from 2009 to 2018, Argentina, Brazil, and Mexico are well distributed in the share of exports that have been affected by protectionist measures. Argentina, for example, was the most protectionist G20 country, based on consideration of the share of exports from the rest of the world to that country. As I will explain in detail in Chapter 5, these three countries are resource-dominated and only Mexico has an important manufacturing sector. I set a regional focus on Latin America, concentrating on differences between Mexico and Argentina/Brazil.

Third, while Argentina, Brazil, and Mexico effectively weathered the GFC, assessments to date completely overlook the role of trade protectionism. For example, Wise et al. (2015, p.1) argue that emerging regions such as Latin America and East Asia showed remarkable resilience when faced with the GFC. As they describe it:

> One of the more surprising features of the 2008-09 global financial crisis was the comparative ease with which emerging economies in Asia and Latin America rebounded. That rebound was a radical departure from the effects of previous crises on these regions, be it the decade-long recession wreaked on Latin America by the 1982 debt shocks, or the financial crisis that dramatically slowed Asian economies in the late 1990s. The quick recovery of emerging economies in 2010–12 was, moreover, instrumental in deterring a full-blown global depression.

This section of my book aims to bring trade protectionism into the framework of Wise et al. (2015). Closer inspection of the data on these three countries' trade measures reveals highly diverse policy responses. Argentina and Brazil, for instance, need to be better integrated into the global economy, while Mexico is perhaps too open for its own good. Recent studies have shown the important direct and indirect effects of current trade disputes on emerging economies, especially those in Latin America.[43] When we analyze less observable trade measures, we find that Latin America has been implementing protectionist measures during the last decade.

This small-N analysis will offer more detail as to whether countries with strong trade ties to the rest of the world via PTAs and GVCs have been differentially affected by protectionist dynamics compared to those with fewer trade ties. For instance, a recent study developed by the Chilean General Directorate of International Economic Relations (DIRECON, 2018) shows that 63% of Chile's exports are designated to go to countries in the Sino–American trade conflict (India, Turkey, the EU, Canada, Mexico and Russia). However, given Chile's strong web of free trade agreements, few of these many tariff increases have been enacted against Chile.

1.4 Historical context and significance of this research

As the historical chapter of this book will further explain, this is a timely project in the field of international political economics (IPE). Although trade protectionism has grabbed the attention of the media and has been at the center of political debates (Beyers & Kerremans, 2007), there have been few articles on trade policy that explore post-GFC protectionism. Figure 1.5 reflects data on Google searches for words related to "trade policy" and "protectionism" since 2008. The figure shows

> search interest relative to the highest point on the chart for the given region and time. A value of 100 is the peak popularity for the term. A value of 50 means that the term is half as popular. A score of 0 means there was not enough data for this term.[44]

As the figure indicates, the "interest" worldwide on news related to "trade policy" and "protectionism" has been significant since 2008.[45] However, since 2008 only nine articles have been published on questions related to "trade protectionism" in the prestigious *American Political Science Review*, and an average of 2.3 articles per year on this topic have been published in the journal *International Organization* (a total of 26 between 2008 and 2019).[46]

Another reason the current research is timely is the high degree of uncertainty that surrounds trade policy, especially since the United States declared a trade war against China in 2018. Prior to the outbreak of the coronavirus (COVID-19) in 2020, this trade war was one of the most pressing challenges to the global economy. The World Trade Uncertainty (WTU) index, is a measure of trade uncertainty introduced by Ahir et al. (2018) to address the impact

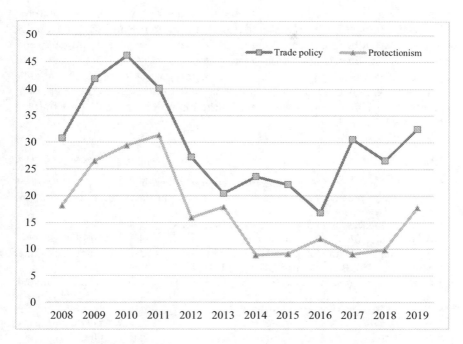

Figure 1.5 Google searches on "trade policy" and "protectionism" (2008–19).

Note: A value of 100 is the peak popularity for the term. A value of 50 means that the term is half as popular. A score of 0 means there were not enough data for this term.

Source: Author's creation based on Google trend data.

of erratic changes in trade policy.[47] It shows how trade uncertainty is rising sharply after 20 years of relative stability.

This uncertainty does not only impact diplomatic relationships among governments. It also affects international actors at every level, from political institutions to corporate and small businesses, to consumers. An uncertain economic environment is not conducive to long term-business decisions. Trade policy impacts consumers, especially since they are most likely to bear the ultimate burden of higher cost processes. When political uncertainty reaches typical business owners and consumers, it shapes public opinion about trade policy and its future.

1.5 Outline of the book

This book proceeds in five more chapters. Chapter 2 offers a historical overview of twenty-first-century protectionism, with an emphasis on how we arrived at this new protectionist juncture. Chapter 3 is a descriptive analysis of the dataset used in this book for the quantitative and qualitative analysis.

Chapter 4 conducts a quantitative analysis that captures the "big picture" of current protectionist trends and tests the main research hypotheses of this book. Chapter 5 concentrates on Latin America as a regional case, and considers three emerging economies in greater detail (Argentina, Brazil, and Mexico); it examines a small number of country cases in depth to qualitatively test some of the main hypotheses discussed in the quantitative chapter. Chapter 6 concludes with a summary of the main findings and contributions of this book project.

Notes

* Some sections of this chapter have been used in Albertoni, N. (2023). The risk of murky trade protectionism in an interconnected and uncertain global economy, *Estudios Internacionales*, 55(205).
1 Author's interview with a union industry leader in Mexico, December 2019.
2 As different studies have shown, from 2008 to 2009 global trade fell by 15%, surpassing the fall in real-world GDP (see Baldwin, 2009; Alessandria, Kaboski, & Midrigan, 2010; Bems, Johnson, & Yi, 2013).
3 As a WTO report shows, in 2016 "of the 2,835 trade-restrictive measures, including trade remedies, recorded for WTO Members since 2008 by this exercise, only 708, or 25%, had been removed by mid-May 2016."
4 WTO, *Report to the TPRB from the Director-General on Trade-Related Developments*, July 4, 2016, www.wto.org/english/news_e/news16e/trdev22jul16e.htm.
5 Different from PTAs, which undoubtedly have fueled the diffusion of trade liberalization, GVCs can be seen as a result of trade liberalization and not a cause of it
6 Keynote speech by President Xi Jinping at opening ceremony of First China International Import Expo, www.xinhuanet.com/english/2018-11/05/c_137583815.htm; see also BBC, Xi Jinping pledges to cut Chinese import tariffs, November 5, 2018, www.bbc.com/news/business-46093478.
7 In a June 2020 report about the effects of COVID-19 on trade, the WTO suggests that the collapse in trade now could be far bigger than in response to the 2008 financial crisis. See WTO (2020), *Trade Falls Steeply in First Half of 2020*, www.wto.org/english/news_e/pres20_e/pr858_e.htm, and "Trade Falls Steeply in First Half of 2020," *Financial Times*, June 23, 2020, www.ft.com/content/e27b0c0c-1893-479b-9ea3-27a81c2506c9?.
8 For more information about firms' trade policy, see Kim, I. S., & Osgood, I. (2019) and Kim, I. S. (2017).
9 Author's interview with a research economist with the WTO, July 2020.
10 G20 members are Argentina, Australia, Brazil, Canada, China, the European Union, France, Germany, India, Indonesia, Italy, Japan, Korea, the Republic of Mexico, the Russian Federation, Saudi Arabia, South Africa, Turkey, the United Kingdom, and the United States.
11 For a list of the 47 LDCs, see: UNCTAD, https://unctad.org/en/Pages/ALDC/Least%20Developed%20Countries/LDCs.aspx.
12 In this section I present a detailed explanation for each type of measure.
13 For more details about how G20 economies' measures have affected LDCs exports, see: https://bit.ly/3959qCa

14 United Nations Statistics Division, Central Product Classification (CPC), https://unstats.un.org/unsd/classifications/unsdclassifications/cpcv21.pdf.
15 In this book, I use the terms "trade policy," "commercial policy," and "international trade policy" interchangeably.
16 OAS SICE, *Foreign Trade System Dictionary of Trade Terms*, www.sice.oas.org/Dictionary/TNTM_e.asp#TNTM.
17 More information on the UN MAST Group's classification of non-tariff measures can be found at: https://unctad.org/en/Pages/DITC/Trade-Analysis/Non-Tariff-Measures/MAST-Group-on-NTMs.aspx.
18 UNCTAD, Classification of NTMs, https://unctad.org/en/Pages/DITC/Trade-Analysis/Non-Tariff-Measures/NTMs-Classification.aspx.
19 Transparency in Trade Initiative (TNT), *Improving Transparency in Trade*, www.tntdata.org/about_tnt.html.
20 Global Trade Alert, www.globaltradealert.org/.
21 In my quantitative analysis, this categorization is used as a dummy variable (1 when it is nontransparent, and 0 when it is transparent).
22 For a more detailed analysis of each instrument, see Evenett & Fritz (2017), pp. 37–41.
23 In this book, I use the terms "response" and "retaliation" interchangeably.
24 WTO, *Regional Trade Agreements*, www.wto.org/english/tratop_e/region_e/region_e.htm.
25 For other studies on why the term "PTA" is preferred over the term "RTA," see, for instance, Hofmann et al. (2019) and Ruta (2017).
26 WTO, *Database on Preferential Trade Arrangements*, http://ptadb.wto.org/?lang=1 and Regional Trade Agreements' Dataset, http://rtais.wto.org/UI/PublicMaintainRTAHome.aspx.
27 WTO, *Article XXIV: Territorial Application, Frontier Traffic, Customs Unions, and Free-Trade Areas*, www.wto.org/english/tratop_e/region_e/region_art24_e.htm.
28 WTO, *What Is the WTO?*, ‹www.wto.org/english/thewto_e/whatis_e/whatis_e.htm›.
29 For an extended analysis of the main functions of the WTO, see Albertoni (2019).
30 GATT (1947), Article I, ‹www.wto.org/SPANISH/DOCS_S/LEGAL_S/gatt47_01_s.htm#articlei›.
31 See, WTO's Glossary, *Free Trade Area*, ‹www.wto.org/english/thewto_e/glossary_e/glossary_e.html› (Accessed Feb, 2020).
32 GATT (1947), Article XXIV, ‹www.wto.org/english/tratop_e/region_e/regatt_e.htm›. For more information about regulatory competition or regulatory harmonization, see Sykes, A. O. (2000, 1999).
33 See Department of Foreign Relations and Trade Australia (2004), *Negociando Acuerdos de Libre Comercio: Una Guía*, ‹www.oas.org/dsd/Tool-kit/Documentosspa/ModuloV/Goode%20Chapter%203%20Reading.pdf›.
34 WTO, *Regional Trade Agreements*, www.wto.org/english/tratop_e/region_e/region_e.htm.
35 To see how this "Wave of Regionalism" evolved in the Middle East and North Africa, see Nugent & Hakimian (2003).
36 Design of Trade Agreements Database, www.designoftradeagreements.org/project-description/.
37 A concept normally related to intermediate good is "intra-industry trade" (IIT), which is a more general way of defining trade within similar industries. The

28 *Trade protectionism in an uncertain global economy*

    Organization for Economic Cooperation and Development (2005) defines IIT as "the trade in similar products ('horizontal trade') with differentiated varieties (e.g. cars of a similar class and price range), and trade in 'vertically differentiated' products distinguished by quality and price (e.g. exports of high-quality clothing and imports of lower-quality clothing)." There could be intra-industry trade in both intermediate and final goods. While IIT can apply to different stages of a good, intermediate goods are normally considered to measure GVCs. See Lüthje (2001) and Peterson & Thies (2015) for studies on intra-industry trade (IIT) and intermediate goods.

38 Bems, Rudolfs Robert Johnson, Kei-Mu Yi (2009), The collapse of global trade: Update on the role of vertical linkages, VoxEU CERP Policy Portal: https://voxeu.org/article/collapse-global-trade-update-role-vertical-linkages.

39 Author's interview with an employee of the University of Chile, April 2020.

40 For instance, if we consider the total number of measures implemented by the United States and China toward Argentina, Brazil, and Mexico, the United States seems to be (disproportionately) more protectionist than China. However, when we consider the actual effect of those measures, the story changes substantially. Indeed, when considering the average share of exports between 2009 and 2017 affected in Argentina, Brazil, and Mexico by protectionist measures implemented by China and the United States, the former is more protectionist than the latter. Apart from being an interesting descriptive finding, this also highlights the relevance of focusing on the effect of protectionist measures rather than just the aggregate number of measures implemented.

41 As will be explained in the following chapters, the database presented in this book combines data from Global Trade Alerts (GTA), the BACI-CEPII database, the Classification Harmonized System (HS), and Broad Economic Categories (BEC). The development of this new dataset at the monthly and the trimester level is part of a joint project with George Gerald Vega, from the USC Center for Applied Network Analysis (CANA).

42 G20, *What Is the G20?* https://g20.org/en/about/Pages/whatis.aspx.

43 Moody's Analytics (2018) estimates the impact of the "Trump Trade War" during 2018–20 and offers different scenarios. Interestingly, under the scenario of 25% tariffs on all Sino–US trade and other "qualitative" actions taken by China against American firms operating there, their results show that protectionism reduces GDP growth from second quarter 2018 to second quarter 2020 in Argentina, Brazil, and Mexico in very different ways: in Argentina, GDP growth is reduced by more than 0.6%, in Brazil 0.3% to 0.6%, and in Mexico less than 0.3%. See Moody's Analytics (2018), *Trump Trade War*, www.moodysanalytics.com/-/media/article/2018/trump-trade-war.pdf. For a review of 17 recent studies on the form and consequences of contemporary trade conflict, see: Evenett & Fritz (2018).

44 Google Trends Data, https://trends.google.com/trends/?geo=US.

45 Altman and Bastian (2019) show that since March 2018, when President Donald Trump announced new steel and aluminum tariffs against China, Google searches for "trade war" spiked to 100, which is the peak popularity in Google searches.

46 In main academic journals of economics, for instance, we see a similar scenario: between 2008 and 2019, there are 11 articles about "trade protectionism" in the *American Economic Review*, and 27 articles in the *Economic Journal*.

47 The index is constructed by using "Economist Intelligence Unit (EIU) Country Reports" to measure uncertainty related to trade for each of 143 countries, on a quarterly basis, from 1996 onward. Data presented is weight averaged. The font in blue indicates the tariff measure taken, and the font in black indicates the narrative of the WTU index. The WTU index is computed by counting the frequency of uncertain words (or the variant) that are near the following words: protectionism, North American Free Trade Agreement (NAFTA), tariff, trade, United Nations Conference on Trade and Development (UNCTAD), and World Trade Organization (WTO). The WUI is then normalized by the total number of words and rescaled by multiplying by 100,000. A higher number means higher trade uncertainty and vice versa. For more information about this index, visit: https://voxeu.org/article/trade-uncertainty-rising-and-can-harm-global-economy.

2 A historical overview of twenty-first-century protectionism
How did we arrive at this point?

2.1 Introduction

This chapter does not attempt to offer an extensive historical overview of trade policy, which has been done masterfully by other scholars (e.g., Irwin, 1998; Bordo, Eichengreen, & Irwin, 1999; Wilkinson, 2006; Canto, 1983; Bhagwati, 1991, 2003; Baldwin, 1988). Instead, my goal is to situate this book in its proper historical context by analyzing the main trade policy milestones of the twenty-first century. This chapter begins with the winding road of trade liberalization since World War II, briefly tracing how we arrived from the early stages of the Bretton Woods System to the current moment of stagnation of the multilateral system and rising protectionism. I then turn to three key events to understand the current new reality: China's accession to the WTO in 2001, the GFC of 2008–09, and the current trade war between the United States and China. I conclude with some final comments on the relevance of my research from a historical perspective.[1]

2.2 The winding road of the world trade system since World War II

The rise of protectionism in the 1930s was believed to be one of the primary causes of World War II (WWII), and global leaders were anxious to prevent this from happening again. As a result, they convened in Bretton Woods, New Hampshire, in 1944 to discuss the need for international institutions to lend order to the world economy. A year later, the majority of these countries reconvened to discuss the establishment of a new International Trade Organization (ITO), but their plan never came to fruition due to isolationist politics in the United States, with the ITO bill never sent by President Harry S. Truman to Congress for final approval. Thus, the lack of support from the United States was the final nail in the ITO coffin. In its place, the General Agreement on Trade and Tariffs (GATT) became the de facto Bretton Woods institution, under which international trade was liberalized in the post-WWII era. Designed solely to govern trade in goods, the GATT was limited in the scope of control it could exert over trade policy.

The GATT's first meeting, held in Geneva in 1947, resulted in the reduction of tariffs and created steps toward the liberalization of global trade. The Cold War incentivized the United States to push its democratic agenda, including liberal trade policies, on a global scale as the liberalization of trade continued through the economic growth of the 1950s and 1960s. In the 1970s, however, economic decline and the emergence of the East Asian newly industrializing economies (NICs) triggered a return to protectionism. Since the GATT restricted the use of tariffs, many countries resorted to nontariff barriers (e.g., quotas, subsidies). The 1982 ministerial meetings of the GATT reached a nadir in its history. It was the first time since WWII that there was a decrease in international trade, which highlighted the shortcomings of the trading system as the number of GATT members increased and the global economy grew more complex. Global leaders became aware of the need for a more effective trade organization, one that would be broader in scope and administrative capability (Grant & Kelly, 2005). The United States led the way in pushing for free trade ideology, heavily influenced by the leadership and economic values of the Ronald Reagan and George H. W. Bush administrations.

The eighth GATT Round in 1986, also known as the Uruguay Round, underscored the need to organize and promote liberalization efforts for an economy moving into the twenty-first century. The inclusion of agribusiness, services, intellectual property, and trade-related investment were discussed, and it became clear that an agreement made solely for goods had become obsolete. The Uruguay Round did not conclude until 1995.[2] During this lengthy session, leaders of the United States, Canada, Japan, and the EU discussed creating an international trade organization to more effectively cover global trade flows not included in the original GATT.

The WTO, officially founded in 1995, diverged from the GATT in fundamental ways in order to address some of the latter's weaknesses. Most importantly, new and binding procedures for settling disputes were implemented, as a lack of such procedures had been a major downfall of the GATT. Especially contentious issues in the Uruguay Round—such as agriculture, intellectual property (IP), and services—were also incorporated into the WTO. In contrast with the provisional nature of the GATT, everything decided upon within the WTO was mandatory for participating nations. By 2003, 146 countries were members of the WTO, and it had dealt with 298 cases.

While the WTO's structure increased efficiency in settling disputes and upholding rules over trade policy, its creation also raised concerns about national sovereignty. Many anti-globalists feared the implications of the WTO and wanted to see its collapse. The first ministerial conference of the WTO was held in Singapore in 1996. At this round, working groups were established around four main issues, which came to be known as the "Singapore Issues." These were transparency in government, trade facilitation, trade-related investment, and competition policy. Although most of these issues were opposed by developing countries, the more powerful bloc of developed nations insisted that any new negotiations must include the "Singapore Issues."

After the Singapore meeting in 1996, the 1999 Seattle ministerial conference, which took place amid massive anti-globalization protests, marked an important milestone for the WTO. With over 40,000 protesters angered by environmental degradation and a lack of labor rights, the WTO's poor incorporation of developing nations only exacerbated this ire. The Seattle meeting was a patent failure. Up to this point, negotiations had followed a "green room" setup, where a few key G7 decision-makers would be in that room negotiating, instead of all WTO member countries. This exclusion of developing nations made decisions less effective, and many saw this as a violation of the multilateral norms upon which the WTO had been founded (Grant & Kelly, 2005; Hopewell, 2016; Jones, 2015). Massive anti-WTO social movements and the developing countries themselves began demanding more transparent and inclusive styles of negotiation (Casey-Sawicki, 2018).

After the Seattle debacle, and without sufficiently addressing those earlier demands, a WTO ministerial was held in Doha, Qatar, in November 2001, and the ninth negotiation round of the GATT/WTO was officially launched. The main objective was to involve developing countries more authentically in global trade negotiations. Doha presented a much less feasible destination for 40,000 protesters than Seattle, especially in the wake of the 9/11 terrorist attacks on the United States. This meeting was born into the Doha Development Round, which sought to address issues on the "old" (agriculture, NTMs, and the market access for manufactured exports from South to North) and "new" (intellectual property rights, services, investment) trade agendas. Developing countries also had the opportunity to discuss the difficulties they had in implementing earlier commitments made under the Uruguay Round (Grant & Kelly, 2005). The targeted completion date of the Doha Round was 2005; however, by 2006, the negotiations were suspended, and the round has not ended to date. Many developing countries had been under the impression that the Doha Round would right previously wrongs around transparency and inclusiveness. They were hoping to see more favorable decisions made regarding market access for agriculture and industrial goods. Yet, the United States and the EU refused to offer significant concessions on both (Bhagwati, Krishna, & Panagariya, 2016). The stagnation of the Doha Round was accompanied by (and in part a consequence of) important events in the multilateral system. One was the decreasing US support of multilateralism and especially of the international trading system over time, something that Allee (2012) attributed to three factors:

> the decline in U.S. hegemony; the role of ideas, and, particularly, the change from the free trade mentality to one that focuses more on the unfair practices of other nations; and the role of domestic interest groups, and, particularly, the increasing effectiveness of import-competing interests.
>
> (p. 235)

The decreasing support of developed nations to the international trading system leads developing countries to have a more active role in the defense of the system. Countries such as Brazil, Russia, India, China, and South Africa (BRICS) have become important supporters of a more balanced agenda between the developing and the developed world. However, as Vickers (2012) said, while these emerging economies "show greater activism in the organization, activism does not equate with leadership" (p. 254). In that sense, it is key to understand the role the G20 developing nations' group (different from the G20 of developed economies) played in the Doha Round, and the high-profile role played by Brazil and India especially.[3] The other two emerging economies with an increasing role in the international trading system, Russia and China, were in different circumstances than those of Brazil and India. Russia did not join the WTO until 2012, and China was concentrating on implementing its 2001 accession commitments. The increasing role of these non-central economies is not only explained by their economic growth, but also their very active trade and investment relations, especially with East Asian countries, which challenge the centralized management of the world trading system by central economies. As Vickers (2012, p. 256) has cautioned, this "shift of systematic influence" signaled a drastic restructuring of the international economic order, and it reflected a "balance of power [that is] more multipolar, even multicultural."

A third significant ministerial conference, albeit short-lived, met in Cancun, Mexico, and erupted in violence.[4] Ministerial conferences held in Hong Kong in 2005 and Geneva in 2008 ended in similar stalemates. The developing nations tried to be involved in the negotiations and advocated for their interests, but gridlock between them and the developed countries prevented much from getting done. Within the context of these aforementioned events, there are at least two relevant pieces of evidence that show how the global trading system is currently in the midst of profound changes: one is the "mega-regional agreements" that facilitate easier consensus by omitting some countries, and the other is the "regionalization and bilateralization of trade," which has led to more RTAs. Moreover, the 2008–09 GFC likely contributed to the "second wave" of protectionism, or the "protectionism resurrection." For example, the WTO has increased restrictive measures by 11% between 2008 and 2016 (Albertoni, 2018, pp. 156–7).[5]

Perhaps most absent in the Doha Round was sound US leadership. In fact, the early 2000s marked the beginning of mini-trade wars by the United States. In 2002, for example, President George W. Bush created temporary tariffs on steel imports. The EU retaliated by placing tariffs on US goods such as Florida oranges and American-made cars. The WTO found that these actions by the United States were in violation with its rules, and they ended 18 months after implementation.

2.3 China's accession to the World Trade Organization in 2001

The most singularly important event in terms of trade policy dynamics during the twenty-first century was China's accession to the WTO in December 2001.

Trade policy experts had downplayed the effect of China's WTO accession because the United States had granted China MFN status as far back as the 1980s (Autor, Dorn, & Hanson, 2016).[6] Yet, studies on the impacts conducted a few years after this occurred demonstrate that China has been the main beneficiary, including "US$31 billion a year from trade reforms in preparation for accession and additional gains of $10 billion a year from reforms after accession" (Ianchovichina & Martin, 2004, p. 3). In addition, among China's commitments in its accession to the WTO were the following: reforming its system of tariffs and quotas to ease the circulation of commodities, changing its practice of state trading to encourage volume control, and introducing critical service sectors, including "telecommunications, distribution, banking, insurance, asset management, and securities to foreign direct investment" (Lardy, 2001). More specifically, Lardy (2001, p. 11) argues that

> the protocol governing its accession sets forth China's commitment to abide by international standards in the protection of intellectual property and to accept the use by its trading partners of a number of unusual mechanisms that could be used to reduce the flow of Chinese goods into foreign markets.[7]

China's accession to the global trading system was also an institutional signal to the rest of the world about its intention to compete under the same rules. In this regard, Lardy (2001) notes that being part of the WTO "impel[s] China to be accountable to an internationally agreed set of rules and bind them to wide-ranging economic and systemic changes in order to meet the commitments they have agreed to undertake as a part of WTO accession."[8] However, China has evaded full compliance with its commitments, and its current trade tensions with the United States have triggered a debate about whether letting China into the WTO was a mistake. Levy (2018) reminds us that during the 15 years of negotiations leading up to China's accession, WTO country members had set several conditions for China's admission, which "involved concessions such as dropping tariffs on many categories of goods, opening up agricultural trade, and allowing in foreign service providers. In contrast, the United States did not need to make any new market-opening concessions."[9]

Autor, Dorn, and Hanson (2016) see China's accession to the WTO as one of the three "China shocks" to the global economy. The first shock occurred in the 1980s and 1990s with the economic opening of China and the takeoff of India's growth, which expanded production based on low-skilled labor. According to Reisen and Stemmer (2018), the second "China shock" spans the time of its accession to the WTO in 2001 up to the 2008–09 GFC, and is based on the "pervasive convergence of poor countries largely due to increasingly China-centric growth and higher raw material prices."[10] The third shock is still underway and started with the 2008–09 GFC. This period has seen a reversal of previous trends "as China is transforming its production and trade patterns toward consumption, away from investment and intermediate trade."[11]

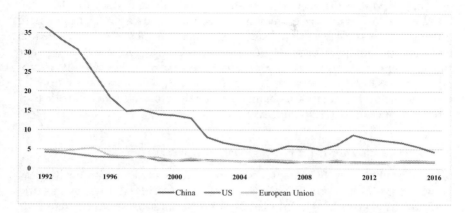

Figure 2.1 The evolution of tariff rates for primary products and manufactured goods imposed by China, the United States, and the EU. Tariff rate, applied, weighted mean, manufactured products (%).

Source: Author's creation based on World Development Indicators.

According to the World Bank (2020a), since its accession to the WTO, China has reduced tariff rates considerably for both primary and manufactured products thereafter. While China's average tariff rate for primary products five years before its accession to the WTO (1996–2000) was 19%, the average was 8% between 2001 and 2006.[12] For manufactured products, the averages were 15% and 7% respectively, before and after the accession. Since the GFC, China's tariff rate reductions have approximated average tariff rates in the United States and the EU (Figure 2.1).

Finally, based on UNCTAD's Non-Tariff Measures dataset,[13] China increased NTMs after its accession to the WTO. While China had an average of 244 NTMs five years before its accession to the WTO (1996–2000), this average jumped to 1,582 between 2001 and 2006.[14] These barriers have made China the "country notifying the second largest number of technical barriers to trade (TBTs)," just after the United States. This is in line with Evenett and Fritz (2018), who have shown that nowadays many countries are increasingly utilizing nontransparent policy instruments (NTMs or "murky" protectionism) as a main trade policy instrument. While China agreed to limit tariffs when it joined the WTO, its trade policy tools simply took on a new form. Garred (2018) found that China has also influenced international trade through export restrictions and value-added tax rebates. This international phenomenon of utilizing various trade policy tools suggests that today's trade war is nothing new to global trade, but rather "the latest example of an ongoing battle whose skirmishes have taken many forms" (Garred, 2019).[15]

Much of Donald Trump's rhetoric throughout his candidacy for the presidency in 2016 framed his protectionist trade policy as a direct response to other global players who were "stealing" American jobs. However, research has found that support for protectionism was not due to globalization or trade shocks. There was not a significant correlation between households in economic distress and support for Trump. Instead, those voters who supported his policies felt the threat of a changing social dynamic at home, and a loss of US dominance abroad (Noland, 2019).

2.4 Global trade after the 2008–09 global financial crisis

Since the 2008–09 GFC, many countries have erected new trade barriers. However, traditional protectionist measures (e.g., tariffs) did not rise as dramatically as expected.[16] New trade policy tools that are less transparent have taken their place. Niu et al. (2018) show that although average tariff rates have fallen since the GFC, there has been a sharp increase in the number of NTMs. These tend to be more restrictive and are clustered in the form of technical barriers to trade as well as sanitary and phytosanitary standards, especially in Central Asia, North America, South Asia, and Europe.[17] Again, this contrasts sharply with global trends over the past 50 years, which saw a sustained opening of national markets. Since 2009, in contrast, G20 governments implemented restrictive measures on 9,041 occasions (Evenett & Fritz, 2018, p. 6).[18] These are all examples of the rise of protectionism during the last decade. Recent studies have analyzed the impact that the 2008 financial crisis had on international trade policy instruments. Countries have overwhelmingly moved toward protectionist policies, with 70% of world trade impacted by these interventions (Evenett, 2019).

While the global crisis induces more restrictive measures, nearly all of the policies implemented post-2008 have fallen within the boundaries of WTO rules. NTMs are more complex, harder to detect, and have "taken over the center stage of trade policy instruments" (UNCTAD, 2010, p. xiii). They also have greater power in influencing modern problems, such as environmental guidelines for the protection of firms and consumers. The counterproductive use of NTMs has gripped the attention of international agencies, which are now working to define, collect information on, and analyze this misappropriation of modern trade policy instruments. These new dynamics of trade protectionism after the GFC will be elaborated upon in the descriptive chapter (3) of this book.

2.5 Bilateral tensions between the United States and China in the present and the past

Since 2016, the United States has been leading trade wars with the world on multiple fronts. Yet, signs of protectionist tension can be found as far back as 2009 during the Obama administration. The United States, for example, limited the number of Mexican trucking firms that could operate within specific areas of the country. At the same time, Barack Obama "softened his tough rhetoric on free trade, warning repeatedly against tit-for-tat protectionism in the midst of an economic crisis" (Alexander & Soukup, 2010, p. 324).[19] Concrete demands for protectionist policies under Trump began with requests filed by the solar panel and washing machine industry in 2017. The US International Trade Commission quickly discovered that foreign imports were harming domestic businesses, and the Trump administration imposed tariffs on solar panels and washing machines in January 2018. This affected approximately $8.5 billion in solar panel imports and $1.9 billion worth of washing machines, largely from China. China countered with tariffs on soybean imports from the United States shortly thereafter, while Korea and China filed WTO disputes against the United States.

The question here is how current trade tensions might differ from previous ones. What explains the length and depth of the current trade slump experienced in the wake of the 2008–09 GFC? Trade tensions or protectionist trends caused by economic shocks that spur the adoption of beggar-thy-neighbor measures are not new in economic history. But why might this time be different from previous trade disputes and protectionist spirals in history? Let us first revisit some similar situations in economic history, which may prove illuminating on the state of protectionism today.

In 1929, when the United States passed the Smoot–Hawley Trade Act, raising tariffs by 60% for more than 3,000 products, at least 60 other nations implemented retaliatory measures against the United States. This almost doubled the world's average level of trade protection and world trade contracted (Boffa & Olarreaga, 2012). Between 1929 and 1933, total global trade decreased by 25% (Canto, 1983), and according to Irwin (1998), 70% of that global trade reduction could be attributed to the Smoot–Hawley tariff and the subsequent retaliatory measures it invoked. However, in 1934, the United States sought to promote economic recovery by reducing tariffs, and the US Congress passed the Reciprocal Trade Agreement Act, which reduced these tariffs (Irwin, 1998). Under the 1934 Trade Act, the executive took command of trade negotiations and the United States signed bilateral trade agreements with 20 countries. Tariffs were eventually lowered to 50% of the rates established by the Smoot–Hawley Act in 1929 (Canto, 1983).

Under section 301 of the 1974 Tariff and Trade Act and the 1988 Omnibus Trade and Competitiveness Act, the US government demonstrated "increased willingness to threaten retaliation against protected foreign markets" (Gould & Woodbridge, 1998, p. 116). During this time (late 1980s and early 1990s), a main objective was to induce macroeconomic reforms and trade opening in Japan. In 1993, President Bill Clinton said, "I am particularly concerned about Japan's growing global current account and trade surpluses and deeply concerned about the inadequate market access for American firms, products, and investors in Japan."[20] This is not too far from what we hear nowadays about China's current account surplus and trade practices. During the 1990s, through the use of various trade and non-trade mechanisms (e.g., antidumping duties and the use of countervailing sanctions), the United States threatened to implement protectionist measures against Korea, Japan, and European countries, seeking to improve US access to these markets (Gould & Woodbridge, 1998). Evenett and Fritz (2018) identify at least three main differences between the 1980s–1990s trade tensions (mostly between the United States and Japan) and current Sino–US trade disputes: Japan is not only a "military ally" of the United States, but the country also poses less of a threat both demographically and economically than China does. Moreover, unlike Japan, China has acted as "the host to the quantum of American foreign investment," which consequently led to "sustained criticism of discriminating against foreign multinationals inside its borders" (p. 116).

It important to make a distinction between the type of protectionism originated by the GFC and that originated by the Trump administration. In an interview I had with a Chilean lawyer and trade negotiator, he said:

> The surge in protectionism is a reality; first as a result of the 2008–09 crisis and later in Trumpian world. But perhaps such protectionism is reduced to certain sectors (steel, aluminum, are examples) and not a widespread phenomenon. Until the Trumpian world, a great deal of protectionism took place as a result of subsidization and trade remedies (particularly antidumping), which may indicate that the appeals for protection were presented as either "I'm too big/strategic to fail" or "It's about fairness not about protectionism."[21]

Beyond the bilateral differences between previous and current trade tensions, there are also major global factors that may be impacting the long-term consequences of current trade disputes and protectionist dynamics. Unlike what happened in the 1980s and 1990s, the high level of trade interdependence through GVCs and PTAs render seemingly bilateral trade conflicts far from solely bilateral; possible systemic consequences can be key explanatory variables in explaining why the current trade recovery is still relatively anemic compared to recovery from previous global trade collapses.[22] As Lamy (2013) states, one of the major changes we see nowadays is the level of interdependency in trade:

> Almost 60 percent of trade in goods is now in intermediates [...] An important consequence of the integration of production networks is that imports matter as much as exports when it comes to contributing to job creation and to economic growth. In 1990, the import content of exports was 20 percent; in 2010, it was 40 percent, and it is expected to be around 60 percent in 2030. This is why enacting protectionist measures in the modern world to protect jobs, such as raising import barriers, can have an inverse reaction in economies that are increasingly reliant on imports to complete their exports.[23]

2.5.1 US–China trade tensions step by step

The US–China trade war has been mounting since Trump hit the campaign trail in 2016. Trump spoke frequently of the US trade deficit, which has been the world's largest since 1975. His move toward protectionism, and specifically policies pointed toward China, was supposed to improve national well-being, yet experts, economic theory, and history have all proved that trade wars will only cause trouble (Thoms, 2019; WEF, 2019). Import tariffs bring economic losses to countries, producers, and consumers (Crowley, 2019), and it is estimated that the US trade war has already lowered gross domestic product (GDP) by 0.6% (Amadeo, 2019). As studies have shown, most of these price increases are passed on to American consumers and not offset by production benefits. At the start of 2018, US tariffs on Chinese imports were 3.1%, while Chinese tariffs on US exports were 8%. In January of 2020, those rates stood at around 23.8% and 25.1%, respectively (Bown & Kolb, 2019). However, in December 2019, China and the United States agreed to pause the tensions as part of a compromise that "requires structural reforms and other changes to China's economic and trade regime in the areas of intellectual property, technology transfer, agriculture, financial services, and currency and foreign exchange."[24]

Trump's legal authority to impose the first round of tariffs came from Section 301 of the US Trade Act of 1974, which states that the president can impose tariffs if the US International Trade Commission finds that imports are causing harm to an industry. However, Section 201 has rarely been used in recent history. The last use was in 2001 when George W. Bush imposed steel tariffs. Trump once again utilized a rarely used section of trade policy, this time, Section 232 of the Trade Expansion Act of 1962, to impose further tariffs. In April of 2017, he instructed the commerce secretary to investigate the steel industry, and by March 2018 he imposed steel tariffs. These tariffs temporarily exempted several countries, including Mexico, Canada, Brazil, Australia, Korea, and the EU. China retaliated shortly after by imposing tariffs on $2.4 billion worth of US goods, which closely matches the $2.8 billion that was affected by the steel tariffs. The steel tariffs continued to follow a tit-for-tat strategy, with the United States raising them for certain countries and those countries then retaliating. Although the tariffs were successful in creating US jobs, they came at a high cost. Each of the 8,700 jobs costs about $650,000 to create. Poor, developing countries were hit the hardest by these tariffs, experiencing a 12% decline in steel exports to the United States and a 15.5% decrease in revenue (Bown & Kolb, 2019). Under Trump's leadership, the United States continued to impose new tariffs throughout 2018 and 2019 to protect industries such as automotive, consumer goods, intermediate goods, and technology. Unsurprisingly, these actions have sparked retaliation from countries on the receiving end, and this explains the current trade war. The mounting tariffs have also done more to deepen the US trade deficit, rather than close it. The deficit reached a 10-year high of $621 billion in 2018, and economists believe that these tariffs have contributed to this gap by hindering economic growth rates for China and Europe.

A trade war between the two largest countries in the global economy also creates a level of uncertainty that has made international leaders uneasy. The role of the dollar-based payment system as the backbone of global commerce also gives America additional ways of influencing trade, which "has been weaponized" (*The Economist*, 2019, p. 13). For instance, a Chinese technology company was banned from doing business with America, which effectively isolated it from the global financial system. As foreign trust in the Federal Reserve declines, global business leaders are looking for alternatives in a "post-American era" (*The Economist*, 2019, p. 14).

While analyzing the US–China trade war can provide valuable insights, it is important to view this in the context of the global trading environment. Evenett (2019) argues that the energy spent on bilateral trade fights may be disproportionate to their actual effect on the global economy. For example, just 2.6% of traded goods have been affected by these bilateral disputes, and US–China trade accounts for only 4.4% of traded goods. Meanwhile, 16.5% of goods are impacted by tariffs of any nature, and 27.2% of world trade is affected by foreign firms trying to compete with subsidized domestic producers.[25] Most of the goods traded globally are influenced by more than a bilateral trade dispute, and this fact should not be overstated by the attention that something like the US–China trade war garners.

2.6 Final comments on twenty-first-century protectionism from a historical perspective

The question raised by this historical review is, to what extent will protectionism be the new norm? Blaming foreign influences for domestic distress is common practice for American politicians, which makes free trade an easy target during election season (Irwin, 2016). Even Democratic US officials, such as Hillary Clinton and Barack Obama, voiced concerns about free trade agreements. Trump claimed his protectionist policies would help Americans, but instead these reckless US actions risked triggering a global trade war that would have adverse effects on all countries (Irwin, 2017). The trade war has already brought an annual loss of $68.6 billion to US producers and consumers, and an aggregate loss of $7.8 billion to the US economy (Fajgelbaum et al., 2019).

In the past decade, "murky" trade policies have further complicated this issue. As countries continue to move toward less transparent instruments, the ways in which we have historically measured their impact are becoming outdated. The opaque nature of those policies implemented over the past decade is a key element to be considered. As Evenett (2019) has said, "for every tariff hike this year, more than 3 trade-distorting subsidies have been imposed. Perspective needed in judging 2019 global trade policy dynamics—US-China is not the only game in town."[26] Interestingly, in 2019, 618 new harmful trade measures were implemented worldwide, with 168 of them corresponding to China and the United States (GTA, 2019).

Yet, these nontransparent trade policies are not getting the media or academic attention needed to properly understand their effects (Evenett, 2019). Most research focuses on tariffs, as we have the most data on these measures, rather than looking at ways in which global trade policy is evolving. As mentioned before in Chapter 1, this lack of appropriate data and research leads to "inadequate scrutiny bias" among leading scholars. They maintain that global trade was unaltered by the financial crisis, yet more comprehensive research on trade distortions could disprove this viewpoint (Evenett, 2019).

This increasingly murky context explains why there is uncertainty about international trade across the globe. As the new Index of Trade Uncertainty shows, it is "rising sharply, having been stable at low levels for about 20 years."[27] This quickly increased in quarter three of 2018, the same time when the US–China tariff war launched from Washington, DC. This index movement has been tracking US–China tensions closely. When officials announced that they were halting tariff escalations at the G20 summit in the fourth quarter of 2018, the index went back down. It then spiked again when China implemented several tariffs on US goods in March 2019. As the world's largest economies, the US–China disputes set trends and frame how foreign officials view the global trade environment. Analysts have cautioned that the trade war is harming the global economy, and several have come together to urge China and the United States to find common ground.[28] Both governments have promised trade talks, yet coming to an agreement will prove to be difficult, especially since the United States has been unclear about what it wants out of these negotiations. Given the lack of communication regarding the two parties' interests, China may likely struggle to formulate a proposal that will be accepted by US negotiators (Evenett, 2019).

Notes

1 This chapter is an extended version of Albertoni, N. (2021). A historical overview of the 21st-century protectionism. *Latin American Journal of Trade Policy*, 4(10), 5–23.
2 For more information about the Uruguay Round, visit: www.wto.org/english/thewto_e/minist_e/min98_e/slide_e/ur.htm.
3 The G20 is a coalition of developing countries "pressing for ambitious reforms of agriculture in developed countries with some flexibility for developing countries." See *Groups in the WTO*, www.wto.org/english/tratop_e/dda_e/negotiating_groups_e.pdf.
4 For more about this ministerial conference in Cancún, visit: www.wto.org/english/thewto_e/minist_e/min03_e/min03_e.htm.
5 As of January 17, 2020, 303 RTAs were in force. See World Trade Organization, "Regional Trade Agreements" [online]. www.wto.org/english/tratop_e/region_e/region_e.htm#facts

42 A historical overview of twenty-first-century protectionism

6 Studies have shown that the possibility of a return to non-MFN tariffs, which averaged 37.0% in the late 1990s and compared to average MFN tariffs of only 3.4% in those years (Pierce & Schott, 2016), "dissuaded Chinese firms from investing in exporting to the U.S. WTO accession removed this uncertainty and encouraged China-U.S. trade" (Autor, Dorn, & Hanson, 2016, p. 11). Also see R. Salam (2018, June). Normalizing trade relations with China was a mistake. *The Atlantic*, www.theatlantic.com/ideas/archive/2018/06/normalizing-trade-relations-with-china-was-a-mistake/562403/.

7 N. R. Lardy. (2001). Issues in China's WTO Accession. *Brookings Institute*. (May 9, 2001). www.brookings.edu/testimonies/issues-in-chinas-wto-accession/.

8 N. R. Lardy (2001). Issues in China's WTO Accession. *Brookings Institute*. (May 9, 2001). www.brookings.edu/testimonies/issues-in-chinas-wto-accession/.

9 P. Levy (2018, April 2). Was Letting China into the WTO a Mistake? *Foreign Affairs*. www.foreignaffairs.com/articles/china/2018-04-02/was-letting-china-wto-mistake.

10 H. Reisen & M. Stemmer (2018). The three acts of the "China Shock." *Shifting Wealth Blog*. http://shiftingwealth.blogspot.com/2018/04/the-three-acts-of-china-shock.html.

11 H. Reisen & M. Stemmer (2018). *The three acts of the "China Shock."* Shifting Wealth Blog. http://shiftingwealth.blogspot.com/2018/04/the-three-acts-of-china-shock.html.

12 *World Bank Open Data*, https://data.worldbank.org/

13 Examples of NTMs are sanitary and phytosanitary measures, technical barriers, quantity control guidelines, and price controls. See United Nations Conference on Trade and Development (UNCTAD), *Non-Tariff Measures Data*, https://trains.unctad.org/Forms/TableView.aspx?mode=modify&action=search.

14 US average NTMs initiated by the United States five years before China's accession to the WTO (1996–2000) were 539. Between 2001 and 2006, this same figure for the United States was 328. See UNCTAD, *Non-Tariff Measures Data*, https://trains.unctad.org/Forms/TableView.aspx?mode=modify&action=search.

15 J. Garred (2019). The persistence of trade policy beyond import tariffs. VoxEU. CEPR.org, July 9, https://voxeu.org/article/persistence-trade-policy-beyond-import-tariffs.

16 See D. Desilver. (2018). *U.S. Tariffs Are among the Lowest in the World—and in the Nation's History*. March 22, Pew Research. www.pewresearch.org/fact-tank/2018/03/22/u-s-tariffs-are-among-the-lowest-in-the-world-and-in-the-nations-history/.

17 An example of a technical barrier to trade is a safety standard for manufactured goods. Sanitary/phytosanitary measures concern safety standards for food or animals.

18 When we refer to restrictive measures, we are talking about any kind of protectionist policy instrument that can take the form of a tariff or an NTM under the classification of the UN MAST classification. which can be found at: https://unctad.org/en/Pages/DITC/Trade-Analysis/Non-Tariff-Measures/NTMs-Classification.aspx

19 See: *The Economist* (2009, April 30) Obama and trade: Low expectations exceeded, www.economist.com/united-states/2009/04/30/low-expectations-exceeded.

20 Public Papers of the President of the United States, William J. Clinton, 1993 (January 20 to July 31). www.govinfo.gov/app/details/PPP-PHOTOS-1993-book1/context

21 Author's interview with a Chilean lawyer and trade negotiator, June 2020.

22 As Bussire et al. (2012) show, one of the distinctive characteristics of the post-2008–09 period was that trade decreased much more than output. In 2009, real world output contracted by 0.7%, whereas real trade flows fell by 11%. These features are surprising because they stand in sharp contrast with past experiences. That is why the dynamics of trade in 2009 became widely known as the "Great Trade Collapse" (Baldwin, 2009).
23 P. Lamy (2013, December 18), Global value chains, interdependence, and the future of trade. VoxEU. CEPR.org. https://voxeu.org/article/global-value-chains-interdependence-and-future-trade.
24 USTR, *United States and China Reach Phase One Trade Agreement,* https://ustr.gov/about-us/policy-offices/press-office/press-releases/2019/december/united-states-and-china-reach.
25 S. Evenett (2019). "For trade war junkies: Why not put the same energy into analyzing & fixing two trade policy problems that implicate much more global trade than the Sino-US trade dispute? ..." [Twitter post, Sept, 2019]. Retrieved from @SimonEvenett: https://twitter.com/SimonEvenett/status/1169553731060297728.
26 S. Evenett (2019, August). "'If it bleeds it leads' I get that. But for every tariff hike this year, more than 3 trade-distorting subsidies have been imposed…" [Twitter post] Retrieved from @SimonEvenett: https://twitter.com/SimonEvenett/status/1165645814267559940/photo/1
27 Hites, Bloom, and Furceri (2019), *New Index Tracks Trade Uncertainty across the Globe,* https://blogs.imf.org/2019/09/09/new-index-tracks-trade-uncertainty-across-the-globe/#.XXdyqn18_Zk.twitter.
28 S. Donnan, Economists Call for Alternative Path to U.S.–China Trade Wars (October 26, 2019), Bloomberg, www.bloomberg.com/news/articles/2019-10-27/economists-call-for-alternative-path-to-u-s-china-trade-wars?utm_source=google&utm_medium=bd&cmpId=google.

3 Understanding trade protectionism piece by piece
Evidence from the data*

If I had to identify a theme at the outset of the new decade it would be increasing uncertainty.

(Kristalina Georgieva, Managing Director, IMF, 2020)[1]

3.1 Introduction

This chapter presents a more detailed analysis of current trade protectionism at the state level and discusses the types of protectionist measures that have been implemented over the last decade (a detailed analysis of the data used for this analysis is presented in the Appendix). For clarity, most of the descriptive analysis at the state level is concentrated in G20 countries, which represent 80% of GWP and three-quarters of global trade.[2] This group of countries also includes the three Latin American cases (Argentina, Brazil, and Mexico) that will be analyzed in detail in subsequent chapters.

3.2 A descriptive analysis at the state level of trade policy dynamics

In this section, I present a detailed descriptive analysis of state-level protectionism over the last decade (between 2008 and 2018). As mentioned, for clarity, I will concentrate on global and regional dynamics. For individual countries, I will mostly focus on G20 economies, which represent 80% of the GWP and three-quarters of global trade. As I previously discussed, trade protectionism has not only increased over the last decade but also changed its form: historical defenders of trade liberalization are protecting their domestic economies more by using less observable trade policy measures (Evenett, 2019; WTO, 2016). These findings raise a number of questions: 1) Which countries are the most protectionist today, determined not only by the number of measures implemented but also, most importantly, by the share of trade (from the rest of the world) that is affected? 2) Which countries have been most affected by protectionism in the past decade? 3) What measures have been

DOI: 10.4324/9781003340393-3

utilized most by countries? 4) What sectors have been most affected by trade protectionism? These questions are answered in the remaining sections of this chapter.

3.2.1 Twenty-first-century protectionism piece by piece: states, sectors, and measures

3.2.1.1 State-level dynamics

From a global perspective, we can see that there has been a clear deficit of trade liberalization in comparison with protectionist measures since 2008 (see Figure 3.1). More specifically, between 2008 and 2019, the total number of new implemented protectionist interventions was 2,646, while there were just 781 liberalizing measures, meaning a "liberalizing deficit" of 1,865 measures.[3] As of the writing this book (May 2020), the Global Trade Alert database reported 390 new protectionist interventions and 197 liberalizing measures between January and May 2020. Most of these trade policy measures have been attributed to the COVID-19 pandemic, which I elaborate on at the end of this chapter.

Figure 3.2 shows the share of global trade that has been affected by protectionist measures around the world. In other words, it demonstrates the extent to which world exports have been influenced by protectionist measures. In general, we can see an important growth of global trade distortions thanks

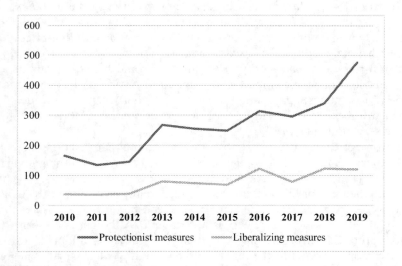

Figure 3.1 New trade policy interventions per year.

Note: GTA tracks policies by 225 countries and jurisdictions; this data is based on reporting-lag adjusted statistics.

Source: Author's creation based on Global Trade Alert, www.globaltradealert.org/

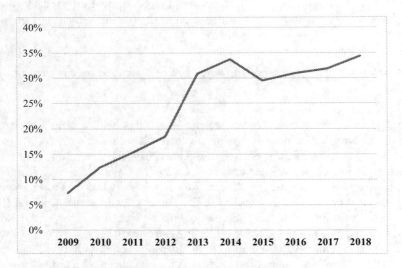

Figure 3.2 Share of world imports distorted by world protectionist restrictions.

Source: Author's creation based on Global Trade Alert, www.globaltradealert.org/

to these protectionist restrictions. The only year where we see a decrease in import distortions is 2015, which is probably explained by the weakness of trade during that year. This was due to a number of factors, including "an economic slowdown of China, a severe recession in Brazil, falling prices for oil and other commodities, and exchange rate volatility" (WTO, 2016a, p. 16).

Upon further examination of particular regions and countries, we can see that protectionism has been more concentrated in Asia and North America. However, it is interesting to note (in Figure 3.3) that when we consider the share of world exports affected by a region's protectionism (average 2009–18), we see a very different story.

North America has affected almost two times more than Asia the share of world exports to that region. We learn at least two things from the graphs in Figure 3.3: 1) the number of measures implemented does not necessarily correlate with the share of bilateral trade affected; 2) many protectionist dynamics nowadays can be more related to signals to defend rather than measures that actually affect to trade. Take Asia as an example. Although Asia seems to be more protectionist in terms of the number of measures adopted, it does not affect world exports to the region in the same way what North America does. This raises the question of the extent to which interdependence factors such as GVCs and PTAs play a role here. For instance, countries with higher dependencies on intermediated goods cannot implement as many protectionist measures as those with lower dependencies.

Trade policy dynamics at the state level also reveal interesting patterns. China, for instance, ranks first in the G20 in terms of the number of protectionist

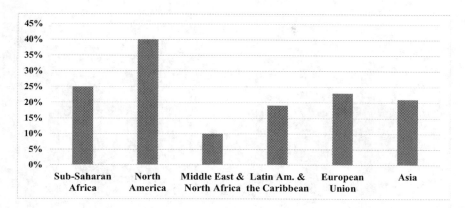

Figure 3.3 Share of world exports to each region affected by each region protectionism measures (Average 2009–18).

Source: Author's creation based on Global Trade Alert, www.globaltradealert.org/

measures implemented, and second in the share of world exports to China that are affected. In comparison, the United States sits in fourth place for the number of protectionist measures adopted and is in sixth place on the share of bilateral trade (from the rest of the world) that is affected. In other words, we may say that the United States has emitted more protectionist signals than actual measures that affect through bilateral trade flows. An extreme case is Argentina, which is one of the "least" protectionist countries in terms of the number of measures implemented, and one of the two "most" protectionist in terms of the share of bilateral trade (from the rest of the world) affected. This suggests that the "few" measures implemented have been very powerful (see Figure 3.4).

In terms of the share of world exports affected by protectionism, Figure 3.5 shows that there is an important difference among the Latin American countries within the G20 (Argentina, Brazil, and Mexico): while Argentina is the most protectionist economy in the G20, Brazil is almost exactly in the middle of the list, and Mexico is among the least protectionist countries.

3.2.1.2 Types of measures implemented

For a deeper understanding of the rise of protectionism post-GFC, I now turn to the type of protectionist measures that have been implemented globally, by region, and by country. As Figure 3.6 shows, the protectionist measures most used during the pre-GFC years (2000–07) are: technical barriers to trade and sanitary and phytosanitary measures, both of them considered (under the GTA classification) transparent measures (see Table 1.4 in Chapter 1).[4] After the crisis (2008–19), we can observe more diversification of measures

48 *Understanding trade protectionism piece by piece*

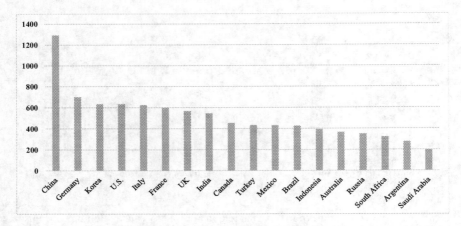

Figure 3.4 Number of protectionist measures of G20 countries toward the rest of the world's imports (average 2009–18, by country).

Source: Author's creation based on Global Trade Alert, www.globaltradealert.org/

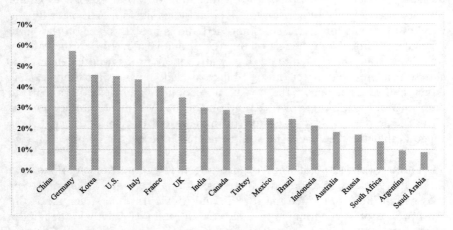

Figure 3.5 Share of world exports to G20 countries affected by protectionism measures implemented from the rest of the world (average 2009–18, by country).

Source: Author's creation based on Global Trade Alert, www.globaltradealert.org/

implemented, where the protectionist measures most used are: contingent trade-protective measures, subsidies, export-related measures, tariff measures, and non-automatic licensing.

In terms of the level of transparency, we can see that pre-GFC (2000–07), 78% of the measures globally have been transparent (e.g., tariff and sanitary and phytosanitary measures), while the other 22% consist of nontransparent measures (e.g., price control).[5] These figures vary significantly after the GFC, when 58% of the measures globally have been transparent and the other 42% consist of nontransparent measures. Although the nontransparent measures are not the majority, they represent a significant portion of protectionist measures between 2009 and 2019. Moreover, the significant increase in nontransparent measures after the crisis also shows an important trade policy substitution between NTMs and tariffs, a topic that, as recent studies have shown, has been under-researched (Beverelli et al., 2019; Niu et al., 2018). We know the more tariffs are lowered via bindings created by WTO rules, the more countries rely on NTMs, but this raises bigger questions about the relationship between trade policy and transparency (Kono, 2006).

When we disaggregate by region, between 2008 and 2019, we can identify a pattern similar to the global one (see figures above). The protectionist measures most used in Latin America were tariff measures and non-automatic licensing;[6] in North America, subsidies; in Asia, subsidies and non-automatic licensing; and in the EU, subsidies (see Figure 1.2, in Chapter 1).

3.2.1.3 A descriptive text analysis of the types of measures implemented

Another way to understand the level of transparency of a given trade policy instrument is to access just how explicit the initiating country is when formally implementing it. As mentioned above, when countries apply a specific trade measure, they are legally obligated to publicize it on a government website or through the press. Technically, the WTO requires that countries publicize a new trade measure before it can be enforced by customs. In any case, governments want to inform citizens of a new policy measure that protects domestic goods from foreign competition (Hollyer et al., 2014). Although governments may want to send economic signals to domestic lobbies, they may also want to keep their policies below the radar of foreign countries. If a foreign trade partner is implementing a protectionist measure against them, governments may enact punitive policies in retaliation. As a result, the way countries communicate their trade policy to each other is relevant and should be considered. One way to do this is to see whether a country mentions a specific trade partner that will be affected by the measure. It could be that instead of implementing a measure against a specific trade partner, countries enact more general measures by only identifying which goods will be protected, rather than which countries will be affected. For example, a measure that states, a "tariff increase on some articles of leather,"[7] which affects all leather exporters to the implementing country, is not the same as a measure that states, "an increase in the fee for registering vehicles imported from the United States."[8] The former is a general trade policy measure that does not specify a specific country, whereas the latter is specific measure toward a specific trade partner.

These dynamics are illustrated in Figure 3.7, where I take all the official documents in which countries announce the implementation of a specific trade measure and download them from the GTA's repository of State Acts

50 *Understanding trade protectionism piece by piece*

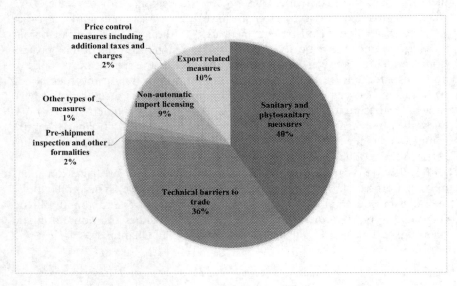

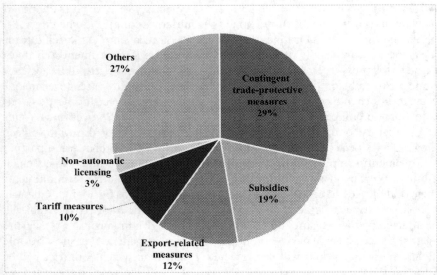

Figure 3.6 Protectionist policy instruments most used globally pre- (2000–07) and post-GFC (2008–19) by types of measure.

Source: Author's creation based on Global Trade Alert, www.globaltradealert.org/

Understanding trade protectionism piece by piece 51

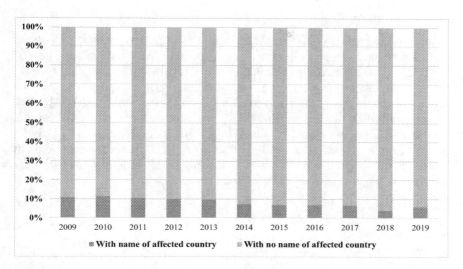

Figure 3.7 Protectionist policy instruments with name of targeted country (2009–19).
Source: Author's creation based on Global Trade Alert, www.globaltradealert.org/

(www.globaltradealert.org/latest/state-acts). I then use the *stringr* package in *R* to study different patterns of the text of those official trade policy documents. I pay specially attention to documents that mention a country (or group of countries) that will be affected by the measure officials are publishing. As we can see, in Figure 3.7, an average of 8% of measures implemented between 2009 and 2019 actually name the country affected in the official document. This suggests that most of the measures have centered on the product they are protecting and not the country that is affected. The fact that most of the measures implemented between 2009 and 2019 were "general trade policy" does not mean that many of them were retaliatory measures. It could happen that countries implement a retaliatory measure without specifying the name of the trading partner but rather a specific product that they are not importing from the country they want to retaliate to. This is something I discussed in Chapter 1 when talking about the complex task of defining policy responses.

3.3 A descriptive analysis of preferential trade agreements and global value chains

Two other variables of interest here are GVCs and PTAs. While I briefly referred to the relevance of these two phenomena in the global economy in Chapter 1, I will now analyze them in more detail.

3.3.1 Preferential trade agreements

As of June 2020, there were 303 PTAs formally notified to the WTO. Of these, 94% are flexible integration agreements (e.g., free trade agreements, partial scope agreements), and the remaining 6% are considered too deep to be integration agreements (e.g., a CU).[9] Europe and Latin America are the two regions with the most trade agreements signed, both within these respective regions and with the rest of the world. Turning to those trade agreements (goods and services) signed by the G20 countries, apart from the EU bloc, Mexico and Turkey are the two countries with the most trade agreements in force. China, Canada, and the United States are in the middle of the list, while Brazil and Argentina are among those countries with fewer than ten trade agreements.

3.3.2 Global value chains

As mentioned before, GVCs are production networks that gather products using parts (semi-finished goods) from around the globe. Today, around 80% of world trade is driven by these production networks (Kolb, 2019). There is probably no better way to describe a GVC than by drawing upon real-life examples. A recent World Bank (2020b) report on GVCs highlights that the bicycle industry offers one of the best examples for understanding the nature of GVCs. Global bicycle production grew from about 10 million units in 1950 to more than 130 million units today. Bicycles are assembled using semi-finished components from all over the world. Take the example of the Bianchi bicycle model: design, prototyping, and conception work are done in Italy, and assembly takes place in Taiwan, using parts and components from China, Italy, Japan, and Malaysia. Shimano of Japan, for example, makes brakes for the Bianchi, while the handlebars are made in China (World Bank, 2020b, pp. 16–17).

Using the latest data, it has been found that

> the overall share of GVC trade in total world trade […] grew significantly in the 1990s and early 2000s, but it appears to have stagnated or even declined in the last 10 years. Still, about half of world trade appears to be related to GVCs.
>
> (World Bank, 2020b, p. 40)

The GFC had an important impact in that it reduced the share of total world trade conducted within GVCs from 52% in 2007 to 43% in 2016 (which is the last year of aggregated data available on GVCs).

It is important to understand that although GVCs span the globe, countries' participation in them is uneven when we consider the types of exports that each country contributes to different GVCs. According to the World Bank (2020b, p. 21):

Some countries export raw materials for further processing; others import inputs for assembly and exports; and still others produce complex goods and services. In addition, some are heavily reliant on GVCs for trade, whereas others export largely domestic goods for consumption. To capture these distinct features of participation, countries are classified into four main types—commodities, limited manufacturing, advanced manufacturing and services, and innovative activities—based on the products they export and their participation in GVCs.[10]

When we study GVC participation in more detail, the World Bank (2020b) has identified a variety of scenarios according to different regions. While Europe is seeing an increase in regional fragmentation, Asia is becoming internationally fragmented but regionally integrated, and Latin America is becoming more integrated across the board. More specifically, the World Bank (2020b, p. 24) explains that:

> In Europe, regional fragmentation of value chains increased through successive rounds of enlargement in which Eastern European countries, including Bulgaria, Hungary, and Poland, progressively joined older members' production networks [...] global fragmentation was equally important, driven mostly by the larger European economies such as France, Germany, and the United Kingdom, whose linkages with countries in Asia such as China or India expanded. In East Asia, linkages are more regional than global and GVCs became more internationally fragmented after 1990 because of both regional and global fragmentation in the 1990s and 2000s, although regional integration dominated. [...] The NAFTA GVCs depend somewhat more on global partners than regional partners, and integration has been increasing on both fronts. [...] In Latin America and the Caribbean, value chains are more globally linked, but they have increased both regionally and globally.

3.4 Final thoughts on rising protectionism vis-à-vis the COVID-19 pandemic

Although this book concentrates primarily on understanding trade protectionism between 2009 and 2019 (in part, due to the amount of data available on the variables of interest), at the moment that I am writing this book, we are in the midst of a global health crisis. The COVID-19 pandemic, which will have an unprecedented impact on the global economy and multilateralism, is causing even more uncertainty in international markets (Baker et al., 2020; Albertoni & Wise, 2020; Pinna & Lodi, 2021). We still have limited data on the trade and economic impact of this pandemic; however, it is important to consider this shock at least as part of this descriptive analysis. After all, the goals of this book are to capture and explain global trade policy dynamics within a highly uncertain context in the world economy. Thus, it is relevant to consider how countries are responding to the COVID-19 pandemic. As the World

Bank (2020) stated in its first *Global Economic Prospects* after the COVID-19 pandemic:

> The COVID-19 pandemic is expected to result in a 5.2 percent contraction in global GDP in 2020—the deepest global recession in eight decades, despite unprecedented policy support. Per capita incomes in the vast majority of emerging market and developing economies (EMDEs) are expected to shrink this year, tipping many millions back into poverty. The pandemic highlights the urgent need for health and economic policy action, including global cooperation, to cushion its consequences, protect vulnerable populations, and improve countries' capacity to prevent and cope with similar events in the future. Once the health crisis abates, structural reforms that enable strong and sustainable growth will be needed to attenuate the lasting effect of the pandemic on potential output.

From the side of the WTO (2020, p. 1), there has been a special concern on the inevitable negative impact the COVID-19 pandemic had already had on global trade, which was expected to fall between 13% and 32% in 2020 because of the pandemic's disruption of "normal economic activity and life around the world."

The WTO (2020) highlights that one of the main challenges of this pandemic is that it happened in a world interconnected by "complex value chains," which can be severely affected in this context of high economic uncertainty. More specifically, the WTO (2020, pp. 1–4) predicted that:

> Trade will likely fall steeper in sectors with complex value chains, particularly electronics and automotive products. […] According to the OECD Trade in Value Added (TIVA) database, the share of foreign value added in electronics exports was around 10% for the United States, 25% for China, more than 30% for Korea, greater than 40% for Singapore and more than 50% for Mexico, Malaysia and Vietnam. Imports of key production inputs are likely to be interrupted by social distancing, which caused factories to temporarily close in China and which is now happening in Europe and North America. However, it is also useful to recall that complex supply chain disruption can occur as a result of localized disasters such hurricanes, tsunamis, and other economic disruptions. Managing supply chain disruption is a challenge for both global and local enterprises and requires a risk-versus-economic efficiency calculation on the part of every company.

Indeed, the impact that the COVID pandemic had on global trade might even surpass the damage inflicted by the 2008–09 GFC. This is why current studies are already suggesting what we could be looking at a "Greater Trade Collapse" (the GFC on trade was called the "Great Trade Collapse") (Baldwin & Evenett, 2020, p. 3). Recent studies have shown that as the pandemic spread across the globe, governments all around the world responded "with a chain reaction of unprecedented trade policy measures" (Joller & Kniahin, 2020, p. 1). Around the world, both import and export measures were quickly implemented to fend off a total collapse in domestic economies, for example, the proliferation of such measures between April and June 2020.[11]

The reason why the collapse would be more catastrophic this time is twofold. For starters, the COVID-19 pandemic impacted every country, whereas the GFC primarily affected the United States and the United Kingdom (Baldwin, 2020). In addition, today's crisis hit both demand and supply, severely limiting the options for remedial economic policies. As Baldwin and Evenett (2020, p. 4) explain:

> While the point-of-impact of the 2008 financial crisis was the US and the UK, today's crisis hit all the world's largest trading nations within a few months. The US, China, Japan, Germany, Britain, France, and Italy—all of which were hit hard by the virus in the first quarter—account for 60% of world supply and demand (GDP), 65% of world manufacturing, and almost as much of world manufacturing exports. While the Great Trade Collapse was primarily caused by a collapse in demand, today's "Great Lockdown," as the IMF is calling it, is a serious supply-side disruption that is affecting all sectors in all of the largest economies in the world. As in 2008, today's trade shock has been accompanied by rising concerns about a return to protectionism.[12]

The COVID-19 pandemic has stopped globalization in its tracks. Understanding what happened in the decade after the GFC will help us forecast what could happen in the post-pandemic era. These extraordinary circumstances offer a natural experiment on the effect of drastically slowed trade on the global economy. As this descriptive chapter shows, one of the contributions of this book is the empirical documentation of the damage that closed markets and trade nationalism can inflict upon the world economy. In essence, this book is a cautionary tale about trade nationalism and the merits of a more open global trade regime. My empirical documentation of the damage currently at play is meant to alert us to what lies ahead in the near future and to better prepare us to cope with the challenges now faced by the global trade regime.

Notes

* Some sections of this chapter have been used in Albertoni, N. (2023). The risk of murky trade protectionism in an interconnected and uncertain global economy, *Estudios Internacionales*, 55(205).
1 IMF Managing Director Kristalina Georgieva Speech at the Peterson Institute for International Economics, in Washington, DC, January 17, 2020, www.imf.org/en/News/Articles/2020/01/17/sp01172019-the-financial-sector-in-the-2020s.
2 The G20 members are Argentina, Australia, Brazil, Canada, China, France, Germany, India, Indonesia, Italy, Japan, the Republic of Korea, Mexico, Russia, Saudi Arabia,

South Africa, Turkey, the United Kingdom, the United States, and the EU. It is "the premier forum for international economic cooperation. The G20 brings together the leaders of both developed and developing countries from every continent."
(See: G20, *What Is the G20?* https://g20.org/en/about/Pages/whatis.aspx.) It is different from the developing nations' G20 group in the WTO, which is a coalition of developing countries formed in 2003 during the Doha Round Negotiations, "pressing for ambitious reforms of agriculture in developed countries with some flexibility for developing countries" (See: *Groups in the WTO*, www.wto.org/english/tratop_e/dda_e/negotiating_groups_e.pdf.

3 Global Trade Alert tracks policies by 225 countries and jurisdictions. It includes state interventions affecting trade in goods and services, foreign investment, and labor force migration: www.globaltradealert.org/global_dynamics/area_all/year-to_2019/day-to_0531.

4 Technical barriers to trade are "measures referring to technical regulations, and procedures for assessment of conformity with technical regulations and standard: Restrictions on toxins in children's toys; Refrigerators need to carry a label indicating their size, weight and electricity consumption level." For a detailed description of each type, see Table 1.3 in Chapter 1. Also, for more information about each classification, see: https://unctad.org/en/Pages/DITC/Trade-Analysis/Non-Tariff-Measures/NTMs-Classification.aspx.

5 Data from UNCTAD's Trade Analysis Information System (TRAINS), http://i-tip.unctad.org/Default.aspx. Given that the structure of the data of TRAINS is different from GTA, it is very complex to conduct a detailed quantitative analysis of pre- and post-GFC years. In any case, this book's main focus is to understand protectionist patterns after the GFC, and by no means does it pretend to claim that the findings of this analysis are generalizable to other economic periods. I talk more about this in Chapter 4.

6 A non-automatic licensing is a "control measures generally aimed at restraining the quantity of goods that be imported. Examples are only hotels and restaurants are allowed to import alcoholic drink; A quota of 100 tons of tuna fish can be imported any time of the year." See: https://unctad.org/en/Pages/DITC/Trade-Analysis/Non-Tariff-Measures/NTMs-Classification.aspx.

7 For instance, in January 2010, the Mercosur members announced a change in import duties that especially affect articles of leather. See: Mercosur, CMC (Consejo del Mercado Común) Decision no. 27/09 of 7 Dec 2009: http://200.40.51.218/SAM%5CGestDoc%5CPubWeb.nsf/B6BA5D474C5B065A032585BC000B9F98/$File/DEC_027-2009_ES_Confecciones.pdf.

8 For instance, in 2016, the Canadian government raised the fees on vehicles imported specifically from the United States. See: www.cbsa-asfc.gc.ca/publications/cn-ad/cn16-30-eng.html.

9 By flexible integration agreements, I mean those cases in which there is a bilateral compromise between countries, which means that the members of such an agreement are free to maintain an independent trade policy with third countries. This is not the case with a CU, under which members are obligated to negotiate together with third countries that are not part of the Union. For more information, see: WTO, *Regional Trade Agreements Database,* http://rtais.wto.org/UI/PublicMaintainRTAHome.aspx.

10 This taxonomy is based on the following criteria by the World Bank (2020b, pp. 22–23):

> Countries are classified based on (1) the goods and services exported, (2) the extent of GVC participation, and (3) measures of innovation. A country's sectoral specialization of exports is based on the domestic value added in gross exports of primary goods, manufacturing, and business services. A country's extent of GVC participation is measured as backward integration of the manufacturing sector as a share of the country's total exports. Higher backward integration in manufacturing is an important characteristic of countries entering or specialized in non-commodity GVCs. Two measures are used to capture a country's innovative activities: (1) intellectual property (IP) receipts as a percentage of GDP and (2) research and development (R&D) intensity, defined as its expenditure of public and private R&D as a percentage of GDP.

11 For more information about trade policy measures generated in the context of the pandemic, see the daily tracker on the ITC Market Access Map: www.macmap.org/covid19.

12 Baldwin (2020), *The Greater Trade Collapse of 2020*, VoxEU.org, April 7, 2020. https://voxeu.org/article/greater-trade-collapse-2020.

4 Protectionism and trade policy responses
A quantitative approach

4.1 Introduction

To test the hypotheses of this book, a mixed-method approach is used—blending both quantitative and qualitative techniques of analysis. This chapter focuses on the quantitative portion of the study where large-N statistical analysis is utilized to present the reader with a "big picture" idea of what the main patterns of protectionism have looked like over the last decade. In this analysis, I include more than 170 countries from regions across the world, which represents, on average, 98% of global trade flows (Evenett & Fritz, 2020). These quantitative insights will serve as a baseline for Chapter 5, where an in-depth qualitative analysis of three country cases—Argentina, Brazil, and Mexico—is conducted. These case studies serve two purposes: first, they allow for the assessment of the validity of my findings from the large-N analysis undertaken in this chapter, and second, they give rise to potentially new and more detailed questions about protectionist responses that can best be identified at the country level.[1]

Before delving into the details, let the main goals of this book be reiterated. In analyzing the explosion of trade protectionism since the 2008–09 GFC, I have uncovered the role that PTAs and GVCs have come to play in the expansion of non-tariff barriers in particular. Ultimately, I argue that PTAs and GVCs, in the current context of high economic uncertainty, have had counterintuitive and contradictory effects on global trade policies. It is true that PTAs and GVCs have fostered healthy patterns of trade interdependences. Both—especially PTAs—have been a force for trade liberalization the world over, and common wisdom has held that the more countries depend on one another, the less likely that protectionist dynamics will arise between them (Baldwin, 2012; Gawande et al., 2015; Jensen et al., 2015; Lamy, 2013). However, a newer, contradictory phenomenon has emerged since the GFC, one where trade protectionism is occurring within the very institutions that have been designed to mitigate it. This phenomenon has barely been discussed or studied (Ahir et al., 2018).

DOI: 10.4324/9781003340393-4

For the remainder of this chapter, various hypotheses will be tested relating to the insertion of non-tariff barriers within PTAs and GVCs, and they will seek to explain how this phenomenon is exacerbated by economic uncertainty. This is approached through a large-N statistical analysis constructed with directed dyad-year data at the state and the industry level. This chapter is divided into three main sections.

First, I analyze my general hypotheses at the state level and probe how countries respond when they are adversely affected by a protectionist measure adopted by another country. At the same time, I ask whether the existence of PTAs and GVCs decreases the likelihood of a protectionist response. In other words, the existence of PTAs and GVCs, ceteris paribus, lowers the probability or severity of bilateral protectionist dynamics:

HYPOTHESIS 1: Direct Retaliation: Countries will retaliate against those nations that initially target them with a protectionist measure.
HYPOTHESIS 2: Conditional Effect of PTAs: PTAs are negatively correlated with protectionist responses.
HYPOTHESIS 3: Conditional Effect of GVCs: GVCs are negatively correlated with protectionist responses.

Second, I focus on the relationship between tariffs and non-tariff measures within PTAs and GVCs. Specifically, I look at whether countries with high trade interconnectivity (i.e., the existence of PTAs and GVCs) will retaliate more with less transparent (NT) measures than with transparent (T) measures.

HYPOTHESIS 4: Conditional Effect of PTAs: PTAs are positively correlated with protectionist non-tariff responses and negatively correlated with tariff responses.
HYPOTHESIS 5: Conditional Effect of GVCs: GVCs are positively correlated with protectionist non-tariff responses and negatively correlated with tariff responses

Again, the different levels of quantitative analysis will be conducted utilizing directed dyad-year data at the state level of analysis. The unit of analysis is dyad countries by year. For the state-level hypotheses, a lagged model is used because it does not assume contemporaneous influence. Rather, it considers the time that the focal country may take—for example, one year—before it decides to retaliate with protectionist policies that its trading partner might levy against it.[2]

4.2 The models

First, to test the hypotheses concerning the likelihood of responses (Hypothesis 1), the conditional effects of PTAs and GVCs in that response (Hypothesis 2,

60 Protectionism and trade policy responses

Hypothesis 3), and the difference between the likelihood of tariff and NTMs responses (Hypothesis 4, Hypothesis 5), the models can be stated as:

$$YAB_{all}, t = \alpha + \beta_1 Y_{BA_{all},t-1} + \beta_2 PTA_{AB,t-1} + \beta_2 GVC_{AB,t-1} + \beta_5 X_{AB_{all},t-1} + \varepsilon_{AB,t-1} \quad (1)$$

$$YAB_{Tariff}, t = \alpha + \beta_1 Y_{BA_{all},t-1} + \beta_2 PTA_{AB,t-1} + \beta_2 GVC_{AB,t-1} + \beta_5 X_{AB_{all},t-1} + \varepsilon_{AB,t-1} \quad (2)$$

$$YAB_{NTM}, t = \alpha + \beta_1 Y_{BA_{all},t-1} + \beta_2 PTA_{AB,t-1} + \beta_2 GVC_{AB,t-1} + \beta_5 X_{AB_{all},t-1} + \varepsilon_{AB,t-1} \quad (3)$$

The main difference between these is the dependent variable. YAB_{all}, t represents all protectionist restrictions by country A on country B at time t, which is measured by the share of bilateral trade affected by protectionist measures in a given year. YAB_{tariff}, t represents protectionist tariff restrictions by country A on country B at time t, and YAB_{NTM}, t represents protectionist non-tariff restrictions by country A on country B at time t. For the three equations, $YBA_{all}, t-1$ represents the protectionist restrictions by country B on country A at time $t-1$; $PTAAB, t$ represents the number of trade agreements in place between A and B; and $GVCAB, t$ represents whether trade between A and B is interconnected through a GVC. XAB, t are control variables consisting of political and economic data regarding A and B such as population weighted distance, normally used for a gravity model. The share of trade positively affected is shown by liberalizing measures by B on A in time $t-1$, bilateral investment treaty between A and B, relative economic difference (B's GDPpc/A's GDPpc), common colonizer, and common official language, among others control measures; whereby α is the intercept and ε is an error term.

4.3 The data

In this section, I concentrate on how the different datasets used for this book are related to the specific variables of interest.[3] Keep in mind that this book is based on several datasets that have been retrieved from public repositories. The four main data sources used were: 1) the Global Trade Alert (GTA), which provides information on state-level trade policy interventions taken since 2008 that are likely to affect foreign trade;[4] 2) BACI-CEPII trade data, which disaggregate data on bilateral trade flows for more than 5,000 products and 200 countries;[5] 3) the International Political Economy Data Resource (IPE), which compiles data from 89 IPE data sources into a single dataset (Graham & Tucker, 2017);[6] and 4) data from the Harmonized System (HS) classification of products, which classifies "traded goods on a common basis for customs purposes."[7]

4.3.1 Measurement of the dependent variables

As mentioned above, the main dataset used for my models derives from the GTA, which provides information on state-to-state—dyad-year—interventions undertaken since 2008 and are most likely to affect foreign trade. This includes "state interventions affecting trade in goods and services, foreign investment and labor force migration."[8] The GTA was launched in 2009 when it was "feared that the global financial crisis would lead governments to adopt widespread 1930s-style beggar-thy-neighbor policies" (Evenett & Fritz, 2020, p. 1). Since it was launched, many studies have relied on GTA data (Evenett et al., 2011; Evenett et al., 2011; Boffa & Olarreaga, 2012; Henn & McDonald, 2014; Georgiadis & Gräb, 2016; Evenett, 2019). It is relevant to note that GTA documents both trade liberalization and protectionist measures, which enables us to measure both sides of trade policy mechanisms and offers control variables to test the real weight of both types of measures when we consider them as explanatory variables. Based on the GTA, in order to measure the dependent variable for the state-level analysis, the following possible outcomes are used:

DV1: All protectionist measures by A on B in time t—the share of bilateral trade affected (Hypothesis 1, Hypothesis 2, and Hypothesis 3);
DV2a & DV2b: Number of Transparent and Nontransparent protectionist measures by A on B in time t—continuous variable (Hypothesis 4 and Hypothesis 5);
DV3a & DV3b: Proportion of Transparent and Nontransparent protectionist measures in total measures by A on B in time t—percentage (Hypothesis 4 and Hypothesis 5).

4.3.2 Measurement of regressors of interest

The measure of PTAs is based on Dür et al. (2014), which contains bilateral data on PTAs from 1948 to 2018 for 203 countries. PTAs have expanded in number and have diversified their content, from the negotiation of 50 PTAs in the 1990s, to 303 as of January 2020.[9] Following the World Bank's definition, Dür et al. (2014) provides a more general description of international trade agreements as "all the agreements that have the potential to liberalize trade" (p. 1).[10] This definition will be used in this book as it is one of the most widely used definitions in the literature (Hofmann et al., 2019; Ruta, 2017). Hence, when referring to a PTA, this includes FTAs, CUs, or partial FTAs, which can take bilateral, for example, two countries; plurilateral, for example, many countries; plurilateral with a third country, for example, EU–Australia Trade Agreement; or region–region, for example, EU-Mercosur Trade Agreement, forms. The diversity of PTA classifications creates a challenge in the term "PTA" itself having any inherent meaning since it could be one of many trade agreements. As mentioned above, as of June 2020, there were 303 PTAs formally notified to the WTO. Of these, 94% are flexible integration agreements, for example, FTAs or partial scope agreements, and the remaining 6% are considered to be deep integration agreements, for example, CUs. This shows that when talking about PTAs, we are in reality talking about FTAs as well.

The measure of GVCs is based on the combination of GTA data and BACI-CEPII trade data, which contains estimates of the composition of trade between countries. As Ruta (2017, p. 175) says, "GVCs [have] radically changed international trade." However, as stated before, it is still very complex to capture bilateral GVC dynamics. One of the better—although imperfect—proxies we have today is the share of intermediate goods between two countries.

Both the GTA and BACI-CEPII enable us to capture these dynamics. For each pair of countries *A and B*—exporter and importer—the data include the product, the HS 2012 code, with an estimate of how much that product accounts for total exports from exporter A to importer B.[11] As mentioned, the classification by BEC is also relied on, which provides "a means for international trade statistics to be analyzed by broad economic categories such as food, industrial supplies, capital equipment, consumer durables and consumer non-durables."[12] Hence, the main variable obtained from *BACI-CEPII trade data* is a percentage that estimates the proportion that a certain product contributes to total exports from country A to country B. Then, combining this percentage with the data provided by GTA, whose product is affected by each protectionist measure implemented from A to B, we can obtain the percentage of trade affected between A and B.[13] Finally, to avoid endogeneity issues, these shares of intermediate goods are calculated using pre-crisis, 2005–07, trade values.

4.3.3 *Control variables*

The control variables include trade liberalizing measures, which are the share of exports positively affected by liberalizing measures and the bilateral investment treaties (BITs) between A and B,[14] from the IPE Data Resource, the Relative Economic Difference—*B's log GDPpc / A's log GDPpc*.[15] They additionally draw from the *GeoDist Database CEPII*, which uses the population weighted distance that is typically employed in a gravity model, Common colonizer, and Common official language.[16] Table 4.1 shows the summary statistics of all the variables considered for the analysis.[17]

4.4 State-level analysis results

The first set of hypotheses presented in this book predict that, in general terms, when a country is adversely affected by another country's protectionist measure, it will systematically respond to that country by adopting its own protectionist measures in return (Hypothesis 1). However, the existence of PTAs (Hypothesis 2) and GVCs (Hypothesis 3) decreases the likelihood of protectionist responses.

Table 4.1 Summary statistics state-level analysis

	VARIABLE NAME	MIN.	MEAN	MAX.
SHARE OF TRADE AFFECTED BY MEASURES	**All protectionist measures** by A on B in time *t* (share of bilateral trade affected, log)	0	0.192	0.693
	All protectionist measures by B on A in time *t-1* (share of bilateral trade affected, log)	0	0.106	0.693
	Nontransparent (*non-tariff*) protectionist measures by A on B in time *t* (share of bilateral trade affected)	0	0.145	0.693
	Transparent (*tariff*) protectionist measures by A on B in time *t* (share of bilateral trade affected)	0	0.085	0.693
Nº OF ALL PROTECTIONIST MEASURES	**Nº of all protectionist measures** by A on B in time *t*	0	5.43	1,661
	Nº of all protectionist measures by B on A in time *t-1*	0	4.87	1,661
	Nº of Nontransparent (*non-tariff*) protectionist measures by A on B in time *t*	0	5.15	1,660
	Nº of Transparent (*tariff*) protectionist measures by A on B in time *t*	0	0.47	74
REGRESSORS OF INTEREST	**Preferential trade agreement (PTA)** *A* and *B*	0	0.006	2
	GVC proxy variable: Percentage of **intermediate goods** in total trade between *A* and *B*	0	0.007	0.57
CONTROLS	**Liberalizing measures** by *B* on *A* in time *t-1*	0	0.99	79
	Bilateral Investment Treaty between *A* and *B*	0	0.004	1
	Population weighted distance (*gravity model*)	35	6,449	19,649
	Relative Economic Difference (*B's GDPpc / A's GDPpc*)	0.51	0.70	0.94
	Common colonizer	0	0.05	1
	Common official language	0	0.13	1

Source: Author's creation.

Table 4.1 shows that, holding all other variables constant, one decimal point increase in the share of bilateral trade affected by import restrictions by *B* on *A* in time *t-1* results in a 0.043 (4.3%) import restriction increase by *A* on *B* in time *t* (Model 1). This positive correlation is statistically significant even when controlling for other bilateral characteristics such as the liberalizing measures by *B* on *A* in time *t-1*, a bilateral investment treaty between *A* and *B*, population weighted distance—the gravity model—the relative economic difference, *B*'s log GDPpc / *A*'s log GDPpc, common colonizer, and common official language (Model 2), and when including countries *A* and *B* fixed effect and time fixed effect (Model 3). These results support Hypothesis 1, which states that

Table 4.2 DV1a: All protectionist measures by A on B in time t

	DV1a: Share of bilateral trade affected (log)		
	Model 1	Model 2	Model 3 A&B fixed effect and time fixed effect
All protectionist measures by B on A in time $t-1$ (share of bilateral trade affected) (*log*)	0.043*** (0.011)	0.070*** (0.010)	0.020** (0.010)
Trade agreements between A and B	−0.094*** (0.012)	−0.110*** (0.010)	−0.050*** (0.010)
% of intermediate goods in total trade between A and B (*GVC proxy variable*)	−0.604*** (0.040)	−0.090* (0.040)	−0.070 (0.040)
CONTROL VARIABLES	NO	YES	YES
Constant	0.200*** (0.001)	−0.390*** (0.01)	9.670*** (0.344)
R2	0.01	0.06	0.39
Adj. R2	0.01	0.06	0.39
Num. obs.	53,831	50,077	50,077
RMSE	0.24	0.23	0.18

Source: Author's creation.

Notes:
***p < 0.001, **p < 0.01, *p < 0.05

countries will retaliate against nations that initially target them with a protectionist measure, which is known as *Direct Retaliation*.

Second, Table 4.2 also shows that the existence of a PTA between A and B is negatively correlated with protectionist responses. In other words, if a PTA exists, then retaliation is less strong than would otherwise be the case. Something similar happens when a GVC exists between A and B. This negative correlation for both variables is statistically significant even when controlling for other bilateral characteristics. Countries A and B and year fixed effects were controlled for because some countries may implement more import restrictions than the average of countries simply to trade more than others, as do the United States and China. Other countries may be targeted with additional protectionist measures related to political concerns and pressures, like the economic sanctions implemented on countries such as Iran and Cuba. When controlling for fixed effects, GVCs do not seem to be as strong as PTAs in restraining protectionist dynamics. This may signal that GVCs are highly concentrated in a few central countries. Many countries do not play a relevant role in GVCs of manufacturing, for example. Some of them do not have much potential at having GVC ties, as is the case with Argentina. Others, though, have important ties, such as Mexico. Both of these cases will be further explained in Chapter 5. This second set of results supports Hypothesis 2, which suggests that PTAs are negatively correlated with protectionist responses, known as the *Conditional Effect of PTAs*.

The second set of hypotheses concentrates on the relationship between Tariffs and NTMs within the institutional context of PTAs and GVCs. Hypotheses 4 and 5 predict that countries with high trade interdependence—with PTAs and GVCs—retaliate more with non-tariff measures, which are less transparent, than with tariff measures. For this set of hypotheses, two different dependent variables were considered to verify the robustness of the results. First, there was the number of transparent (**DV2a**) and nontransparent (**DV2b**) protectionist measures levied by A on B in time t, the continuous variable. Second, was the proportion of transparent (**DV3a**) and Nontransparent (**DV3b**) protectionist measures out of total measures created by A and used on B in time t as a percentage.

Table 4.3 shows that, holding all other variables constant, one unit of increase in the number of import restrictions by B on A in time $t-1$ increases the number of tariff restrictions by A on B in time t by 0.230 (Model 1a). The number of non-tariff restrictions in time t also increases by 0.490 (Model 1b). Second, it shows that, when we use an interaction term between having a PTA and being affected by a protectionist measure in $t-1$, there is a negative relationship with tariff retaliation (Model 2a). This means that when a PTA exists between A and B, and B implements a protectionist measure toward A, the latter responds not with tariff measures (Models 2a and 4a), but rather with non-tariff protectionist measures (Models 2b and 4b). This same pattern holds with GVCs (Models 3a, 4a, 3b, 4b). In other words, having a PTA or GVC is negatively correlated with tariff responses, while positively correlated with non-tariff responses (Models 3b and 4b). These results are consistent with the expectations of Hypotheses 4 and 5: both PTAs and GVCs are negative, statistically significant predictors of tariff responses, but positive, statistically significant predictors of non-tariff responses.

Finally, Table 4.4 supplements the previous results by considering the proportion of transparent and nontransparent protectionist measures in total measures by A on B in time t as the dependent variable. I find very similar results regarding the effect of GVCs in both Transparent (Model 3a) and Nontransparent (Model 3b) protectionist measures, even when considering different control variables (Models 4a and 4b). Additionally, I find similar results regarding the effect of PTAs in both Transparent (Model 2a) and Nontransparent (Model 2b). However, this statistical significance diminishes when the control variables are included (Models 4a and 4b). These results are mostly consistent with the expectations of Hypothesis 5: GVCs are negative,

Table 4.3 The relationship between tariff and non-tariff measures with PTAs and GVCs (DV2a and DV2b)

	DV2a: **Tariff protectionist measures** by A on B in time t (**number of measures**) (log)				DV2b: **Non-tariff protectionist measures** by A on B in time t (**number of measures**) (log)			
	Model 1a	Model 2a	Model 3a	Model 4a	Model 1b	Model 2b	Model 3b	Model 4b
Protectionist measures by B on A in time t-1 (num/ of measures) (log)	0.230*** (0.000)	0.230*** (0.000)	0.230*** (0.000)	0.181*** (0.000)	0.490*** (0.004)	0.486* (0.004)	0.520*** (0.010)	0.500*** (0.010)
Interaction term: Trade agreements * Protect. measures in t-1		−0.041* (0.020)		−0.040* (0.020)		0.130** (0.048)		0.141** (0.050)
Interaction term: % of intermediate goods (GVC) * Protect. measures in t-1			−0.224*** (0.030)	−0.360*** (0.031)			0.010*** (0.001)	0.010*** (0.001)
CONTROL VARIABLES	NO	NO	NO	YES	NO	NO	NO	YES
Constant	0.110*** (0.000)	0.110*** (0.000)	0.113*** (0.002)	−0.482*** (0.024)	0.352*** (0.005)	0.352*** (0.005)	0.360*** (0.005)	3.01*** (0.060)
R2	0.23	0.23	0.24	0.28	0.20	0.20	0.20	0.26
Adj. R2	0.23	0.23	0.24	0.28	0.20	0.20	0.20	0.26
Num. obs.	51,872	51,872	51,872	50,441	51,872	51,872	51,872	50,441
RMSE	0.45	0.45	0.45	0.44	1.07	1.06	1.06	1.03

Source: Author's creation.

Notes:
*** $p < 0.001$, ** $p < 0.01$, * $p < 0.05$

Table 4.4 The relationship between tariff and NTMs with PTAs and GVCs (DV3a and DV3b)

	DV3a: Proportion of Tariff protectionist measures by A on B in time t (%)				DV3b: Proportion of Non-tariff protectionist measures by A on B in time t (%)			
	Model 1a	Model 2a	Model 3a	Model 4a	Model 1b	Model 2b	Model 3b	Model 4b
Protectionist measures by B on A in time $t-1$ (num/ of measures)	0.053*** (0.001)	0.054*** (0.001)	0.230*** (0.000)	0.100*** (0.000)	0.130*** (0.001)	0.146*** (0.001)	0.154*** (0.002)	0.150*** (0.010)
Interaction term: Trade Agreements (PTAs) * Protect. measures in $t-1$		−0.041*** (0.012)		−0.002 (0.002)		0.0005* (0.0003)		0.0002 (0.002)
Interaction term: % of intermediate goods (GVC) * Protectionist measures in $t-1$			−0.074*** (0.020)	−0.001*** (0.000)			0.003*** (0.000)	0.003*** (0.001)
CONTROL VARIABLES	NO	NO	NO	YES	NO	NO	NO	YES
Constant	0.080*** (0.001)	0.078*** (0.001)	0.080*** (0.001)	−0.710*** (0.020)	0.146*** (0.001)	0.144*** (0.001)	0.148*** (0.001)	−0.970*** (0.020)
R2	0.05	0.05	0.05	0.05	0.14	0.14	0.14	0.20
Adj. R2	0.05	0.05	0.05	0.05	0.14	0.14	0.14	0.20
Num. obs.	51,872	51,872	51,872	50,077	51,872	51,872	51,872	50,441
RMSE	0.27	0.27	0.27	0.30	0.36	0.36	0.36	0.36

Source: Author's creation.

Notes:
***p < 0.001, **p < 0.01, *p < 0.05

68 *Protectionism and trade policy responses*

statistically significant predictors of tariff responses, while they are positive, statistically significant predictors of non-tariff responses.

4.5 Political and economic magnitude of findings at the state-level analysis

The empirical results presented above are merely statistical relationships between the variables of interest. As such, the political and economic magnitude of the findings cannot be inferred directly. However, careful interpretation of the econometric findings can shed light on how interconnectedness through a PTA or GVC may affect the dynamics of bilateral protectionism. From a quantitative perspective, the main goal here is first to establish the existence of the relationship between the main variables of interest and then to explore them in detail through country case studies presented in Chapter 5. However, as a political scientist, I am also particularly interested in the political economy magnitudes of these results, which is one of the areas in which further research can build upon the results presented in this book. I will talk more about this in Chapters 5 and 6.

Let us return to the results presented in Table 4.3, where Hypotheses 1, 2, and 3 are tested. This first set of results shows interesting stories from an economic perspective. As discussed earlier, both the DV and the main IV present the share of bilateral trade affected by protectionist measures by one country against another. This characteristic of the variables of interest—which is a percentage between 0 and 100 representing the share of value traded between two countries affected by protectionist measures by year—already gives a rough estimate of how much of the value between two trading partners is affected through retaliation. However, it still has not been determined how much this trade retaliation actually hurts the partner and what the economic magnitude is of the effect of an existing PTA. To get to the bottom of this, I take a closer look at the coefficients and interact them with the maximum, minimum, and average of the variables of analysis presented in Table 4.1. In doing so, the following results were found:

- If the share of trade affected by protection measures from B toward A in time $t-1$ increases 100%, from 0% to 100%, retaliation from A toward B increases 2%, on average based on Model 3 of Table 4.3.
- If the share of trade affected by protectionist measures from B toward A in time $t-1$ increases by one percentage point, such as from 1% to 2%, retaliation from A toward B increases 0.020%, on average. Even though this is not nearly a one-to-one relationship, it still indicates that retaliation dynamics exist.

From Table 4.1, we know that the average of all protectionist measures by B on A in time $t-1$, which is the share of bilateral trade affected in terms of log, is 0.106 (10.6%). With this data in mind, the average protectionist measure

Protectionism and trade policy responses 69

response can be presented, which is 0.21% (0.106*0.020*100). The interpretation here is if country B has no protectionist measures in place, and it simply introduces the average protectionist measures across the same, which is 10.6%, then, ceteris paribus, country A will verily retaliate with 0.21%.

The interesting part of the main analysis presented above is the impact of having a PTA in place in bilateral protectionist dynamics. What Table 4.3 exhibits is that having a PTA in place, ceteris paribus, means that the retaliation is 5% smaller than not having it. This is a considerable effect size when compared to the 2% effect of the protectionist measure. In other words, if county B protectionism toward A impacts, in the share of trade increases from 0% to 100%, A will increase protectionism toward B by 2%. If this result is turned around and B goes from 100% to 0% protectionism toward A, then A will only reduce its protectionist measure toward B, on average, by 2%. This is three percentage points less than the reduction effect in the protectionism of PTAs, or a decrease of 60%.

Let us think about these results from a political perspective. The main political outcome here is that PTAs seem to be effective in deterring a spiral of protectionism and help prevent a tit-for-tat dynamic in exactly the way that they are designed to do. Hence, instead of dismantling them, countries should work to deepen trade-related constraints through trade agreements. However, the results presented in Tables 4.3 and 4.4 introduce two key elements related to the real effect of PTA in the context of murkier protectionism. If there is a trade agreement in place, when B introduces one new protectionist measure against A, retaliation from A to B of tariff measures is negative, as demonstrated by Models 2a in both Table 4.3 and Table 4.4. However, if there is a trade agreement in place when B introduces one new protectionist measure toward A, retaliation from A to B of non-tariff measures is positive. This has very important policy implications: given that non-tariff measures are not easily observable, countries with PTAs tend to respond much more with non-tariff measures than with tariff measures. Here is a step-by-step description of what can be the political dynamics that explain the findings:

1. Country B implements a protectionist measure toward A. There is a PTA in place between the two countries.
2. If the measure implemented by B is transparent or nontransparent, the affected sector normally notices that measure before the government. For example, if it is a consumption subsidy on domestic products, the affected sector in country A will notice that by a decrease in their exports to B.
3. Once the affected sector in country A notices the protectionist measure, it will pressure its government to ask country B to do something in response.
4. Country A's government, in order not to escalate the tensions with B but to give a response to its domestic industry, will have much more incentive to implement a non-tariff measure in response. This protectionist measure would probably be to defend the sector affected domestically.

Finally, on the effect of GVCs, no dependable results were found to draw some analysis on the economic magnitude of them. This is likely due to the limitations behind GVC measures. As different studies have shown, it is still a very complex task to measure them (World Bank, 2020b), not only from the measurements themselves but also due to the lack of consensus still existing about the right measure to use. This is something that policymakers note also. For instance, in an interview I had with a former Mexican government undersecretary, they said:

> For example, in Latin America the big problem is that it depends a lot on commodities and not on products with more added value. Then each reality depends on the explanation of why they have not also fared in a globalized world. That is why it is very complex to generalize.[18]

To contemplate this complexity the interviewee talks about, in this book, I rely on intermediate goods as my main variable of analysis, following a similar logic of studies by the World Bank (2020b); and the WTO (2020). Using intermediate goods as GVCs proxies is still imperfect because as soon as countries trade in intermediate products and add some value along the chain, they are included in a GVC. As such, it is taxingly difficult to say which countries are partners in a GVC and which ones are not. In general, GVC data quality is still limited, as well as the data reported by multinationals. Take, for example, the case of the value chain of an iPod from Apple. Studies have shown that in exports from China to the United States, the iPod's final price was reported at only 2% of the represented value added in China (Dedrick et al., 2010).[19] More generally, when analyzing GCVs, we should be skeptical about the reports of multinationals due to transfer pricing, and limited information about the actual value added, as there are plenty of tax and accounting issues, making it a work of art and science to find the true value added at each station along the GVC. So, not by averaging, the results on GVCs have to be taken as conclusive rather just preliminary evidence until more detailed and publicly available data becomes obtainable.

If we take the case of the US–China trade war as an example, we can see that the results above are in line with the bilateral tension between the two countries. Chong and Li (2019) evaluate the domino effect of the United States setting higher tariffs and China setting higher tariffs in response, and take the worst-case scenario of bilateral trade between China and the United States dropping by 27% (Peluffo, 2020, p. 10).

For all these reasons it is important to put the quantitative results in context. The fact that a coefficient is highly statistically significant, still does not tell too much about the real economic and political significance. This is why in Chapter 5, an in-depth analysis of three specific country cases is conducted to elucidate the political and economic magnitude of the empirical findings.

This analysis will be centered in Latin America on three countries in particular—Argentina, Brazil, and Mexico—for a more detailed analysis that

Protectionism and trade policy responses 71

will answer questions about how much an increase in protectionism has an effect on the economy and take into account country-specific variables. An example of this includes, how many jobs are at stake with protections? What share of GDP is really affected by recent protectionist dynamics? Likewise, I study the profile of the trade between specific countries and their main trading partners, from the perspective of what underlying factors are traded. For example, if it is mainly manufacturing being targeted, such as in the case of Mexico, then jobs get lost through retaliation. If it is resources or services, it may well be that only capital incomes fall through the retaliation by trading partners but not a significant number of jobs are directly affected.

Notes

1 This chapter is an extended version of Albertoni, N. (2023). The risk of murky trade protectionism in an interconnected and uncertain global economy, *Estudios Internacionales*, 55(205).
2 Data from the GTA show that, in general, it takes time (sometimes many months) for governments to formally implement trade policy measures. Moreover, it shows how this time has quickened since the last GFC. However, we can see that, to collect an important threshold of data (around 1,000 policy interventions), they have taken a minimum of 187 days in the past four years. This may suggest that most of the recent protectionist dynamics are more political threats than in real measures. All this is to say that a period of one year is the time in which retaliation dynamics move beyond mere anecdotal evidence.
3 In the Appendix, the structure of different datasets considered in this book are introduced and the different patterns these reflect in the quantitative analysis.
4 For more details about the GTA, visit: www.globaltradealert.org/.
5 For more details about BACI-CEPII trade data, visit: www.cepii.fr/CEPII/en/bdd_modele/bdd_modele.asp.
6 For more details about the IPE Data Resource, visit https://doi.org/10.7910/DVN/X093TV.
7 For more details about the GTA, visit www.globaltradealert.org/; for the Harmonized System (HS), visit: https://unstats.un.org/unsd/tradekb/Knowledgebase/Harmonized-Commodity-Description-and-Coding-Systems-HS.
8 Global Trade Alert, www.globaltradealert.org/.
9 WTO, *Regional Trade Agreements*, www.wto.org/english/tratop_e/region_e/region_e.htm.
10 For other studies on why the term "PTA" is preferred over the term "RTA," see, for instance, Hofmann et al. (2019) and Ruta (2017).
11 The raw data is publicly available at www.cepii.fr. BACI-CEPII uses the HS 2002 version, so I merged it with the equivalent code in the HS 2012 version. See: UN Statistics Division, *Correlation and Conversion Tables Used in UN Comtrade*, https://unstats.un.org/unsd/trade/classifications/correspondence-tables.asp.
12 *UN Statistics Division, Classification by Broad Economic Categories*, https://unstats.un.org/unsd/tradekb/knowledgebase/50089/classification-by-broad-economic-categories-rev4. See Table 1.5 in Chapter 1. It shows the three basic classes of goods categorized in the BEC. As explained above, a concept normally related to intermediate good, is "intra-industry trade" (IIT), which is a more general way of

defining trade within similar industries. The OECD (2005) defines IIT, as "the trade in similar products—horizontal trade" with differentiated varieties, for example, cars of a similar class and price range, and trade in "vertically differentiated" products distinguished by quality and price, for example, exports of high-quality clothing and imports of lower-quality clothing. There could be IIT in both Intermediate and final goods. While IIT can applied to different stages of a good, intermediate goods are normally considered to measure GVCs. See Lüthje (2001) and Peterson &Thies (2015) for studies on IIT and intermediate goods.

13 Based on these new measures, further studies can interact this with the share of trade between A and B of total trade of A, to get a "back-of-the-envelope" calculation for the income effects of retaliation, which will be further discussed later.

14 UNCTAD (2018) International Investment Agreements Database, http://investmentpolicyhub.unctad.org/IIA/IiasByCountry#iiaInnerMenu.

15 The International Political Economy Data Resource (IPE), which compiles data from 89 IPE data sources into a single dataset (Graham & Tucker, 2017); visit: https://doi.org/10.7910/DVN/X093TV.

16 T. Mayer & S. Zignago (2011), Notes on CEPII's distances measures: the GeoDist Database CEPII Working Paper 2011-25, www.cepii.fr/CEPII/en/bdd_modele/presentation.asp?id=6.

17 Given the high concentration in zero values in the main variables of interest, I use $log(x+1)$ transformation, which is widely used among data scientists (Bellégo & Pape, 2019).

18 Author's interview with a former Mexican government undersecretary, January 2020.

19 For an extended discussion about Dedrick et al.'s findings, see H. R.Varian, An iPod has global value: ask the (many) countries that make it, *New York Times* (June 28, 2007), www.nytimes.com/2007/06/28/business/worldbusiness/28scene.html.

5 A comparative approach
Protectionism and trade policy responses in Latin America

5.1 Introduction

This chapter moves away from the large-N analysis undertaken in Chapter 4 and concentrates on three country case studies in the Latin American region: Argentina, Brazil, and Mexico.[1] As mentioned throughout this book, I have used a mixed-method approach to test the hypotheses and causal claims presented in earlier chapters. Chapter 4 consisted of a quantitative analysis based on large-N data sets. In this chapter, I undertake comparative case-study research, which combines qualitative and quantitative information derived from within-country data. As different studies on policymaking have shown, the case-study approach helps "directly analyze and reconstruct the process of political decision making," in which actors' interests and political and economic factors play a key role (Mukherjee, 2016, p. 23). Case analysis helps us ascertain causal mechanisms in more detail than can be gleaned from large-N analyses (Collier et al., 2004; King et al., 1994). As Mukherjee (2016, p. 23) states, "a contextual comparison of individual cases also ensures that the generalizations made from the large-N analysis are not too sweeping."

Hence, these small-n case studies not only complement my quantitative findings but also offer a robustness test of the large-N statistical analysis presented earlier. As Seawright (2016, p. 42) notes, "an integrative multimethod design provides a family of compelling strategies for linking qualitative and quantitative components of an overall design, while also enhancing the quality of causal inference." I chose Mexico, Brazil, and Argentina as my country cases because they represent 72% of total regional exports and 64% of total imports (UN Comtrade, 2019). My task is to better understand their trade policy performance and illuminate how they were affected by and have responded to protectionism since the GFC.

As a main departure point, I build upon Wise et al.'s (2015) *Unexpected Outcomes*, which argues that emerging regions such as Latin America and East Asia showed remarkable resilience when faced with the GFC. This phenomenon differed from previous historical cases in the 1980s and 1990s and may have played a role in "deterring a full-blown global depression" (p.1). I take this framework further and explore how the industrial characteristics of my

DOI: 10.4324/9781003340393-5

three country cases shape the likelihood of a response to rising global protectionism. Within each country, I analyze specific industry-level cases that have been directly or indirectly affected by current protectionist trends and I examine the political economy dynamics that are playing out in each case. Recent studies have shown important direct and indirect effects of post-GFC trade disputes in emerging economies, especially in Latin America.[2] In light of this, I probe whether countries that have strong trade ties with the rest of the world via preferential trade agreements have been more affected by less transparent protectionist dynamics than those with fewer formal trade ties. In other words, one of the essential research questions will be the extent to which trade interconnectivity increases the risk of being harmed by nontransparent protectionism.

A study developed by the Chilean General Directorate of International Economic Relations (DIRECON, 2018) shows that 63% of Chile's exports were designated to countries in the core and periphery of the US–Sino trade conflict—India, Turkey, the EU, Canada, Mexico, and Russia. Given Chile's strong web of FTAs, many tariff increases will not be implemented against Chile by its various trading partners.[3] This does not mean that the country has escaped the effects of non-tariff protectionist measures, however. Indeed, Chile was affected by 2,124 measures between 2009 and 2019, 79% of which have been "murky" instruments implemented by countries that comprise the rest of the world, that is, countries with which Chile trades in the absence of an FTA.[4] What happened in Argentina, Brazil, and Mexico? Have they been affected by protectionism over the last decade? And if so, how did they respond to it?

This chapter is organized as follows: I begin with an explanation of my case selection strategy and Latin America's relevance. Second, my fieldwork method is described, including my interviews with key social, economic, and political actors involved in the making of Latin American trade policy. Third, I present an in-depth analysis of the three cases of interest. I conclude with some finals thoughts on this comparative analysis of protectionism and trade policy responses in Latin America.

5.2 Case selection: why Latin America and why these three countries?

Latin America, in general, and my specific three countries of interest are relevant for both theoretical and methodological reasons. First, from a theoretical point of view, the latest studies and political debates on recent trade dynamics have focused on the United States, China, the EU, Canada, and Japan. Less has been written on the effects of protectionist global dynamics in emerging regions since the GFC. This fixation on central economies, though pertinent, overlooks the fact that emerging countries such as Brazil, Mexico, and Argentina have also been impacted by the rise of trade protectionism over the past decade (Zandi et al., 2018; Evenett & Fritz, 2018). Moreover, the literature has paid little attention to how these Latin American countries have reacted to this increasingly adverse global trade environment. Second, I selected these three Latin American emerging economies because they are also part of the G20 group of countries and thus representative of this larger group, which is the premier forum for international financial and economic cooperation.[5]

From a regional perspective, Latin America has emerged as an interesting "median" case in the non-developed world with regard to protectionist and liberalizing trade policy measures (Seawright & Gerring, 2008). As Figure 5.1 shows, Latin America stands between Asia and Africa, two non-developed regions, in both total numbers of protectionist and liberalizing measures between 2008 and 2018 (left axis) and the share of RoW's exports to the region affected by protectionist measures (right axis). As a regional "median" case in the non-developed world, the current literature has paid scant attention to the impact and responses to protectionist dynamics in Latin America (Seawright & Gerring, 2008).

Also relevant is the fact that Argentina and Brazil, two of my three case countries, are members of the Southern Cone Common Market (Mercosur), which is a regional integration project established in 1991 by Argentina, Brazil, Paraguay, and Uruguay. Mercosur comprises more than 270 million people, and its combined GDP is US$ 5.8 trillion, making this Southern bloc equivalent to the fifth-largest economy in the world. According to the Treaty of Asuncion—the founding document of the bloc—Mercosur's main goal was to establish a common market by December 31, 1994. This involved "the free movement of goods, services and factors of production between countries through […] the elimination of customs duties and non-tariff restrictions on the movement of goods, and any other equivalent measures."[6] Yet, 30 years since its founding, the formation of a common market has eluded bloc members. That is why Mercosur is normally defined as an "imperfect customs union," or simply a "free trade agreement" (Felter et al., 2019; Albertoni, 2016, 2019b). To date, the members have agreed to eliminate some customs duties, to implement a

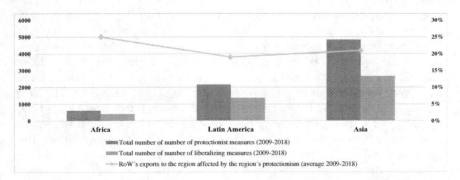

Figure 5.1 Latin America as a median case in the non-developed world in terms of protectionist measures.

Source: Author's creation based on Global Trade Alert www.globaltradealert.org/

common external tariff on certain products originating outside of Mercosur, and to adopt a common trade policy toward outside countries and blocs (Felter et al., 2019).

Mexico, too, conducts most of its trade policy strategy through bilateral and unilateral policies. Having joined the North American Free Trade Agreement (NAFTA) with Canada and the United States in 1994, Mexico maintains an independent trade policy toward non-NAFTA trade partners. These differences are relevant in terms of my comparative case analysis because they offer sub-regional (Argentina and Brazil) and bilateral (Mexico) perspectives regarding the respective trade policy dynamics of these countries. The selection of these three cases also shows "diversity" within both the G20 and the Latin American region. Figure 5.2 shows how the three countries at hand are distributed in terms of share of world exports to the countries affected by protectionist measures in the G20 and Latin American countries. For both subgroups, Argentina has been the most protectionist, Brazil is in second place, and Mexico is the least protectionist of the three selected countries.

When we consider trade measures implemented by the G20, which represent 80% of GWP and three-quarters of global trade from 2009 to 2019,[7] Argentina, Brazil, and Mexico are well distributed in terms of both the number of protectionist measures that each country has implemented as a G20 member and the share of the world's exports to each country that has been affected by protectionist measures within the Latin American region. Argentina has been the most protectionist country within the G20; Brazil falls in the middle of the list of G20 countries; and Mexico was the second least protectionist of the G20 economies.[8]

The countries at hand also represent an interesting mix in terms of their main economic and trade indicators. Table 5.1 shows the economic differences and commonalities between the three countries. First, when considering average growth of GDP between 2008 and 2018, Argentina registered the highest growth rate during those ten years (43%), ranking it 91st out of 196 countries in terms of GDP growth.[9] Both Mexico's and Brazil's GDP growths rates were 10%, ranking them 143rd and 144th in terms of GDP growth, respectively, over this same time period. We see a very different scenario in terms of growth of GDP per capita, which is a more comparative figure that compensates for population differences. Argentina, again, is the country that has grown more in terms of per capita GDP growth (29%) from 2008 to 2018, ranking 83rd out of the 196 countries in this variable; Brazil's per capita GDP growth was 1% over this same period, ranking it 144th; and Mexico had a negative per capita GDP growth rate of −3.43%, ranking 159th in the 196-country sample.

Second, the three countries have different markets as their main export destinations. Argentina's main destination is Brazil, which is 18% of its total exports; for Brazil, China is the main destination (26%); and for Mexico, the United States is the main export destination (70%). While China is in the top three destinations for Argentina and Brazil, it is not one of Mexico's main

Protectionism and trade policy responses in Latin America 77

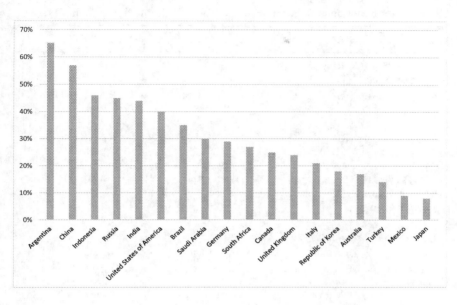

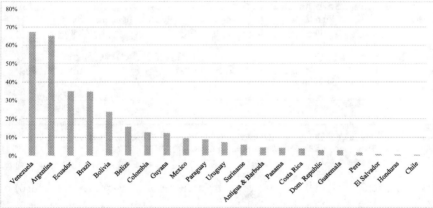

Figure 5.2 Distribution of the three case countries in the G20 and Latin America (Av. 2009–18).

Share of world exports to **G20 countries** affected by protectionist measures.
Share of world exports to **LatAm countries** affected by protectionist measures.
Source: Author's creation based on GTA, 2019.

destinations. Mexico demonstrates an important concentration of exports to the United States, while Argentina and Brazil have better diversification in terms of destinations. Significant variations also arise when considering the origin of imports for the three countries. Argentina's main origin is Brazil, which is 24% of its total imports; for Brazil, China is the main origin (20%);

Table 5.1 Main economic and trade characteristics of Argentina, Brazil, and Mexico

	ARGENTINA	BRAZIL	MEXICO
ECONOMIC FIGURES			
GDP GROWTH (Av. 2008–18)	44% (RANKING 91 OF 196)	10% (RANKING 143 OF 196)	10% (RANKING 144 OF 196)
GDP PC	$11,684 (RANKING 66 OF 196)	$8,921 (RANK 82 OF 196)	$9,673 (RANKING 79 OF 196)
GDP PC GROWTH (Av. 2008–18)	29.5% (RANKING 83 OF 196)	1.02% (RANKING 141 OF 196)	−3.43% (RANKING 159 OF 196)
TRADE FIGURES			
Main Export Destinations	Brazil: 18% China: 7% US: 7%	China: 26% US: 12% Argentina: 6%	US: 70% Canada: 4% Germany: 2%
Main Import Origins	Brazil: 24% China 17% US: 13%	China: 20% US: 17% Germany: 6%	US: 57% China: 13% Germany: 4%
Main Exporting Sectors	Soybean Meal: 15% Corn: 6% Trucks: 6%	Soybeans: 14% Crude Petroleum: 10% Iron Ore: 8%	Cars: 11% Vehicle Parts: 7% Trucks: 6%
Main Importing Sectors	Cars: 8% Vehicle parts: 5% Soybeans: 4%	Refined Petroleum: 7% Vehicle Parts: 4% Crude Petroleum: 3%	Refined Petroleum: 8% Vehicle Parts: 7% Office Machine Pts: 4%

Source: Author's calculation of country rankings based on the Observatory of Economic Complexity, 2018, https://oec.world/en/profile/country/

and for Mexico, the United States is the main import origin (57%). Third, in terms of sectoral representation in international trade, we can see a very similar pattern between Argentina and Brazil. In both cases, the main export sector is related to soybeans. Mexico is a more industrialized economy in which the three main exporting sectors are cars (11%), vehicle parts (7%), and delivery trucks (6%). In the main import sectors, we can see that Argentina is more dependent on industrial goods, with cars registering 8% and vehicles parts 5% as its two main importing sectors. Mexico's import sectors are refined petroleum (8%) and vehicle parts (7%).

Regarding institutional factors such as rule of law, effectiveness of government, and regulatory qualities, there are no major differences between the three countries of interest. For this analysis, we are comparing cases that deal with similar structural challenges. In the three periods of analysis, Mexico had better performance in terms of the effectiveness of governments and regulatory quality. During the three periods of analysis, Brazil had better performance in terms of rule of law. Argentina has the worst performance in all three periods for the three variables.

Finally, the region in general, and the three countries specifically, have their differences and commonalities in terms of PTAs and GVCs, two variables central to this analysis. In terms of PTAs, Mexico, with 22 PTAs, is second only to the EU countries in the number of PTAs it has signed up to 2019. Brazil and Argentina (Mercosur) are among the least integrated countries in terms of PTAs, as Mercosur's common trade policy mandates that the four countries negotiate outside PTAs as an entire bloc.

To show how my three selected countries stand in comparison with other countries in terms of GVCs, WTO data on "Trade in Value-Added (VA) and Global Value Chains (GVCs)," will be used, which provide "an overview of the key indicators that can be derived from trade in value-added statistics."[10] Some of the measures presented in the WTO's profiles in VA and GVCs are the interconnection of national economies within GVCs and the level of trade in merchandise and services in intermediate products.[11] The GVC participation index specifically provides "an estimation of how much an economy is connected to global value chains for its foreign trade." There are two methods of GVC participation, including "upstream and downstream links in international production chains":

> Individual economies participate in global value chains by importing foreign inputs to produce the goods and services they export (backward GVC participation) and also by exporting domestically produced inputs to partners in charge of downstream production stages (forward GVC participation).[12]

The measure of trade in intermediate products and services shows the share in total trade of "tangible and intangible products utilized as inputs in production, excluding fixed assets. Trade statistics on intermediate products reflect the exchanges of parts, components, accessories, and intermediary services taking place within international production chains."[13] As explained in earlier chapters, the definition of intermediate goods is based upon the United Nations' Broad Economic Categories (BEC) classification, which groups commodities by main end-use, distinguishing between consumption, capital, and intermediate goods. Figure 5.4 shows how the three selected countries are distributed in terms of the GVC Participation Index, which combines backward and forward GVC participation:

> Backward GVC participation refers to the ratio of the "foreign value-added content of exports" […] to the economy's total gross exports. This is the "buyer" perspective or sourcing side in GVCs, where an economy imports intermediates to produce its exports. Forward GVC participation corresponds to the ratio of the "domestic value added sent to third economies" […] to the economy's total gross exports. It captures the domestic value

80 *Protectionism and trade policy responses in Latin America*

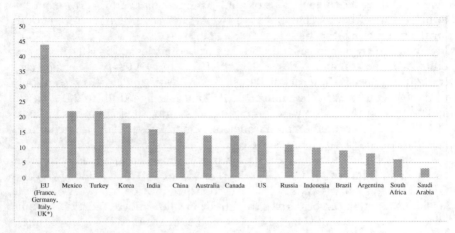

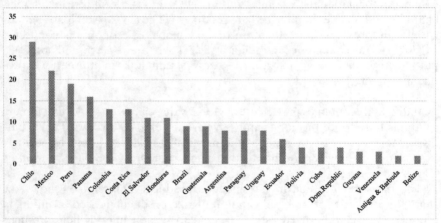

Figure 5.3 How are the three selected countries distributed in the G20 and in Latin America on preferential trade agreements?

Number of PTAs of G20 countries until 2019.
Number of PTAs of Latin American countries until 2019.
Source: Author's creation based on WTO's Regional Trade Agreements Database, http://rtais.wto.org/

added contained in inputs sent to third economies for further processing and export through value chains. This is the "seller" perspective or supply side in GVC participation.[14]

As we can see, in terms of GVC participation, the three countries present interesting variation, both among themselves and between the average of developing and developed economies. Mexico appears to be in a better

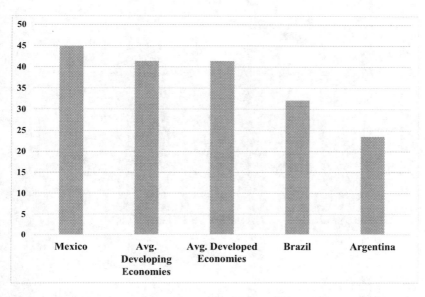

Figure 5.4 The GVC Participation Index (% share in total gross exports, in 2015).

Note: The last publicly available data by country is for 2015.

Source: Author's creation based on WTO, *Trade in Value Added and Global Value Chains*, www.wto.org/english/res_e/statis_e/miwi_e/countryprofiles_e.htm

position in terms of GVC interconnectivity, while Brazil and Argentina fall below average when compared with the rest of the world. In Figure 5.5, when we consider trade in merchandise intermediate products, we see that Brazil and Mexico are the two countries in which imports of intermediate goods have a higher representation in total imports. In comparison, Argentina and Brazil have a higher representation of intermediates in total exports.

Considering the differences at hand, I used a "diversity" approach as the main case selection technique. Seawright and Gerring (2008) state that in case selection and analysis, the "diverse" method serves to "exemplify diverse values" of the dependent and independent variables, and is imperative when we are conducting an "expiratory or confirmatory" analysis in which we want to illuminate the full range of variation on the dependent and independent variables (p. 297). As shown, diversity as the case selection technique fits the three cases mentioned above from both a regional and a global perspective. Taking three different Latin American country cases, which are "medians" in the non-developed world (see Figure 5.1), helps us understand regional patterns as well as trade policy dynamics in other non-developed regions. Simultaneously, the three countries selected shed light on G20 dynamism. As different figures above show, the three countries selected are well distributed within the G20,

82 Protectionism and trade policy responses in Latin America

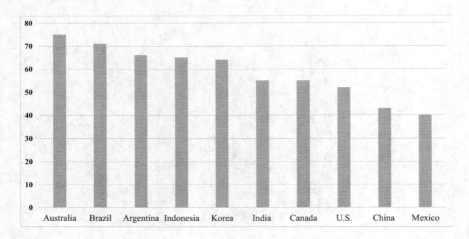
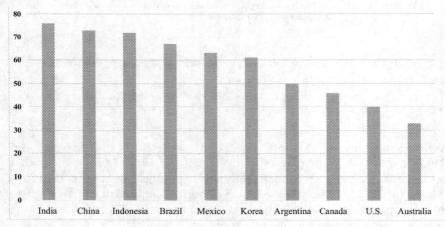

Figure 5.5 Trade in merchandise intermediate products (2017).

Exports of intermediates (% in total exports).
Imports of intermediates (% in total imports).

Source: Author's creation based on Source: WTO, *Trade in Value Added and GVC*, www.wto.org/english/res_e/statis_e/miwi_e/countryprofiles_e.htm.

in key variables of interest. The diverse position of the countries of interest at the regional and global levels, lends logic to the case analysis presented in this chapter (Gerring & Cojocaru, 2016; Seawright & Gerring, 2008).

As mentioned, another key element regarding case selection is that it aims to complement the large-N statistical analysis presented in Chapter 4. In this regard, considering the six types of case studies suggested by Lijphart (1971, p. 691)—theoretical, interpretative, hypothesis-generating, theory-confirming, theory-infirming, and deviant—the present case study has theory-confirming goals. Hence, having selected these cases, it is important to note that this is not simply country case analysis but rather country-sector analysis—meaning that the country-sector that reflects the impact of protectionist measures emanating from the rest of the world will be the focus here. Particular attention will be paid to the following research questions:

1) Who are the domestic economic actors involved in developing a trade policy response?
2) When they are adversely affected by a trade partner, how might they lobby for protectionist responses?
3) Do they promote diplomatic approaches before retaliation, such as bilateral working groups, to pressure the implementing country to lower trade restrictions?
4) Do representatives from the affected export sector coordinate with other traditional protectionist sectors, like importers, to demand retaliation?

My intention in posing these questions is to add important insights to the trade policy literature by demonstrating that both export and import sectors may coordinate to demand protectionism when faced with adverse policies from trade partners. As the trade literature has extensively demonstrated, the exporting sector typically lobbies for trade openness, while import-competing industries tend to lobby for protection (Roosevelt, 2016). Can we say that both sectors find an equilibrium and together lobby for protection when faced with a protectionist policy response? The primary group that will be interviewed in this book is the main industry lobby—such as in Brazil, the National Confederation of Industry—as well as other actors, including economic interest groups such as trade chambers, unions, and exporter associations.

Before delving into the details of each country case, let me mention what I expect to see in each country in light of my quantitative results reported in the previous chapter. First, if my theoretical intuitions are correct, I expect that when they are adversely affected, all three countries will systematically respond to protectionist measures imposed by another country (H1). However, the existence of PTAs and GVCs can decrease the likelihood of a protectionist response (H2 and H3). Thus—considering Figures 5.3, 5.4, and 5.5—I would expect that: Mexico, which is more interconnected to the world through PTAs and GVCs, would be less responsive to protectionism than Argentina and Brazil, which are less interconnected to the rest of the world. Second, I expect that countries with high trade interdependencies, such as Mexico, will retaliate more with NTMs, which are less transparent, than with tariff measures.

5.3 Fieldwork: interviews with key trade policy actors in Latin America

Between fall 2019 and summer 2020, I developed a list of relevant actors to interview in each country of interest. I then designed a semistructured questionnaire to guide my fieldwork interviews with key social, economic, and political actors relevant to trade policy. Apart from gathering these insights on the topic of interest, another goal was to collect data on specific sectors that have been affected by protectionist measures. In particular, the interviews helped me pinpoint some of the factors that prompted policy makers to adopt more restrictive trade policies in the wake of the 2008–09 GFC. This fieldwork also allowed me to understand the policymaking processes that undergird my large-sample analysis. Due to the coronavirus pandemic. I conducted most of these interviews via Zoom or Skype.

5.3.1 Interview design and methodology

As mentioned before, my research design has two steps. First is the large-N quantitative analysis presented in Chapter 4 based on dyad-year data at the state and industry levels, that encompassed different countries from different regions across the world.[15] The second part of my research design, which this chapter focuses on, is based on a more in-depth analysis of three emerging economies in Latin America: Argentina, Brazil, and Mexico. The following sections consist of a country narrative of trade policy performance amid current protectionist trends for each of the three cases. In doing so, this section offers a robust examination of these country cases according to the different levels of analysis offered above. Again, a qualitative interview method is used to flesh out those factors that prompted policymakers to adopt more restrictive trade policies in the wake of the 2008–09 GFC.

Interviewees primarily consist of industry leaders, "elites" from government, academia, the media, and research institutions. The sample size consists of at least one to two individuals from each category in each country. Contact information for the participants came through the standard snowball method. When I conduct an interview, I ask for suggestions for future interviewees. Additional contacts came from other known contacts or subjects in or familiar with the region. Twenty-four individuals were selected for interviews who came from various backgrounds and professions as listed in Table 5.2. Once an email address or other forms of contact information were obtained, an email was sent to potential subjects briefly describing the research, what would be required of the meeting including when and where, the list of talking points based on the general themes of the research, and the informed consent disclosure.[16] If subjects agreed, they were asked for approximately 30 to 60 minutes for an individual, one-time interview.

Talking points for these meetings were based on my extensive literature review on those factors that prompted policymakers to adopt restrictive trade policies. Participants chose the location, day, and time for the conversation via Skype or Zoom. Handwritten notes were taken for all meetings, and further impressions and notes were recorded with typewritten notes.[17] The list of interviewees was divided into five main groups: 1) Global trade perspectives and 2) Latin American perspectives; and experts and key actors from 3) Argentina, 4) Brazil, and 5) Mexico. Table 5.2 includes a short biographical description.[18]

Table 5.2 List of interviewees

Interview ID	Short Bio
	GLOBAL TRADE PERSPECTIVES
001	Research economist with the World Trade Organization.
002	Chilean lawyer and trade negotiator.
	LATIN AMERICAN PERSPECTIVES
101	Researcher of the Catholic University of Chile.
102	Former Chilean government minister.
103	Former Ecuadorean government minister.
104	Employee of the University of Chile.
105	Former Colombian government vice minister.
106	Economist and former Peruvian government minister.
	MEXICO
201	Employee of COPARMEX, the Mexican Employers' Association.
202	Employee of Tenaris Mexico.
203	Former Mexican government undersecretary.
204	Industrial union leader in Mexico.
205	Mexican trade policy expert.
	ARGENTINA
301	Former Argentinean government minister.
302	Former Argentinean government secretary.
303	Argentinean economist, employee of the Center iDeAS/UNSAM.
304	Former Argentinean trade policymaker.
305	Former Argentinean trade policymaker.
306	Argentine specialist in international trade relations and economic integration.
	BRAZIL
401	Employee of the Foudaçao Getulio Vargas, Rio de Janeiro.
402	International Trade and Public Policies expert.
403	Former Brazilian government secretary.
404	Employee of the University of International Business and Economics in Beijing, China.

Source: Author's creation.

5.4 A brief background of Latin America's trade policy evolution

The modern economic history of Latin America has seen numerous reforms since the mid-1980s. External shocks have periodically hampered the economic success of the region. The widespread and prolonged reliance on import-substitution-industrialization (ISI), which originated in the 1960s, was a main drag on these economies.

> [ISI] represents a shift away from the outward orientation to export promotion, to an inward-looking orientation. ISI was designated to replace imports with domestic production under the guiding hand of the state. Governments used activist industrial, fiscal, and monetary policy to achieve growth.
>
> (Franko, 2018, p. 615)

ISI measures wreaked havoc on regional fiscal accounts and induced periodic balance-of-payments crises.

In the 1970s, international bank lending was directed toward Latin America under the auspices of sovereign borrowing. However, oil stocks prices in 1973–4 and again in 1978–9 fueled global inflation. When the US Federal Reserve responded with high interest rates, this sparked a debt crisis in Latin America that caused commercial banks to halt new lending to the region. The 1980s saw the collapse of the prevailing ISI model, as countries could no longer afford the subsidies and tax breaks. Nor could they generate the foreign exchange needed to pay for increasingly costly imports (Gereffi, 2014).

After almost three decades of an ISI strategy based on high tariffs to protect national industries, many Latin American countries in the 1980s launched ambitious reforms based on trade liberalization, privatization, and deregulation. These were in line with the Washington Consensus (WC), a set of policy instruments that Washington institutions such as the World Bank and the IMF prescribed for developing countries after the lost decade that followed the 1982 debt crisis. The WC advocated a package of policies to achieve economic recovery (fiscal discipline, public expenditure priorities, tax reforms, financial liberalization, exchange rates, FDI, privatization, deregulation, property right, and trade liberalization). On trade liberalization specifically, the policy recommendations were the following (Williamson, 1990, pp. 14–15):

> Quantitative trade restrictions should be rapidly replaced by tariffs, and these should be progressively reduced until a uniform low tariff in the range of 10 per cent (or at most around 20 per cent) is achieved. There is, however, some disagreement about the speed with which tariffs should be reduced (with recommendations falling in a band between three and ten years), and about whether it is advisable to slow down the process of liberalization when macroeconomic conditions are adverse (recession and payments deficit).

In the mid-1980s, there was no Latin American country with a positive current account balance, and regional capital "dried up to the debt crisis, current account deficits become unsustainable without external financing" (Williamson, 1990, p. 234). Conditionality tied to emergency loans from the IMF throughout Latin America promoted this trade liberalization. Mexico was the first of my three case countries to move from trade protectionism to trade liberalization, which it did in the context of acceding to the GATT in 1986. However, these reforms were not uniform throughout Latin America, and many countries still protected certain industries. Some trade liberalization efforts were quickly counteracted with protectionist policies in the form of NTMs meant to reduce imports (IDB, 2018). Such are frequently designed to protect domestic losers from liberalized trade who demand compensation from losses when trade is liberalized. As such, domestic actors that represent these losing commercial interests also have an influential role in the trade

Table 5.3 Weighted mean tariff rate applied to all products (%)

Country	Mid-1980s	Late 1980s	Mid-1990s	2000–07	2008–19
Latin America	50	34	12	8	5
Argentina	28	44	14	8	7
Bolivia	20	19	10	7	5
Brazil	80	51	13	9	8
Chile	36	15	11	5	3
Colombia	83	48	11	10	6
Costa Rica	53	n/a	12	4	2
Ecuador	50	40	11	9	6
El Salvador	23	n/a	9	6	3
Guatemala	50	n/a	11	6	2
Honduras	n/a	42	18	7	6
Mexico	34	11	14	8	3
Nicaragua	54	n/a	17	4	2
Panama	n/a	33	n/a	7	8
Paraguay	71	19	9.4	7	4
Peru	64	68	16	9	2
Uruguay	32	27	10	5	5
Venezuela	30	33	12	13	10

Source: Data from IADB and World Bank, https://data.iadb.org/ and https://data.iadb.org/

policymaking process. These trade reforms in Latin America also increased exposure to global volatility, especially in terms of commodities. For commodities, terms of trade are contingent on constant and unpredictable price fluctuations. Ultimately, in many countries throughout the region, trade policy choices were not made at the national level but instead were rooted in the rules of membership in the WTO (IDB, 2018).

In part, thanks to the numerous trade reforms of the 1980s and 1990s, the average tariff rate in Latin America decreased significantly. For instance, the regional average tariff was nearly 50% in 1985, with rates as high as 80% in Brazil and Colombia. By the mid-1990s, the average tariff had come down to 12% and to 10% in 2002. Interestingly, as Table 5.3 shows, tariffs in Latin America have been consistently decreasing since the mid-1980s. A former Chilean government minister is worth quoting on this topic:

> Tariffs in the region are less and less relevant as protection measures. In fact, except Venezuela, Mercosur remains the set of countries that have the highest applied tariff in the region at a level of around 10%. Effective protection and tariff escalation with a high peak are where a relevant level of protection is found. It is precisely formal non-tariff barriers and discriminatory administrative practices that really aim to manage trade.[19]

While tariffs have decreased in the last several decades, exports and imports of goods and services have increased consistently since the 1960s (Figure 5.6).

88 *Protectionism and trade policy responses in Latin America*

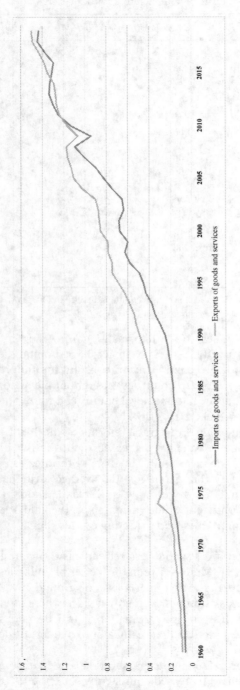

Figure 5.6 Latin America exports and imports trends (1960–2019) in trillions.
Note: Exports of goods and services (constant 2010 US$), trillion dollars.
Source: World Bank national accounts data, and OECD National Accounts data files.

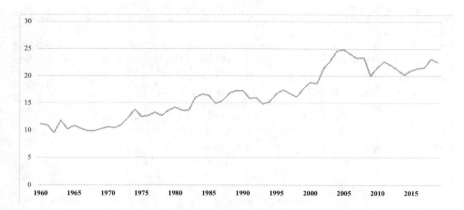

Figure 5.7 Latin America exports of goods and services (% of GDP).
Note: Exports of goods and services (constant 2010 US$), trillion dollars.
Source: World Bank national accounts data, and OECD National Accounts data files.

In addition, exports as a share of GDP have also witnessed significant growth since the 1980s (Figure 5.7).

At the same time, as Moreira et al. (2019, p. 118) state, "since trade is liberalized, there is no guarantee that it will remain liberalized." Indeed, these authors distinguish between two types of policy trajectories since the liberalization of trade in the 1980s and 1990s:

> Chile, Colombia, Costa Rica, and Mexico, have continued to reduce trade barriers, signed preferential trade agreements with an increasing number of regional and extra regional partners, and persisted in maintaining and deepening open trade [...] Argentina, Brazil, and Venezuela, have resurrected some trade barriers or come up with new ones.
>
> (p. 118)

Another important factor for understanding Latin American trade policy dynamics is the composition of trade in terms of sectors and destinations. As Table 5.4 shows, Latin America's main trading partners for both imports and exports are the United States, China, Canada, and Brazil. As well, the structure of exports and imports by product groups shows that the region is still a raw materials provider and a capital goods consumer. One pressing challenge is for the region to add value to its exports.

To fully understand trade policy in Latin America, specific attention must be given to the political economic context that periodically invokes backlash against free trade. Here, we must consider the mechanisms behind policymaking in the region. Within the executive branch of government, trade negotiations generally fall under the responsibility of Ministries of Foreign Trade

Table 5.4 Main trade characteristics of Latin America (2019)

Trade Policy Information	Data
Top 3 export destinations	US (43%) China (12%) Canada (3%)
Top 3 import origins	US (31%) China (18%) Brazil (5%)
Exports by product groups	Raw materials (30%) Intermediate goods (19%) Consumer goods (22%) Capital goods (23%)
Imports by product groups	Raw materials (7%) Intermediate goods (22%) Consumer goods (31%) Capital goods (37%)
Main products exported	Vehicles (13%) Mineral fuels (11%) Machinery (9%)
Main products imported	Electrical machinery (14%) Machinery (13%) Mineral fuels (12%)

Source: Author's creation based on World Bank-World Integrated Trade Solutions (WITS), https://wits.worldbank.org/countrysnapshot/en/LCN

or External Relations. Occasionally, when countries have ministries delegated to both of these roles, there can be tension between them in the policymaking process. Examples are found in the cases of Costa Rica (Monge-González & Rivera, 2018) and Mexico (Córdova Bojórquez et al., 2018). Further, when other ministries have constituents affected by trade policy, officials may seek out an administrative role in the implementation of trade policy (Moreira et al., 2019).

In terms of the legislative branch, most countries require approval to pass trade legislation. In some countries, the legislature's ability to introduce amendments before passing negotiations can slow this process (Moreira et al., 2019). Further, the level of the legislature's involvement in trade policymaking can lead to different policy outcomes. For instance, legislatures that are strongly influenced by domestic business interests can produce more protectionist policies if this meets the demands of their constituents. Moreover, incumbent legislators seeking reelection may respond to popular sentiment on trade policy among those they represent (Conconi et al., 2014). The legislature can also serve an important role in providing checks and balances on executive power in the trade policymaking process. This role ultimately provides countries with a more consistent and predictable policy that is less susceptible to rapid, partisan changes.

The private sector in Latin America plays a pivotal role in the formulation of trade policy. Consistent with economic theory, more productive firms tend to enjoy open trade policies due to their comparative advantage, while less productive firms push to maintain trade barriers (IDB, 2018). Latin American producers, not consumers, have the largest stake in these policy negotiations and are the most politically engaged. Therefore, political mobilization and organization mostly occurs at the level of producers. Domestic producers primarily seek representation through conventional lobbying efforts directed toward the executive and legislative branches at both the national and the local level.

With the regional context in mind, the following subsections briefly analyze variables of interest in this book from a regional angle. Regional interconnectedness is analyzed through the lens of PTAs and the kinds of protectionist tools that policymakers are deploying withing this context.

5.4.1 Latin America regional integration

Latin America is very well interconnected in terms of regional agreements. Recent studies have shown that "excluding those agreements that cover less than 80 of products, there are currently 33 LAC-to-LAC PTAs in force, including the four original blocs discussed earlier (CACM, Mercosur, CAN, and CARICOM)." This means that 80% of regional trade flows today are under some type of preferential agreement (Mesquita Moreira, 2018, p. 15). In general terms, Latin America is much more connected regionally than with the rest of the world. However, there is a lack of harmonization of the trade rules. There are many subregional agreements, but there is a lack of coordination among them. That is why some studies have suggested that for better integration, one of Latin America's major policy alternatives is "to build bridges among the existing RTAs—strive to achieve some form of convergence or gradual harmonization of the various RTAs in the Americas and to implement cumulation of production among them" (Estevadeordal et al., 2009, p. x). In the interview I conducted with a researcher of the Catholic University of Chile, they said:

> The restrictions in the region have a relevant component of non-tariff barriers, where the lack of regulatory convergence and excess administrative requirements end up making the integration process difficult. Undoubtedly, internal structural reforms are necessary to maximize the benefits derived from trade.[20]

Table 5.5 lists the most important regional agreements since the 1960s. Most of them have trade and economic objectives, such as creating a free trade zone or a common market. Others focus on political and social issues, for example, through the creation of regional intergovernmental organizations—such as the Bolivarian Alternative for Latin America and the Caribbean (ALBA) and the Union of South American Nations (UNASUR). All of these have been crucial for regional integration in Latin America.[21] As the table shows, one of the first steps toward Latin American integration was taken when Argentina, Brazil,

Table 5.5 List of the regional agreements in Latin America

Regional bloc and original treaty	Members and type of agreement
Latin American Free Trade Association (LAFTA)/Latin American Integration Association (LAIA), Treaty of Montevideo 1960/1980.	Members: 13 members [a] Type/objective: FTA (TM60) common market (TM80)
The Caribbean Community and Common Market (CARICOM), Treaty of Chaguaramas 1973.	Members: 15 Caribbean nations and dependencies[b] Type/objective: trade and economic integration, common market
The Latin American and Caribbean Economic System (SELA), SELA, Panama Convention 1975.	Members: 28 countries of Latin America and the Caribbean Type/objective: creation of a regional intergovernmental organization
Rio Group, 1986, Declaration of Rio de Janeiro	Members: signed by Argentina, Brazil, Colombia, Mexico, Panama, Peru, Uruguay, and Venezuela
The Central American Integration System (SICA), 1991, succeeded the Central American Common Market (CACM), 1960	Members: created by Costa Rica, El Salvador, Guatemala, Honduras, Nicaragua, and Panama. Subsequently, Belize and the Dominican Republic joined as a full members. Type/objective: creation of an institutional framework for regional integration in Central America
The Southern Cone Common Market (Mercosur), Treaty of Asuncion 1991.	Members: Argentina, Brazil, Paraguay, Uruguay, and Venezuela (joined in 2012, suspended in 2017) Type/objective: trade and economic integration, CU
The North American Free Trade Agreement (NAFTA), 1994.	Members: Canada, the United States, and Mexico Type/objective: trade and economic integration, FTA
The Andean Community of Nations (CAN), succeeded the Andean Pact (1969), 1994.	Members: Bolivia, Colombia, Ecuador, and Peru Type/objective: trade and economic integration, CU. Called the Andean Pact until 1996 and came into existence when the Cartagena Agreement was signed in 1969
The Bolivarian Alternative for Latin America and the Caribbean (ALBA), ALBA Establishment Agreement, 2004.	Members: 11 countries[d] Type/objective: intergovernmental organization
The Dominican Republic–Central America FTA (CAFTA–DR), 2004	Members: United States, Costa Rica, El Salvador, Guatemala, Honduras, Nicaragua, Dominican Republic Type/objective: trade and economic integration, FTA

Table 5.5 (Continued)

Regional bloc and original treaty	Members and type of agreement
Petro Caribe, Puerto La Cruz, Venezuela, 2005.	Members: 18 members[e] Type/objective: a regional project to promote energy sector cooperation
The Union of South American Nations (UNASUR), succeeded the South American Community of Nations (2004), 2008.	Members: 12 South American nations[f] Type/objective: political/intergovernmental organization
CELAC (Comunidad de Estados Latinoamericanos y Caribeños), 2011.	Members: 33 countries in the Americas excluding Canada and the United States[g] Type/objective: political integration with some features of economic integration.
Pacific Alliance (PA), Lima Declaration, 2011.	Chile, Colombia, Mexico, and Peru Type/objective: trade and economic integration, FTA.

Source: Albertoni and Rebolledo (2018) based on the original treaties and the information provided on their web page.

Notes: [a]LAIA: Argentina, Bolivia, Brazil, Chile, Colombia, Cuba, Ecuador, Mexico, Paraguay, Panama, Peru, Uruguay, and Venezuela. [b]CARICOM: Antigua and Barbuda, the Bahamas, Barbados, Belize, Dominica, Grenada, Guyana, Haiti, Jamaica, Montserrat, Saint Lucia, Saint Kitts and Nevis, Saint Vincent and the Grenadines, Suriname, and Trinidad and Tobago. [c]SELA: Argentina, Bahamas, Barbados, Belize, Bolivia, Brazil, Chile, Colombia, Costa Rica, Cuba, the Dominican Republic, Ecuador, El Salvador, Grenada, Guatemala, Guyana, Haiti, Honduras, Jamaica, Mexico, Nicaragua, Panama, Paraguay, Peru, Suriname, Trinidad and Tobago, Uruguay, and Venezuela. [d]ALBA: Antigua and Barbuda, Bolivia, Cuba, Dominica, Ecuador, Grenada, Nicaragua, Saint Kitts and Nevis, Saint Lucia, Saint Vincent and the Grenadines, and Venezuela. [e]Petro Caribe: CARICOM (excluding Barbados, Montserrat, and Trinidad and Tobago), Venezuela, Cuba, and the Dominican Republic. Haiti and Nicaragua joined the union at the third summit. Guatemala joined in 2008 but left the organization in November 2013. [f]UNASUR: Argentina, Bolivia, Brazil, Chile, Colombia, Ecuador, Guyana, Paraguay, Peru, Suriname, Uruguay, and Venezuela. [g]CELAC: Mercosur, UNASUR, SELA, ALBA. CELAC is the successor of the Rio Group and the Latin American and Caribbean Summit on Integration and Development (CALC).

Chile, Mexico, Paraguay, Peru, and Uruguay signed the Treaty of Montevideo in 1960 (TM60), which established the Latin American Free Trade Association (LAFTA). Between 1961 and 1967, Colombia, Ecuador, Venezuela, and Bolivia also joined. The main objective of LAFTA was to create a free trade zone among the countries of Latin America over 12 years. Note that during this decade, the region's economic model was based on ISI, as defined earlier. Hence, the main idea behind integration at that time was to encourage the economies of scale needed for industrialization (Tussie, 2009). During the 1980s, its members transformed LAFTA into the Latin American Integration Association (LAIA) through a revised 1980 Treaty of Montevideo (TM80), the main objective being to create a Latin American Common Market over an extended period. In the 1990s, Latin America started a new phase in its economic integration history defined by a proliferation of regional agreements (Albertoni & Rebolledo, 2018, pp. 99–112). As Table 5.5 shows, more than ten regional initiatives were developed between the 1970s and the beginning of the twenty-first century.

5.5 Trade protectionism from a regional perspective

Overall, Latin America has been very responsive to global protectionism in the last decade. Figure 5.8 shows that there is a positive relationship between protectionist dynamics in *t-1* (from the RoW toward Latin America) and what happened in time *t* (Latin America toward the RoW). In conjunction with the regional integration that has increased over the past decades, the Latin American region has also experienced some policy reversals in the liberalization process. That is why the IDB recently has let it be known that "the pace towards open markets has not been steady" (IDB, 2018, p. 1). More specifically, these policy reversals have "led to tariff increases or the establishment of non-tariff barriers including the pervasive use of instruments like antidumping, import license requirements, and quantitative restrictions on imports" (IDB, 2018, p. 1).

In an interview with a former Colombian government vice minister, on Latin American protectionism, he noted:

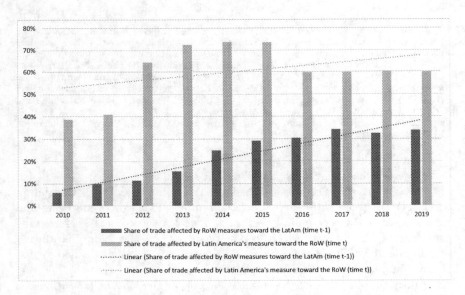

Figure 5.8 How responsive is Latin America to trade protectionism?

Note: Share of country's total exports affected (*t-1*) versus share of world export to the country affected (time *t*) by protectionist measures (Average 2009–19). This is an average of share of trade affected in Argentina, Brazil, and Mexico.

Source: Author's creation based on the Global Trade Alert, www.globaltradealert.org

Without no doubt trade interconnection has generated less transparency in trade policy. Likewise, Latin America has been less successful than Europe, for example, in making its trade policy complex in such a way that it continues to protect without making it very obvious. The commercial policy officials today, seeing that in Europe they have applied increasingly transparent measures, feel that if we from Latin America apply some, it is more to level the playing field.[22]

Given the region's high interconnectivity through regional agreements, we would expect that Latin America as a region would not protect intra-regionally because most countries have at least some types of trade agreement with one another. Remarkably, the data show that Latin American has actually been consistently more protectionist. Moreover, 47% of the measures implemented within the region have been "murky instruments," while the share of "murky instruments" leveraged by Latin America toward the G20 countries is 33%. Figure 5.9 shows Latin America trade policy measures within the region and toward the G20 countries between 2008 and 2019. Although the region has been more protectionist against G20 countries overall—with 1,578 measures versus 1,022 measures in the region—the proportion of nontransparent murky measures is almost the same: 530 murky measures against G20 and 490 murky measures within the region. Latin America has implemented considerably more liberalizing measures toward the G20 than it has intra-regionally.

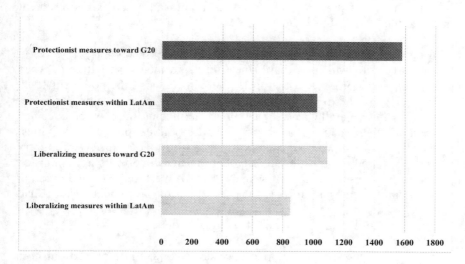

Figure 5.9 Latin America trade policy measures within the region and toward the G20 (2008–19).

Note: When considering the G20, I removed Argentina, Brazil, and Mexico given that they are Latin American countries.

Source: Authors' creation based on GTA.

In the interview I conducted with a former Mexican government undersecretary, they observed that "the difference of Latin America with other blocs, such as the European Union and ASEAN, is that, within these blocs, they have managed to liberalize trade. Unfortunately, the region has not achieved that. Intra-regional trade is very small."[23]

Figure 5.9 shows that Latin America's interconnectivity through regional trade agreements does not seem to be a decisive factor in deterring protectionism or murky instruments, that is, nontransparent measures. On the prevalence of NTM in Latin America, Cadestin et al. (2016, p. 39) state the following:

Measures arising from national regulation, such as sanitary and phytosanitary (SPS) measures and technical barriers to trade (TBT), have grown in importance globally in recent years while the usage of more traditional NTMs such as, for example, quantitative restrictions and non-automatic licensing has declined. The incidence of NTMs in Latin American countries is no higher than, for example, in Europe or Asia but there is important heterogeneity across Latin American countries, ranging from more than 40% coverage ratios in Argentina, Brazil, and Chile to less than 20% in some countries in Central America. This means that traders in different countries in the region face very different challenges in dealing with NTMs.

Additionally, during my fieldwork in Latin America, trade policymakers also highlighted that PTAs do not deter less transparent trade measures. For instance, in an interview with an economist and former Peruvian government minister, they stated that:

It did happen in the Peruvian case of applying protectionist measures in countries with which we have free trade agreements. [...] Indeed, when protection is not given at the tariff level but rather at the non-tariff level, through subsidies to local companies, the defense process requires an investigation that generally takes some time. Governments must be well informed enough not to yield to power groups under political pressure. They must make decisions based on proven evidence for the good of the entire country and not based on private interests. During my three years as a minister, I fought for transparent management. Every time I met with the different actors in the sector, I informed the press about the agreements made. I had to negotiate and sign the Pacific Alliance and the TPP, and I had very positive experiences and, fortunately, few of the others.[24]

Another perspective on the relevance of regional trade protectionism is whether there exists a pattern between the destinations of exports of intermediate goods by region and the types of measures implemented. As depicted in Figure 5.10, since 2008, Asia and the United States have consistently been the leading destinations for Latin American intermediate goods. Between 2008 and 2018, we can say that in terms of possible GVC linkages—measured by

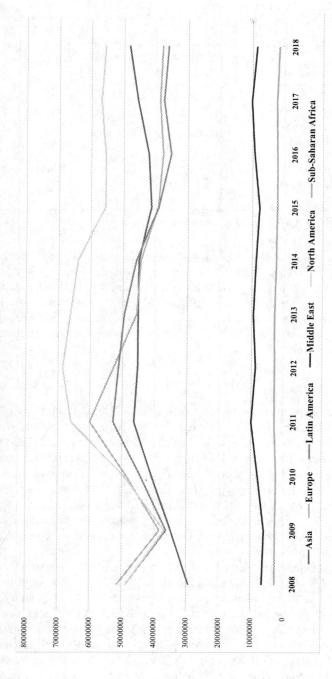

Figure 5.10 Latin America exports of intermediate goods by region.

Note: Exports in US dollars by thousands.

Source: Author's creation based on World Bank–World Integrated Trade Solutions (WITS), https://wits.worldbank.org/countrysnapshot/en/LCN

Table 5.6 Latin America intermediate goods destinations and types of measures implemented toward those destinations (2008–19)

	North Am.	Asia	Europe	Lat. Am.	M. East	Africa
Total number of protectionist measures implemented between 2008 and 2019	850	1,054	1,221	1,022	353	202
Total number of murky protectionist instruments implemented between 2008 and 2019	450	306	342	480	166	117
Share of protectionist measures that use murky instruments	53%	29%	28%	47%	56%	58%

Source: Author's creation based on GTA, www.globaltradealert.org/

intermediate goods exports—the order of regional importance has been: North America, Asia, Europe, Latin America, the Middle East, and Africa.[25] Interestingly, Table 5.6 shows a similar order regarding the total number of murky protectionist instruments implemented from Latin America toward other regions. In other words, regions where Latin America is exporting more intermediate goods are also those where Latin America has also implemented murkier instruments.

5.6 Country case studies

This section concentrates on my three case studies. The methodology used to analyze each case study draws on Frieden (2000), who argues that the following components are necessary to consider when conducting a political economic analysis of a given country case: knowledge of the recent history, identification of key actors and their goals, specification of actors' policy preferences, as well as the aggregation of actors into groups and social institutions. The underlying goal of this analytical framework is to better understand policy outcomes, how government policies—for instance, trade policy retaliation—are adopted, and their associated results (whether, how, and when actors decide to reject, reform, or build political institutions).

I begin with the case of Mexico. I then turn to Brazil and Argentina. Again, as members of Mercosur (which aims to be a CU), Brazil and Argentina are not entirely free to make unilateral trade policy decisions. As explained earlier, Mexico offers us the opportunity to study trade policy dynamics in a country where unilateralism has been the main trade policy approach. Argentina and Brazil shed light on cases that operate regionally and need to coordinate with other regional partners to define and carry out trade policy. Moreover, despite this regional characteristic in the trade policy of Mercosur countries, my analysis shows that Argentina and Brazil have engaged in some trade policies that have their own unique dynamics. For the three cases, I contextualize each country's trade policy evolution and identify the key actors involved. I then focus on specific protectionist policies and their impacts and responses (H1) from the perspective of the types of trade policy instruments utilized (H4 and H5), the effects of PTAs (H2 and H4), and how GVCs (H3 and H5) shape trade policy responses.

5.6.1 The case of Mexico

In the last several decades, Mexico's trade policies have undergone significant change. After almost three decades of ISI policies, Mexico initiated a trade liberalization process that resulted in its 1986 accession to the GATT and its entry into NAFTA, with Canada and the United States in 1994. This section recounts Mexico's trade policy evolution and the key actors at play. Following this contextualization, I focus on the specific impact of and responses to rising trade protectionism since the 2008–09 GFC.

5.6.1.1 Mexico's trade policy evolution and key actors involved

After 30 years of high growth under ISI, which was embedded in the country's stabilizing development model, Mexico was one of the first countries in Latin America to embrace trade liberalization. As Table 5.3 shows, the weighted mean tariff rate applied to all products was 34% in the mid-80s in Mexico, while the average in Latin America was 50% (Brazil reached 80% at the same time). In the 1980s, Mexico lowered its tariffs to 11%, while the regional average was 34%. Upon Mexico's accession to NAFTA, its average tariff was 14%. Over the past two decades, Mexico has been substantially more open to trade, with an average tariff of 8% between 2000 and 2007, and 3% between 2008 and 2018. The regional average has been 5% over the same period (see Table 5.3). This fast reduction in Mexico's tariffs explains, in part, why this country is one of the most open economies in the developing world today (Zabludovsky & Pasquel, 2010). Pastor and Wise (1994, pp. 462–3) identify three phases in Mexico's trade policy from the 1980s to the 1990s: first, was a "loosened restrictive import regime" under the administration of President Miguel de la Madrid (1982–8) implemented during the "debt crisis and continuing balance-of-payments shortfall"; second, a "new four-step tariff reduction schedule" was instated to "eliminate all official prices for imports and exports" and "promote external competition as a way to restrain domestic prices"; third, was a process of "fine-tuning" of these tariff initiatives.

Zabludovsky and Pasquel (2010) define the 1980s in Mexico as the decade of "unilateral" trade policies, in which there are two main events: the reforms implemented for the recovery from the 1982 debt shocks and the GATT accession. In the late 1980s, the administration of President Carlos Salinas de Gortari (1988–94) intensified the reform process, the main goals being to harness "the unilateral liberalization of the 1980s […] taking advantage of the accession to GATT in order to expand Mexico's export markets in North America, Europe and East Asia" (Garciadiego & Hernández, 1994, p. 16). However, this approach shifted in the early 1990s in response to the fall of the Berlin Wall in 1989. In response to this new world order, President Salinas concluded that Mexico had "to take advantage of its geographical proximity to the largest economy in the world and become part of a trading bloc. Such thinking prompted Mexico's proposal to the United States to negotiate a free trade agreement in the early 1990s" (Salinas De Gortari, 2002, pp. 47–8). After four years of negotiations, on January 1, 1994, NAFTA entered into force, marking a radical turning point in Mexico's trade policy. As Zabludovsky and Pasquel (2010, p. 92) state, "NAFTA creates the opportunities for negotiating similar agreements with other Latin American nations, the European Union, the European Free Trade Agreement (EFTA) countries, Israel and Japan [...] [It] also strengthen Mexico's presence in other multilateral and regional forums."[26] Thus, between 1990 and 2019, Mexico negotiated 14 FTAs with over 50 countries (60% of world product) and joined various multinational organizations such as the Asia Pacific Economic Cooperation (APEC) forum in 1993, the OECD in 1994, and the Pacific Alliance in 2014. Mexico also joined the Comprehensive and Progressive Agreement for Trans-Pacific Partnership (CPTPP), signed in 2018.[27] Table 5.7 shows the main trade

Table 5.7 Mexico trade agreements, blocs, and international forums (1992–2020)

Date of Entry into Force	Agreement
1992	FTA with Chile
1993	APEC[a] (21 members)
1994	NAFTA (Mexico, Canada, and the United States)
	OECD[b] (37 member)
1995	FTA with Costa Rica
	FTA with Bolivia
	FTA with Venezuela
1998	FTA with Nicaragua
	FTA with Uruguay
2000	FTA with Israel
	FTA with EU[c]
2001	FTA with EFTA
	FTA with Guatemala, Honduras, and El Salvador
2005	FTA with Japan
2012	FTA with Peru
2015	FTA with Panama
2016	Pacific Alliance (Mexico, Peru, Colombia, and Chile)
2020	USMCA (Canada–Mexico–United States)

Source: Zabludovsky & Pasquel (2010) and OAS Foreign Trade Information System, www.sice.oas.org

Notes: [a]APEC, 21 members, www.apec.org/About-Us/About-APEC; [b]OECD, 37 members, www.oecd.org/about/members-and-partners/; [c]EU, 27 members, https://europa.eu/european-union/about-eu/countries_en

policy agreements signed by Mexico since the early 1990s. Nowadays, 82% of Mexico's total exports are sent to countries with which it has standing trade agreements.[28]

Another way to understand Mexico's trade policymaking is to explore the actors involved. There are at least four key actors that participate in Mexico's trade policymaking process: the executive, the Senate, state actors, and private/nonstate actors. As Pastor and Wise (1994, p. 182) highlight: "an organizational overhaul, particularly at the level of the state, played a strong role in facilitating the successful implementation of Mexico's trade reforms." In an interview I conducted with a Mexican trade policy expert, they stated that, in Mexico very "influential sectors [that] have lobbied the government, not only to respond but also to protect and safeguard their interests." More specifically, they continued:

Depending on the government and the technical capacity of its officials, these supports have been aligned with international commitments or have taken unorthodox forms, such as making the entry of merchandise more difficult by modifying customs requirements. For example, in the case of sugar in Mexico, the sector asked the government to protect access to the American market. At the same time, products competing with sugar—such as fructose—were proposed to be subject to retaliatory measures. When conflicts escalated to the USMCA negotiation, the same sectors demanded that access to the American market be protected, while protecting the local market.[29]

Table 5.8 shows a summary of the key actors involved in Mexico's trade policymaking.

I interviewed an executive of COPARMEX, the Mexican Employers' Association, about the negotiation process:

COPARMEX actively participates in the "Attachment Room," which is a group that has been created to favor the participation of the business sector in the negotiation processes of free trade agreements in which Mexico is involved. In this group, we work in coordination with the federal government to know and jointly propose the terms of negotiation of any free trade agreement to be concluded by our country. This group has representatives of accredited companies in Mexico, from all productive sectors, as well as those responsible for the area and/or foreign trade issues of the various organizations and business chambers that exist in Mexico. In addition, we work closely with the Ministry of Economy, specifically with the undersecretary of foreign trade, to learn about the plans, programs, and projects that are promoted by the federal government to boost the foreign trade of Mexican companies. We maintain a representation chair in these spaces, and we participate in the various events that are held by the federal government in this area.[30]

102 *Protectionism and trade policy responses in Latin America*

Table 5.8 Main actors involved in the development of Mexico's trade policy

State actors	The participation of state actors in trade negotiations is regulated by the constitution. The Mexican constitution states that any legislation that emanates from an international agreement entered into by the president and approved by the Senate becomes supreme law of the land and is, therefore, part of Mexican domestic law (Mexican Constitution:1475/98) (Zabludovsky & Pasquel, 2010, p. 99)
The executive	There are a number of agencies the executive is involved in with regard to the negotiation and implementation of international trade agreements. The Ministry of the Economy is in charge of the negotiation process and aided by the following ministries: Ministry of Agriculture, Ministry of Foreign Affairs, Ministry of Finance, Ministry of Interior, and officials from the Central Bank.
The Senate	Once a PTA is negotiated, it has to be signed by the executive and ratified by the Senate to become Mexican legislation.
Private and nonstate actors	The following institutions are normally consulted during trade negotiations: Confederation of Industrial Chambers of Mexico (CONACIM); the Employer's Confederation of the Mexican Republic (COPARMEX); the Coordinator for Foreign Trade Business Organizations (COECE); the Confederation of National Chamber of Commerce (CONCANACO).

Source: Zabludovsky & Pasquel (2010, pp. 99–108) and OAS Foreign Trade Information System, www.sice.oas.org

Regarding their position on trade protectionism, they said:

We advocate fair trade, based on the guidelines of multilateralism and dispute settlement mechanisms established in each FTA, as well as those promoted by the WTO. However, we must also recognize that Mexico has a lot of experience in tariff and non-tariff measures (depending on the circumstances), carousel strategies that have been used in the past to guarantee fair conditions, as well as to defend free market principles, commercial reciprocity, most favored nation treatment, etc. We have noticed that applying these types of measures often results in issues of illegality and lack of ethics. For this reason, COPAMEX is in favor of tariff policies which benefit national economies by allowing the strengthening of their industries by becoming much more competitive within the international market, which in the end brings greater benefits to their entrepreneurs, their workers and, therefore, to the economy of each country.[31]

Finally, when I asked them about how they react as an institution when they are affected by a protectionist measure from a close partner, they said that, in this situation:

Tariff policies are synonymous with legality and ethics, values that COPARMEX defends and demands, so the position we take on this issue is the search for negotiations through the corresponding instances and mechanisms for dispute resolution, in order to ensure that our country can participate freely within the international market, demonstrating in this way the capacity and competitiveness of our industries, products, and services offered inside and outside the country.[32]

Finally, as mentioned, Mexico has been very active in GVC participation, and not necessarily as an intermediate goods exporter but rather as a capital goods exporter. Many products are thus at the end of the "factory line." A recent study by *The Economist* (2020, p. 1) explores how well Latin America is prepared for post-COVID-19 trade dynamics with regard to GVCs:

> Mexico seems best placed to increase its position in the U.S. supply chain, but there are issues here too. In the very near term, the problem will center around the country's slow emergence from the health and economic effects of Covid-19. More fundamentally, Mexico will struggle without government policy to actively promote supply chain shifts, and without policy that attracts investment more broadly.

Mexican exports have been growing consistently in terms of intermediate, consumer, and capital goods. The top ten destinations of intermediate, consumption, and capital goods (average share in total exports between 2008 and 2018) represent, on average, 83% of total exports of Mexico's intermediate goods between 2008 and 2018. Table 5.9 shows five key players in Mexico's

Table 5.9 Top destinations of intermediate, consumption, and capital goods (average share in Mexico's total exports between 2008 and 2018)

Consumption goods	% in total exports	Intermediate goods	% in total exports	Capital Goods	% in total exports
US	79%	US	65%	US	87%
Canada	3%	Canada	3%	Canada	3%
Germany	3%	China	2%	China	1%
Colombia	2%	UK	2%	Brazil	1%
Brazil	2%	Colombia	3%	Germany	1%
China	1%	Belgium	2%	Netherlands	1%
Chile	1%	Brazil	3%	Colombia	1%
Argentina	1%	Guatemala	1%	France	1%
Guatemala	1%	Switzerland	2%	Japan	0.5%
Panama	1%	Spain	1%	UK	0.4%

Source: Author's creation based on World Bank-World Integrated Trade Solutions (WITS), https://wits.worldbank.org/countrysnapshot/en/LCN

exports and potential GVC dynamics. The United States is the major destination by far for all three categories. However, Canada, China, Colombia, and Brazil also appear as consistent destinations in the three categories.

5.6.1.2 Impacts of Mexico's trade protectionism and economic responses

Here, I concentrate on three main issues. First, I focus on how protectionist dynamics from Mexico's main trading partners have affected Mexico in the last decade. For this task, I concentrate on those countries with whom Mexico has close trade relationships. Second, I analyze how Mexico has affected these close partners with its own protectionist dynamics. For both cases, I analyze the types of measures countries have used and the specific sectors that have been affected. Finally, I test the differences between "cross" and "within" sectoral dynamics in Mexico's retaliation.

In light of the descriptive evidence presented, I predict that when Mexico is adversely affected by a protectionist measure adopted by another country, it will systematically respond to that country by adopting protectionist measures in return (H1). However, the existence of PTAs (e.g., NAFTA, Pacific Alliance) decreases the likelihood of a protectionist response (H2). As I stated before, I expect that Mexico has been generally less affected by those countries with which it has a PTA. Finally, I believe that Mexico will retaliate more with NTMs (less transparent) than with tariff measures.

Figure 5.11 reflects Mexico's total exports affected (in *t-1*) versus world export to Mexico affected (time *t*) by protectionist measures (Average 2009–19). As we can see, Mexico has been very responsive to protectionist measures. Overall, this confirms H1, which states that, broadly speaking, when a country is adversely affected by a protectionist measure adopted by another country, it will systematically respond to that country by adopting protectionist measures in return.

Figure 5.12 shows that, in the last decade, Mexico's share of exports has been consistently more impacted by those countries with whom Mexico has no FTA. On average, between 2009 and 2019, 14% of Mexico's exports were affected by close trading partners and 21% by those countries with no trade agreement with Mexico. In other words, having a PTA leads to a 6% reduction in Mexico's exports.

In Figure 5.13, we can see the share of close and not close trading partners' exports to Mexico impacted by Mexico's protectionism. Since 2014, countries with no trade agreements with Mexico have been consistently more impacted by Mexico's protectionism than those with an FTA with Mexico. This is exactly in line with the results presented in Table 4.3, where we can see from a large-N analysis that the existence of a PTA between *A* and *B* is negatively correlated with protectionist dynamics.

At the same time, my earlier results in Chapter 4 showed that GVCs do not seem to restrain protectionism along the same lines as do PTAs. In Figure 5.14, I apply the same exercise to those close trading partners through potential GVC

Protectionism and trade policy responses in Latin America 105

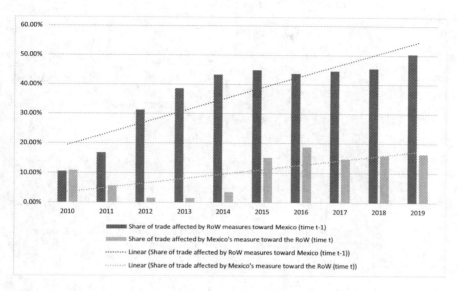

Figure 5.11 Share of Mexico's total exports affected (t-1) versus world export to Mexico affected (time t) by protectionist measures (Average 2009–19).

Source: Author's creation based on the Global Trade Alert.

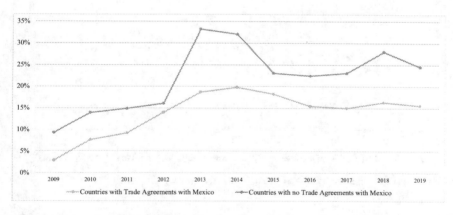

Figure 5.12 Share of Mexico's exports impacted by close and not close trading partners' protectionism.

Source: Author's creation based on Global Trade Alert, www.globaltradealert.org/

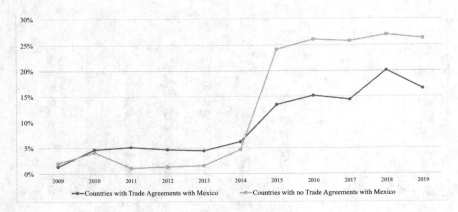

Figure 5.13 Share of close and not close trading partners' exports to Mexico impacted by Mexico's protectionism.

Source: Author's creation based on Global Trade Alert, www.globaltradealert.org/

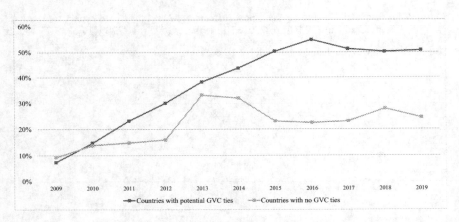

Figure 5.14 Share of Mexico's exports impacted by GVC ties versus no GVC ties.

Source: Author's creation based on Global Trade Alert, www.globaltradealert.org/

ties with Mexico (e.g., United States, Canada, China, Colombia, Brazil, as shown in Table 5.9). Interestingly, we see a very different scenario. On average, between 2009 and 2019, 36% of Mexico's exports were affected by close trading partners and 21% by those countries that have no PTA with Mexico. These results show that GVCs do not seem to restrain protectionism as PTAs do. The case of Mexico thus confirms H2 on the negative relationship between protectionist dynamics and PTAs. Moreover, it does not confirm H3, in line with the quantitative results presented earlier (Model 3, Table 4.3).

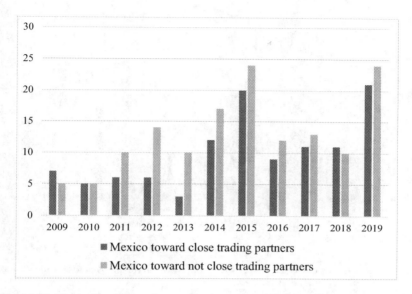

Figure 5.15 Mexico's number of protectionist measures implemented toward close and not close trading partners.

Source: Author's creation based on Global Trade Alert, www.globaltradealert.org/

Relying now on the number of protectionist measures implemented, Figure 5.15 shows that since 2011, Mexico has consistently implemented more protectionist measures against countries with which it has no trade agreements than toward close trading partners (e.g., with a PTA in force). The same occurred with those measures that affected Mexico (Figure 5.16). It has been consistently more affected by countries with which it has no trade agreements. The only exception is in 2019, when the trade war between the United States and China spread to Mexico and then-US president Trump threatened to impose an extraordinary escalating tariff on Mexico if it did not try harder to address the problem of migration flows from Central America.[33] Although much of it was undocumented, this bilateral tension was at the rhetorical level, there were numerous nontransparent measures implemented by the United States toward Mexico.[34]

Focusing now on the level of transparency of trade measures, in Figure 5.17 we can see that the share of protectionist interventions that rely on nontransparent instruments used by Mexico toward close trading partners is much higher (on average, 47% between 2009 and 2019) than with countries that have no trade agreement (32% on average, between 2009 and 2019) with Mexico. Furthermore, the share of nontransparent protectionist interventions toward Mexico by close trading partners (82%) is higher than by countries with which it has no trade agreements (80%) (Figure 5.18). This is in line with

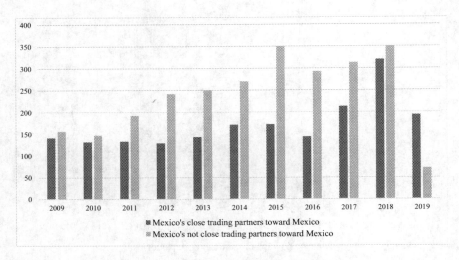

Figure 5.16 Number of protectionist measures toward Mexico by close and not close trading partners.

Source: Author's creation based on Global Trade Alert, www.globaltradealert.org/

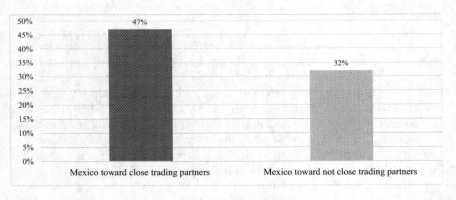

Figure 5.17 Share of nontransparent protectionist interventions by Mexico toward close and not close trading partners (average 2009–19).

Source: Author's creation based on Global Trade Alert, www.globaltradealert.org/

research proposition *B* (H4), which states that we would expect to see more nontransparent protectionist dynamics between close trading partners (e.g., through PTAs).

Table 5.10 concentrates on sectoral dynamics in Mexico, which shows a cross-sectoral retaliatory dynamic. This can be explained by the fact that most of the sectors affected are embedded in GVCs, such as fabricated metal

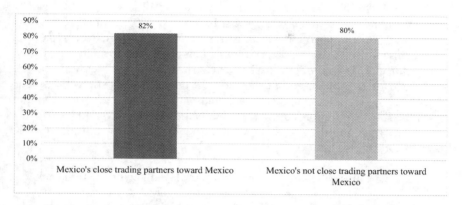

Figure 5.18 Share of nontransparent protectionist interventions toward Mexico by close and not close trading partners (average 2009–19).

Source: Author's creation based on Global Trade Alert, www.globaltradealert.org/

Table 5.10 Sectors most affected in and by Mexico (2009–19)

Sectors Most Affected in Mexico (by Main Trading Partners' Protectionism)	Sectors Most Affected by Mexico's Protectionism (toward Main Trading Partners)
By Close Trading Partners	
Products of iron or steel→	Products of iron or steel
Other fabricated metal products	Cereals
Basic iron & steel	Sugar & molasses
Motor vehicles, trailers & semi-trailers	Food products
Prepared & preserved fruits & nuts	Wearing apparel, except fur apparel
By Countries with No Trade Agreements with Mexico	
Motor vehicles, trailers & semi-trailers	Products of iron or steel
Computing machinery & parts	Other fabricated metal products
Electric motors, generators & transformers	Cereals
Electricity distribution & control apparatus	Basic iron & steel
Pharmaceutical products	Wearing apparel, except fur apparel

Source: Author's creation based on Global Trade Alert, www.globaltradealert.org/

products, basic iron and steel, and products made of iron or steel.[35] Hence, a retaliatory dynamic from within would severely impact consumers of Mexico's key products. As the table shows, one of the sectors most impacted in Mexico by recent protectionism has been the steel sector. During my fieldwork, I interviewed an employee of Tenaris Mexico, one of the most important global manufacturers and suppliers of steel pipes and related services.[36] They noted that the current protectionism against the steel sector can be explained by China's oversupply of steel and its impact on global trade:

The problem of excess capacity has been under discussion in the OECD Steel committee for the last ten years. In the year 2001, China became part of the WTO and negotiated a transition period of 15 years to complete its reforms and become a market economy. This did not happen because China did not modify its model. The US reacted with different measures, but by the end of the Obama administration did not apply drastic actions. The [Mexico's] steel sector has been affected with [section] 232 [Investigation on the Effect of Imports of Steel on US National Security] and section 301 [of the Trade Act of 1974]. Now we live under administrated trade (quotas, tariffs, tariff-rate quota).[37]

Figure 5.19 illustrates the percentage of employed persons within each key sector out of the total workforce in Mexico. In Figure 5.20, we can see that the industry sector was by far the most affected. When I link these two figures by sector and the total number of employed persons in Mexico, we can approximate the number of employed people who are affected by protectionism in Mexico. More specifically, an average of 12.3 million people working in the industrial sector were exposed to 12,406 protectionist measures from the rest of the world between 2009 and 2019 (90% of total measures that impacted Mexico); 27.3 million worked in the service sector, which were exposed to 862 measures (6% of total measures that impacted Mexico); and, 5.9 million people worked in the agricultural sector, which was exposed to 500 measures (4%). In sum, 90% of the protectionist measures that affected Mexico were against a sector that represents, on average, 25% of employed persons in Mexico.

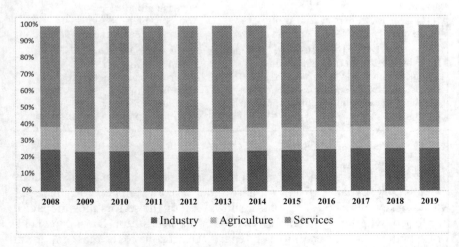

Figure 5.19 Mexico's employment in industry, agriculture, and services (% of total employment).

Source: Author's creation based on Global Trade Alert, www.globaltradealert.org/

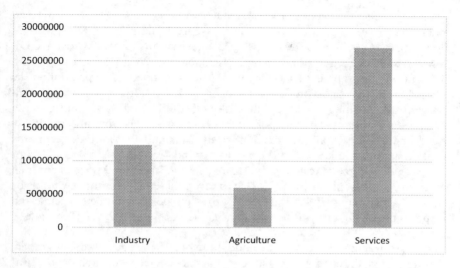

Figure 5.20 Total number of measures affecting Mexico by main economic sectors (2009–19).

Source: Author's creation combining data from International Labour Organization, ILOSTAT database and Global Trade Alert.

5.6.1.3 Political economy insights based on the case of Mexico

The case of Mexico raises some interesting questions. For example, how have these protectionist measures interacted with the ongoing development strategy? Contrary to the case of Mercosur, NAFTA has integrated Mexico into powerful GVCs. However, because of Mexico's role as an assembler rather than an innovator, and its overdependence on the US market, NAFTA has hampered Mexico's exports diversification and become a trap that prevents the country from retaining high value added. What are the implications for policy reform?

During the 1970s, Mexico's ISI development strategy had gone into crisis. The scarcity of fiscal resources, rising inequality, a dual agricultural sector, and an external debt crisis all stymied economic growth. These realities reflected the disconnection between Mexico's socioeconomic and political systems (Riguzzi & de los Ríos, 2012). In the late 1980s, Mexico WClicy recommendations from Washington, with mixed results. Since then, Mexico experienced two additional economic crises in the past decades. First, was the 1994 peso meltdown, which can be explained by a reliance on short-term flows of portfolio capital to achieve internal macroeconomic stability. This new financial context also reflected the perils of a rapid opening of the capital account, as advocated by the WC. Investors were incentivized to look for high returns in Mexico, but this created an asset bubble that exploded into a joint currency and banking collapse. The second major crisis was that during the 2008–09 GFC, Mexican policymakers misread the shock from Wall Street and raised interest rates in 2009 for fear of inflation. This delayed recovery and drove Mexican GDP lower than that of any other emerging economy in 2009 (Wise et al., 2015). The current development trajectory of Mexico is defined by its position in the United States–Mexico–Canada Agreement (USMCA). In short, Mexico´s unilateral trade opening and trilateral FTA with the United States and Canada has been a disincentive for its policymakers to foster solid forward and backward linkages for small and medium-sized firms and the domestic economy overall. Mexican linkages to GVCs must expand beyond North America. For instance, from Japan, Germany, and Korea has incorporated Mexican contract assemblers into sophisticated GVCs. However, these account for low levels of trade/FDI. The country's average GDP growth since 2000 has been anemic and its per capita GDP growth is strongly negative. As Wise (2020, p. 195) states:

> as warning signs went unheeded and more promising routes were not taken, Mexico lost the economic dynamism that had carried it through the postwar era up to through the 1970s. However, the low growth and paltry per capita gains that have persisted since the early 1980s were far from predetermined. These policy failures have been self-inflicted.

Mexico's restart to protectionist measures is testimony to these policy failures.

Although the three main pillars of the WC, liberalization, privatization, and deregulation, were quickly and rigorously adopted post-1988 in Mexico (Wise, 2020), Mexico is currently facing a major reversal of its previous progress and gains with trade liberalization. In other words, just as a wave of liberalization occurred as a result of Mexico's strong political and economic ties with the United States and its eagerness to join NAFTA, current protectionist responses are a reaction to rising US protectionism and a more "anti-trade" narrative that has emerged since the GFC. As an employee of the University of Chile observes, "today [in Mexico] there is much less consensus on the advantages of trade openness that seemed very evident in all countries."[38] In the same vein, a former Mexican government undersecretary has observed:

> [After the liberalization reforms,] something that was not well calculated is that trade policy should have been accompanied by internal policies that addressed certain structural problems that were specific to each country ... I think that the impulse towards the outside was very strong but unfortunately it was not accompanied by other types of policies that also explain why so much inequality has been generated. So, in a context where this commercial opening and neoliberal policies did not seem to be the model to follow, there were no policies that addressed productive development to achieve more education, innovation, greater competition in the markets to have more accessible prices for the entire population.[39]

The data I have reviewed thus far suggests that Mexico "has been a laggard in terms of institutional reform and aggregate and per capita growth" Wise (2020, p. 191). The lack of an industrial competition policy to complete trade policy reforms is the reason for a large part of Mexico's underperformance. Moreover, policymakers must strive to secure better access to markets beyond North America. In 2013, Mexico started this process by introducing an ambitious program of reform in 11 different sectors, including (WTO, 2017b, p. 2):

> The implementation of reforms around competition policy, tax policy, energy, financial services, and telecommunications, which walled for the amendment of the Constitution. A review of taxation was provided in order to improve tax collection. The measures adopted included an expansion of the base for income tax collection, fewer exemptions on payment of value added tax (VAT), revised taxation for the mining sector, and the introduction of "green" taxes. These led to a growth in tax revenue, from 9.7% of GDP in 2013 to 13.1% in 2015, while government finances became significantly less dependent on oil revenue. Despite these efforts, the public sector deficit rose from 2.3% of GDP in 2014 to 3.2% in 2015 and is forecast to be 3.5% in 2016. The efforts at reform have, nonetheless, managed to install a general climate of macroeconomic stability, although Mexico is still facing major challenges, particularly to the wide disparity in income, insecurity, and shortcomings in governance, as well as high dependence on a single market.

What this book suggests is that Mexico's dependence on the US market is not just about trade. That is, NAFTA was more than just trade for Mexican producers and decision-makers; it also was a tool to "stabilize the policy environment" (Pastor & Wise, 1994, p. 489). However, more than a quarter century later, this stabilizing tool has become increasingly counterproductive for both domestic politics and US–Mexico political and economic relations (Puyana, 2018). In this context, it is crucial for Mexico to craft a new and more proactive trade agenda, especially toward China. As Wise (2020, p. 191) states:

> at the turn of the new millennium it was China that had become more problematic for Mexico, as reflected in the acerbic comments made by Xi Jinping[40] while visiting the country prior to assuming the Chinese presidency in March 2013. Until the mid-1990s the two countries had enjoyed a cordial bilateral relationship on issues ranging from academic exchanges to science and technology collaboration.

At the same time, the modernization of trade agreements signed already (beyond NAFTA), may be required. Interestingly, in April 2020, Mexico concluded negotiations with the EU to modernize and update the 1997 EU–Mexico Economic Partnership, Political Coordination and Co-operation Agreement (Rodríguez-Piñero, 2020). The modernization of this agreement with the EU can be a good road map to be continued by Mexico with other countries with which it has PTAs (Japan, Israel, Chile, Peru, Colombia, Bolivia, Central America). Mexico has attracted less Chinese FDI that small states like Chile and Ecuador, and its trade deficit with China accounts for 80% of Latin America's total trade deficit. Rather than leverage the Sino–Mexico relationship to balance against US trade and investment dominance, the country's leaders have spurned Chinese overtures. The "renegotiation" of NAFTA to the USMCA in late 2018 was imposed upon Mexico and Canada by the Trump administration. The USMCA is historic in that this is the first time the United States has actually raised trade barriers in the context of a PTA. With the advent of the Biden administration in 2021, Mexican policymakers should now push to modernize the USMCA along the lines of the updated EU–Mexico PTA. Among other things, the modernization of the EU–Mexico trade agreement includes the following (Rodríguez-Piñero, 2020, p. 1):

1. In the area of agricultural goods, more than 85% of tariff lines would be fully liberalized, while sectors such as dairy and meat would remain subject to restrictions such as quotas and tariff rate quotas.
2. In addition, it includes chapters on rules of origin, trade facilitation, trade remedies, technical barriers to trade, and sanitary and phytosanitary rules.
3. Regarding services, modernization would make it easier for EU firms to do business in Mexico (including in the maritime transport, telecommunications, and financial sectors), while protecting both parties' right to regulate.
4. The modernized agreement would also include chapters on dispute settlement, anti-corruption measures, trade and sustainable development (TSD), transparency, energy and raw materials, small and medium-sized enterprises, subsidies, competition, good regulatory practices, and animal welfare and antimicrobial resistance as well as annexes on motor vehicles and wine and spirits.

5.6.2 Mercosur and a brief contextualization of trade policy in Argentina and Brazil

In contrast to the case of Mexico, Argentina and Brazil have been part of the same trade bloc (with Uruguay and Paraguay), the Southern Common Market (Mercosur), since the early 1990s. This means that these two neighbors have shared a trade policymaking institutional framework for 30 years (see section 5.2 of this chapter for more detail on Mercosur's decision-making institutions).[41] Again, Mercosur was founded in 1991 with the signing of the Treaty of Asuncion.[42] Venezuela became a full member in July 2012 (but was suspended in 2017 when an authoritarian regime came to power), while Bolivia has been in the process of becoming a full member since 2012. Chile, Colombia, Ecuador, and Peru have remained associate members. Today, Mercosur is the most important bloc in South America, with more than 275 million inhabitants and a gross product of US$ 3.5 trillion (making it equivalent to the fifth-largest economy in the world).

By 1986, after years of rivalry, Argentina and Brazil simultaneously transitioned to democratic rule. Newly elected presidents sought to enter into a cooperative relationship by creating the Argentine–Brazilian Economic Integration Program (ABEIP; PICAB in Spanish), aimed at economic and political cooperation. The political side of ABEIP tried to strengthen these infant democratic regimes, which had emerged after long periods of military rule in both countries. From an economic perspective, ABEIP sought to expand and diversify trade between the two countries with a special focus on agribusiness and the automotive sector (Manzetti, 1993).

When Presidents Carlos Menem in Argentina and Fernando Collor de Mello in Brazil took office (in 1990 and mid-1989, respectively), free market ideas about trade liberalization and integration where now becoming accepted in the region. As Manzetti (1993, p. 104) points out, during those years, "both (countries) re-affirmed their commitment to, and desire to push forward with even greater zeal, the integration effort. Indeed, economic integration was a key component of both their foreign policies." In 1990, after several meetings, Collor de Mello and Menem signed the Buenos Aires Act, which established the objective of creating a common market by the end of 1994. When Argentina and Brazil started to formalize this agreement, Paraguay and Uruguay joined the proposal. Finally, on March 26, 1991, the foreign ministers of the four countries signed the Treaty of Asunción, which defined the common market as:

> The free movement of goods, services and factors of production between countries through, inter alia, the elimination of customs duties and non-tariff restrictions on the movement of goods, and any other equivalent measures; the establishment of a common external tariff and the adoption of a common trade policy in relation to third States or groups of States, and the co-ordination of positions in regional and international economic and commercial forums; The co-ordination of macroeconomic and sectorial policies between the States Parties in the areas of foreign trade, agriculture, industry, fiscal and monetary matters, foreign exchange and capital, services, customs, transport and communications and any other areas that may be agreed upon, in order to ensure proper competition between the States Parties; the commitment by States Parties to harmonize their legislation in the relevant areas in order to strengthen the integration process.[43]

Based on the conceptual underpinnings of a common market, the main objectives of the Treaty of Asunción were as follows (Manzetti, 1993, p. 105):

1. Across-the-board-tariff reductions to replace the sector-by-sector approach used by the ABEIP.
2. The coordination of macroeconomic policies in accordance with the tariff reduction schedule, and the elimination of non-quantitative restrictions.

3. The establishment of a common external tariff for trade partners outside Mercosur, with the objective of increasing the competitiveness of the member countries.
4. The development of accords for specific sectors of the economy in order to optimize the use and mobility of production factors and achieve efficient economies of scale.
5. The implementation of an institutional framework to solve trade litigation.

After sluggish progress in the 1990s, the Common Market Council (CMC) passed Decision 32/00 in 2000. This was as a new impetus to deepen economic integration between Mercosur members. During the summit of Buenos Aires in June 2000, the members "re-launched" the process of integration in order to strengthen the bloc both internally and externally. Known as the "Re-launching Agenda of Mercosur" (CMC decisions 22/00 to 32/00), the strategy sought to identify Mercosur's bottlenecks and to generate proposals to resolve them. In June 2001, a CMC meeting took place in Asunción and emphasized the need to make progress in the following key areas (European Commission, 2007, pp. 6–7):

a) reformulation of the system of dispute settlements;
b) identification and elimination of intra-regional barriers to trade (internal);
c) elaboration of common trade disciplines to prevent the imposition of trade-distorting measures (internal);
d) creation of a Free Trade Area of the Americas (external);
e) creation of an Inter-Regional Association Agreement with the EU (external).

Despite the many challenges Mercosur still faces—most of them derived from asymmetries among the four main partners—after the EU, it is nevertheless one of the longest lasting, most sophisticated, and deep regional integration initiatives. Mercosur as a bloc currently has trade agreements with the countries listed in Table 5.11. Around 60 of Mercosur's total exports go to countries with which the bloc has negotiated these agreements (UN COMTRADE, 2019).[44]

5.6.3 *The case of Argentina*

Keeping in mind the context of Mercosur, which is the basis upon which Argentina develops its trade policy, this section concentrates on the economic impact and policy responses of Argentine trade protectionism. First, I will briefly trace Argentina's trade policy evolution beyond its 1991 accession to Mercosur. Argentina's trade policy has been a roller coaster since the Peronist era in the 1950s. The Menem administration (1989–99) quickly adopted the WC policy reforms and moved to reduce and streamline trade barriers with the new Mercosur bloc. After an unprecedented economic depression between 1998 and 2002 (the economy shrank 28% during that period), due to the

Table 5.11 Mercosur trade agreements

Date of Entry into Force	Agreement
1996	Mercosur—Chile
1997	Mercosur—Bolivia
2004	Mercosur—Colombia–Ecuador–Venezuela
2005	Mercosur—Peru
2006	Mercosur—Mexico
2007	Mercosur—Israel
2008	Mercosur—Cuba
2009	Mercosur—India
2010	Mercosur—Morocco
2016	Mercosur—Southern African Customs Union (SACU)[1]
2017	Mercosur—Colombia
	Mercosur—Egypt
2019	Mercosur—EU[2]

Source: OAS Foreign Trade Information System, www.sice.oas.org; and Mercosur www.mercosur.int/relacionamiento-externo/red-de-acuerdos/

Notes: [1] Botswana, Eswatini, Lesotho, Namibia, and South Africa.
[2] Reached an agreement in 2019, still not signed.

haphazard and reckless implementation of market reforms, Argentina swung back toward extremely protectionist trade policies during the administration of Nestor Kirchner (2003–07) and Cristina Fernandez (2007–15).[45] This approach too, was a failure and led to a "return to the world" (*volver al mundo*) strategy during the Mauricio Macri administration (2015–19) that followed.[46]

Pita (2017, pp. 35–9) distinguishes between two main periods of trade policymaking during the Kirchner and Fernandez administrations:

> Internal and external turbulence (2007–2011), in which Kirchner's response to the growing inflationary problem was simply to sweep the problem under the rug, postponing any economic solution. In January 2007, he decided to understate the true inflation rate in the official statistics [given] a brief, yet intense, worldwide recession lasting approximately from spring of 2008 to winter of 2009 […] there were problems, but there were also successes: economic growth, high salaries, cheap tariffs, exchange rate appreciation, expansion of public spending, fiscal deficit, and the financing of this deficit through the Central Bank.[47]

In an interview I had with a former Argentinean government secretary, they recalled:

> Argentina was already, in 2008, one of the most closed economies in the world, both by level of tariffs and by volume of trade. This closure was deepened in 2011–2015 with exchange controls, para-tariff barriers and the DJAI system, prior import control, which was punished in a WTO panel

initiated by the United States, the EU and Japan. The result was a 30% drop in exports between 2011 and 2015, and the loss of about 5,000 of 15,000 exporting companies. This greater protectionism was not a response to the 2008 crisis, but a strategy to sustain an artificially low (appreciated) exchange rate that led to the loss of reserves. In this ultra-closed context, any request for protection from the private sector was generally met, generating higher costs for consumers (prices up to three times higher than in the US for toys, clothing, electronics and appliances) and loss of competitiveness for industries dependent on imported inputs. The government that assumed power in 2015 sought to implement a gradual opening of the economy, based on free trade agreements, initially with partners that did not represent a risk to Argentine production, and ensuring long terms of tariff reduction (EU-Mercosur, deepening of Mercosur and regional agreements such as Colombia, Chile and Mexico).[48]

Very different from his two immediate predecessors, Macri

considered the inward-looking orientation of the previous government a limitation to economic development. During the presidential campaign, Macri and his political coalition advanced an idea of a more open economy, publicly presented with expressions such as an "intelligent integration to the world" (*integración inteligente al mundo*).

(O'Farrell et al., 2018, p. 12)

In my interview with a former Argentinean government minister during the Macri administration, they highlighted this idea of more trade openness:

Contrary to what is observed in some countries of the world, with protectionist advances, our government has decided to integrate itself into globalization, multilateralism, and commerce [...] In these four years we have opened more than 250 markets for products from agriculture, livestock, and fisheries [...] we find that there are many tools to help [...] International agreements such as EU–Mercosur, multilateral agencies such as the WTO, and global forums such as the G20 are some examples. They are platforms from which a country can generate many instances of negotiation and interaction with others, to promote dialogue and trade. Undoubtedly, these institutional tools make the effects of a protectionist trend soften, and for our country they are essential.[49]

Despite these noble intentions, recent studies have identified some protectionist tools that were adopted during the Macri administration. O'Farrell et al. (2018, p. 12) summarizes these trade policies as follows: 1) lower tariff barriers, within the limits imposed by Mercosur CET; 2) replacement of the system of non-automatic import licenses (NALs) implemented by the previous administration for a new scheme of licenses that respected the rules of the WTO (and

Table 5.12 Top destinations of intermediate, consumption, and capital goods (average share in Argentina's total exports between 2008 and 2018)

Consumption goods	% in total Consumption goods exports	Intermediate goods	% in total Intermediate goods exports	Capital goods	% in total Capital goods exports
Brazil	40%	Brazil	10%	Brazil	50%
Chile	12%	US	6%	Chile	5%
US	8%	India	5%	Mexico	5%
Uruguay	5%	Canada	4%	US	5%
Paraguay	4%	Netherlands	4%	Germany	3%
Netherlands	2%	Spain	4%	Venezuela	3%
Venezuela	2%	China	3%	Uruguay	3%
Bolivia	1%	Vietnam	3%	Colombia	2%
Mexico	1%	Indonesia	3%	Paraguay	2%
Colombia	1%	Switzerland	3%	Peru	2%

Source: Author's creation based on World Bank-World Integrated Trade Solutions (WITS), https://wits.worldbank.org/countrysnapshot/en/LCN

that would be progressively dismantled); 3) changes in the methodology of antidumping measures; and 4) increased use of technical regulations in replacement of non-tariff barriers to trade, such as non-automatic import licenses.

One useful way to understand Argentina's protectionism during the time period of my study (2008–19) is to analyze the different types of products exported. Argentina's export of intermediate, consumption, and capital goods has been declining since 2008, which reflects the impact of the blanket protectionism embraced by the Kirchner and Fernandez administrations. In contrast with Mexico, Argentina is weakly connected to GVCs as an exporter of both capital and intermediate goods. Table 5.12 shows the five key destinations for Argentina's exports and potential GVC dynamics. Brazil is by far the major destination for Argentina's consumption and capital goods. Chile, the United States, Uruguay, and Paraguay also appear as consistent destinations in all three product categories. Interestingly, China is not among its main trading partners in any of the three categories.

5.6.3.1 Argentina's trade protectionism: economic impacts and responses

In this section, I first concentrate on how protectionist measures imposed by Argentina's main trading partners have affected Argentina over the past decade. In this regard, I concentrate on those countries with which Argentina has close trade relationships through trade agreements and potential GVC ties (Table 5.12). Second, I analyze how Argentina has responded to these close partners and the effects of its own protectionist measures. Here, I study the types of measures countries have used and the specific sectors that have been

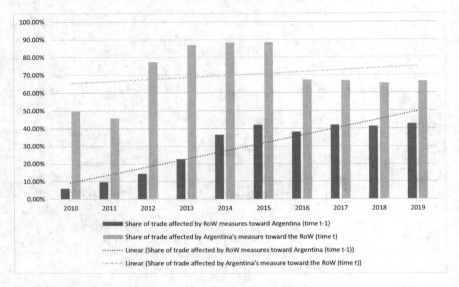

Figure 5.21 Share of Argentina's total exports affected (t-1) versus world export to Argentina affected (time t) by protectionist measures (Average 2009–19).

Source: Author's creation based on Global Trade Alert.

affected. Finally, I explore how trade protectionism has impacted Argentine employment in industry, agriculture, and services.

In light of the descriptive evidence I have in hand, I expect to find the following: first, if my theorical intuitions are correct, I expect that Argentine policymakers will systematically respond to adverse protectionist measures adopted by another country and adopt protectionist measures in return (H1). Second, the existence of PTAs (e.g., Mercosur) decreases the likelihood of a protectionist response overall (H2). Again, I expect that, as a member of Mercosur, Argentina has been less affected by those countries with which the bloc has PTAs. Third, I expect that Argentina will retaliate more with (less transparent) NTMs than with tariff measures.

Regarding my first assumption, Figure 5.21 shows the share of Argentina's total exports affected (in t-1) versus how world exports to Argentina are affected (in t) by protectionist measures (on average by year between 2009 and 2019). As we can see, Argentina has been especially responsive to protectionist measures up until 2015. Since 2016, the first year of Macri's administration, the level of protectionism targeted toward Argentine exports has remained the same, but its protectionist responses have decreased. Overall, until 2015, the case of Argentina confirms H1, which states that when a country is adversely affected by a protectionist measure adopted by another country, it will systematically respond to that country by adopting protectionist measures in return.

Protectionism and trade policy responses in Latin America 121

In Table 5.12, I show Argentina's main trading partners through trade agreements. The following two figures discriminate between close (e.g., PTA) and not close trading partners. Figure 5.22 shows that up until 2014, Argentina's share of exports was more impacted by protectionism on the part of not close trading partners. Since 2014, Argentina has been similarly impacted by protectionist measures of close and not close trading partners. This can be explained by the increasing protectionism of Brazil, as this is the key destination of Argentine exports. On average, between 2009 and 2019, 50 of Argentina's exports have been affected by close trading partners and 47 by those countries with which it has no trade agreements. In other words, for the case of Argentina, PTA membership has not reduced protectionist measures but rather increased them. Figure 5.23 shows the share of exports from close and not close trading partners impacted by Argentine protectionism. Remarkably, the pattern of protectionism between close and not close trading partners moves in tandem. This evidence for Argentina does not support the results from the large-N analysis presented in Table 4.3, where we saw that the existence of a PTA between A and B is negatively correlated with protectionist dynamics. This can be explained by the fact that Argentina does not have PTAs with Chile or the United States, two other key market destinations for its exports. Moreover, Brazil, the top trading partner of Argentina, has become increasingly protectionist, despite its Mercosur membership. From a policy perspective, this result shows that countries like Argentina would do well to sign more trade agreements, especially strategic ones, that is, enter into agreements with those countries with which Argentina has trade complementarities.[50] However, Argentina is hampered from doing this because of its membership in Mercosur. In the final section of this chapter, I concentrate on how modernizing reforms could allow greater flexibility for this CU.

Considering the number of measures implemented (and not the share of trade affected), Figure 5.24 shows that Argentina has consistently implemented more protectionist measures against countries with no trade agreements than toward close trading partners (e.g., with a PTA in force). Even more consistent is the effect of protectionist measures by countries with no trade agreements on Argentina (see Figure 5.25). This evidence for Argentina supports the results from the large-N analysis, where the existence of a PTA between A and B is negatively correlated with protectionist dynamics.

As for the level of transparency in protectionist interventions, in Figure 5.26 we can see that the use of nontransparent instruments by Argentina toward close trading partners is much higher (33 on average between 2009 and 2019) than for countries with which it has no trade agreements (24). This is in line with research proposition B (H4), which states that we would expect to see more nontransparent protectionist dynamics between close trading partners (e.g., through PTAs; Figure 5.27). An Argentinean economist and researcher of the Center iDeAS/UNSAM spoke with me about this phenomenon:

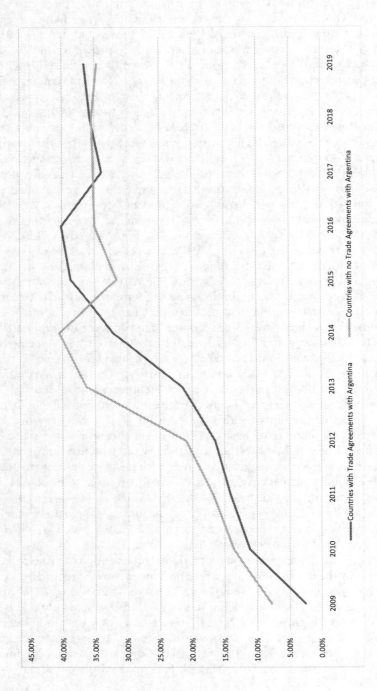

Figure 5.22 Share of Argentina's exports impacted by protectionism from close and not close trading partners.

Source: Author's creation based on Global Trade Alert, www.globaltradealert.org/

Protectionism and trade policy responses in Latin America 123

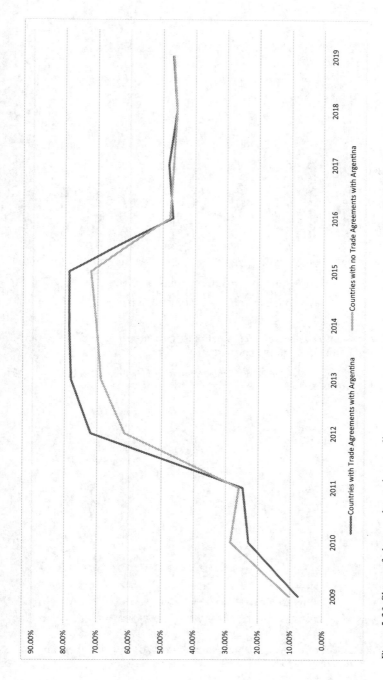

Figure 5.23 Share of close and not close trading partners exports to Argentina impacted by Argentina's protectionism.

Source: Author's creation based on Global Trade Alert, www.globaltradealert.org/

124 *Protectionism and trade policy responses in Latin America*

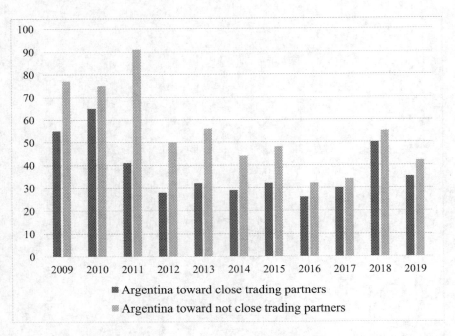

Figure 5.24 Argentina's number of protectionist measures implemented toward close and not close trading partners.

Source: Author's creation based on Global Trade Alert, www.globaltradealert.org/

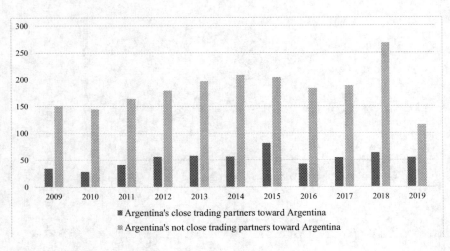

Figure 5.25 Number of protectionist measures toward Argentina by close and not close trading partners.

Source: Author's creation based on Global Trade Alert, www.globaltradealert.org/

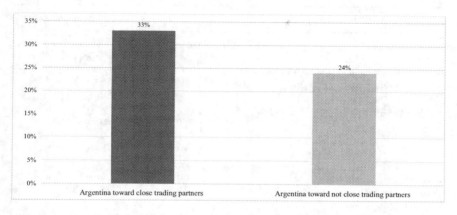

Figure 5.26 Share of nontransparent protectionist measures by Argentina (Mercosur) toward close and not close trading partners (average 2009–19).

Source: Author's creation based on Global Trade Alert, www.globaltradealert.org/

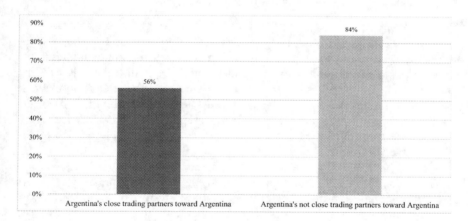

Figure 5.27 Share of nontransparent protectionist measures toward Argentina (Mercosur) by close and not close trading partners (average 2009–19).

Source: Author's creation based on Global Trade Alert, www.globaltradealert.org/

In Argentina, these discussions are less subtle, and the logic is "in a protectionist world, we have to be protectionist," while in Mexico, for example, they tell you "although NAFTA was not all that good, we increased exports and jobs." And while the previous government (of Macri) did not share this protectionist vision, the government now [of Alberto Fernandez] agrees more in this regard. [51]

Table 5.13 Most affected sectors in and by Argentina (2009–19)

Most affected sectors in Argentina	Most affected sectors by Argentina
Close Trading Partners	
Cereals	Motor vehicles, trailers & semi-trailers
Motor vehicles, trailers & semi-trailers	Other fabricated metal products
Sugar & molasses	Other general-purpose machinery & parts
Pharmaceutical products	Prepared & preserved fish, crustaceans
Pumps, compressors, hydraulics & engines	Wearing apparel, except fur apparel
Not Close Trading Partners	
Products of iron or steel	Other fabricated metal products
Pharmaceutical products	Motor vehicles, trailers & semi-trailers
Fruits & nuts	Domestic appliances & parts
Prepared & preserved fruits & nuts	Other general-purpose machinery & parts
Motor vehicles, trailers & semi-trailers	Wearing apparel, except fur apparel

Source: Author's creation based on Global Trade Alert, www.globaltradealert.org/

Finally, Table 5.13 concentrates on sectoral dynamics for the case of Argentina. Here, there are important within-sector retaliation dynamics in the industrial sector, including motor vehicles, trailers & semi-trailers. Recall that H7 says we would not expect to find much within-sector retaliation in those sectors with high levels of industrialization. The reverse finding for Argentina can be explained by the fact that it is poorly integrated into GVCs. With regard to these sectoral dynamics, the Argentinean economist and employee of the Center iDeAS/UNSAM continued:

The sectors where Argentina has problems are the same sectors where everyone has a problem: clothing (textiles), footwear, which are more automated sectors, that generate employment, and today are most exposed to competition internationally. The largest sectors, automotive, iron and steel, are the ones with more problems abroad, where Argentina exports. But above all, the most problematic is that of iron and steel. In this sector there are two important companies: Techin and Acindar. Techin (mostly Argentine capital), which is the largest, does two types of things: flat pipes and tubes that are not traded goods. These companies have private and public reactions (to protectionism). On the private ones, since they are transnational, they invest in other countries to break through the barriers. For example, they put a plant in the US, in Asia. On the other hand, in the domestic market they ask to be protected against Chinese and Russian competition, and against global overproduction and low prices.[52]

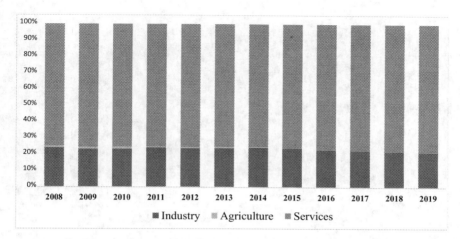

Figure 5.28 Argentina's employment in industry, agriculture, and services (% of total employment).

Source: Author's creation based on Global Trade Alert, www.globaltradealert.org/

Figure 5.28 illustrates the percentage of workers in each sector out of the total number of employed persons in Argentina. In Figure 5.29, I divide Argentinean employment into the three main sectors of the economy (industry, services, and agriculture), and we can see that the industry sector has been most affected by protectionist measures. More specifically, between 2009 and 2019, an average of 2.5 million people worked in the industrial sector, which was exposed to approximately 5,800 protectionist measures from the rest of the world (80% of total measures that impacted Argentina). Over 33 million people worked in the services sector, which was exposed to 850 measures (5% of total measures that impacted Argentina), and 0.2 million people worked in the agriculture sector, which was exposed to 862 measures (6%). In sum, 80% of the protectionist measures that affected Argentina were against the industrial sector, which represents, on average, less than 1% of employed persons in Argentina. Interestingly, although protectionism in the industrial sector is highest, it has less impact on the workforce. Moreover, if we consider that Brazil is the top destination of Argentinean exports, and that, on average, 43% of its exports to Brazil were impacted by protectionist measures (Global Trade Alert, 2020), this alerts us to some serious bottlenecks within Mercosur.

5.6.4 *The case of Brazil*

This section investigates the economic impacts and responses of trade protectionism in the Brazilian case. As in the case of Argentina, I analyze Brazil's trade policy as a country, beyond its membership in Mercosur.

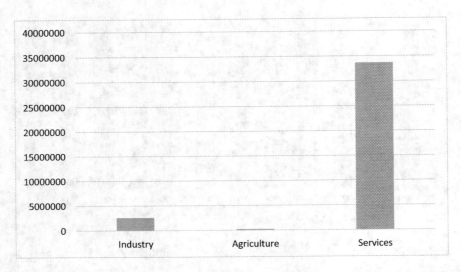

Figure 5.29 Number of protectionist measures affecting Argentina by main economic sectors (2009–19).

Source: Author's creation combining data from INDEC, International Labour Organization, ILOSTAT database, and Global Trade Alert.

Brazil has maintained a relatively closed economy compared to other countries in Latin America. From the 1930s to the late 1960s, the Brazilian economy was dominated by an import substitution industrialization model. Under this model, Brazil established successful automobile and steel production industries, marked by import barriers, subsidies, and state sponsorship. However, after 50 years of these protectionist policies, Brazil's role in global trade was disproportionately low given its population.

To be sure, Brazil was not immune to the Latin American debt crisis of the 1980s. The neoliberal WC policies that emerged in the 1990s led to privatization and trade liberalization throughout the region. However, foreign trade strategies in Brazil maintained a protectionist industrialization agenda compared to those of neighboring countries. Further, these WC policy changes were not followed up with further tariff reductions in Brazil, and non-tariff barriers to trade have increased since then. This agenda, coupled with passive involvement in preferential trade agreements, has hindered exports, economic growth, and allowed protectionism to flourish.

Brazil's historic lack of exposure to global trade fostered the economic success of certain industries that remained protected even after the trade reforms of the 1990s. Overall, manufacturing in Brazil represents a smaller portion of GDP than it did under import substitution industrialization. Industrial sectors like automobiles and capital goods that thrived under Brazil's import substitution strategy receive a large share of FDI, mainly because they have retained preferential treatment. Analysis of the prominent actors and sectors in Brazilian trade policymaking reveals the roots of protectionism in the country. Special interest groups are able to assert their political influence due to their ample resources for lobbying and because of the substantial number of workers in the industrial sector. Other, more competitive sectors that emerged under export-oriented strategies, predominantly agriculture, have failed to effectively challenge this historic industrial protectionism. In the time period of this study, exchange rate overvaluation has also favored industry over agriculture.

The institutional framework in which trade policy is made sheds further light on how domestic actors have managed to maintain protectionist policies in Brazil. Structural changes have occurred within civil society and state institutions due to two main forces: the unilateral nature of post-debt crisis liberalization and Mercosur. The liberalization that followed the 1980s debt crisis led to the mobilization of civil society, especially in the business sector. This was later influenced by the launching of hemispheric negotiations for a Free Trade Area of the Americas (FTAA), to be completed by 2005. Ultimately, Brazilian internal institutional restructuring, which concentrated power in the Ministry of Development and Foreign Trade, gave rise to greater influence and political power within the industrial sector as a force in Brazilian trade policymaking.

Another important Brazilian entity is the Foreign Trade Chamber (CAMEX), an interministerial body that coordinates different institutions involved in the trade policymaking process. Originally formed in 1995 under the office of the president, the Foreign Trade Chamber was moved to the Ministry of Development and Foreign Trade. Specialized bodies in the Foreign Trade Chamber advise their local business councils on specific policy issues, which cover all areas of trade, including tariff policy, trade defense, trade negotiations, and trade facilitation.

Meanwhile, in the 1990s, consultation and coordination mechanisms were developed to account for the new relevance of trade policy negotiation even though these changes ran counter to Mercosur and the ongoing FTAA negotiation. On tariff policy, existing "exception mechanisms" enabled the shift of product-specific tariffs between levels, which are for lobbyists a pathway to exert influence. Additionally, special import regimes have the ability to exempt or suspend certain tariffs. This process is costly and bureaucratic, favoring larger, richer companies that can bear the burdensome costs. These two mechanisms in particular, render Brazilian trade policymaking vulnerable to the demands of special domestic interests seeking protection.

In 2001, the Foreign Trade Chamber was given the discretion to apply trade defense measures on investigations conducted by the Department of Trade Defense. The conclusions from the Department of Trade Defense are legally binding and the Foreign Trade Chamber must adopt them. Exceptions to these legally binding recommendations exist in cases of public interest arising in the private sector or with another CAMEX member. Within the government, many public entities that are not directly involved with trade issues were brought into the discussion and formulation process. These mechanisms incorporated representatives from civil society as well.

Indeed, the mobilization of civil society in trade policy incentivized stronger connections between public and private actors. In the public sector, mechanisms to strengthen these connections were implemented. In the executive branch, the National FTAA Secretariat was created under the Ministry of Foreign Affairs to monitor hemispheric negotiation groups. These groups sometimes allowed participation by the private sector. In the legislative branch, Congress must ratify negotiated trade agreements. This can give the private sector a voice in the policymaking process. For instance, the Congress rejected a commitment made to the WTO to eliminate import duties under pressure from the Textile Parliamentary Front.

Finally, Figure 5.30 and Table 5.14 show Brazil's export of different types of products (intermediate, consumer, and capital goods). Figure 5.30 indicates that, after a sizeable decrease in 2008, Brazil's exports of intermediate, consumer, and capital goods have been growing in the last decade. Table 5.14 shows that Mercosur countries, the United States and the Netherlands (China only for intermediate goods) are important destinations for intermediate, consumption, and capital goods.

5.6.4.1 Brazil's trade protectionism: economic impact and responses

Figure 5.31 indicates the share of Brazil's total exports affected (in t-1) versus world exports to Brazil affected (time t) by protectionist measures (average by year between 2009 and 2019). As we can see, Brazil has been very responsive overall to protectionist measures since 2012, which marked the first year of Dilma Rousseff's (Worker's Party) presidency. Since then, the level of impact of protectionism toward Brazilian exports has remained the same, but the responses have increased. Overall, the case of Brazil confirms H1 which states that, in general terms, when a country is adversely affected by a protectionist measure adopted by another country, it will systematically respond to that country with protectionist measures in return.

Considering the information above about Brazil's main trading partners (Table 5.14) through trade agreements, the following figures distinguish between "close" (e.g., PTA) and "not close" trading partners. First, Figure 5.32 shows that during the period of analysis, Brazil has been similarly impacted by protectionism on the part of close and not close trading partners. This can be explained by the increasing protectionism of key trade partners (China, the United States, and Mercosur), which are the main destinations for Brazilian exports. Figure 5.33 shows the share of Brazil's protectionism and its effect on close and not close trading partners. We can see that there is little difference in the impact of Brazil's protectionism between close and not close trading partners.

Protectionism and trade policy responses in Latin America 131

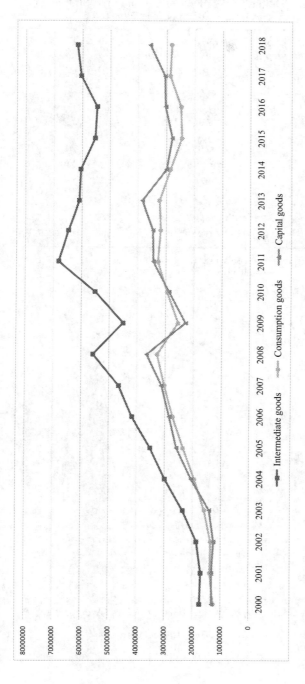

Figure 5.30 Brazil export of intermediate, consumer, and capital goods between 2000 and 2018 (in thousand US$).

Source: Author's creation based on World Bank–World Integrated Trade Solutions (WITS), https://wits.worldbank.org/countrysnapshot/en/LCN

132 *Protectionism and trade policy responses in Latin America*

Table 5.14 Top destinations of intermediate, consumption, and capital goods (average share in Brazil's total exports between 2008 and 2018

Consumption goods	% in total Consumption goods' exports	Intermediate goods	% in total Intermediate goods exports	Capital goods	% in total Capital goods exports
Argentina	20%	US	15%	US	23%
US	14%	Netherlands	9%	Argentina	13%
Netherlands	7%	China	9%	Netherlands	12%
Paraguay	4%	Argentina	7%	Mexico	6%
Mexico	3%	Germany	3%	Singapore	4%
Belgium	3%	Italy	3%	Chile	4%
Singapore	3%	UK	3%	Panama	4%
Uruguay	3%	Canada	3%	Germany	4%
Chile	3%	India	2%	Colombia	2%
Colombia	2%	Korea	2%	Paraguay	2%

Source: Author's creation based on World Bank-World Integrated Trade Solutions (WITS), https://wits.worldbank.org/countrysnapshot/en/LCN

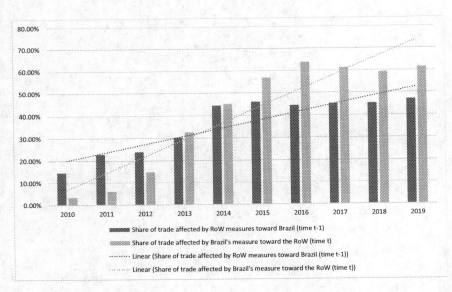

Figure 5.31 Share of Brazil's total exports affected ($t-1$) versus world export to Brazil affected (time t) by protectionist measures (Average 2009–19).

Source: Author's creation based on the Global Trade Alert.

Protectionism and trade policy responses in Latin America 133

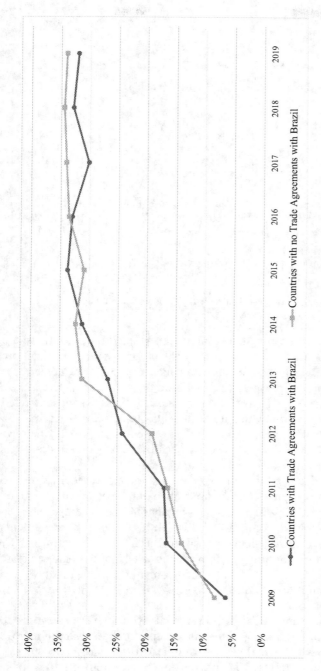

Figure 5.32 Share of Brazil's exports impacted by close and not close trading partners' protectionism.

Source: Author's creation based on Global Trade Alert, www.globaltradealert.org/

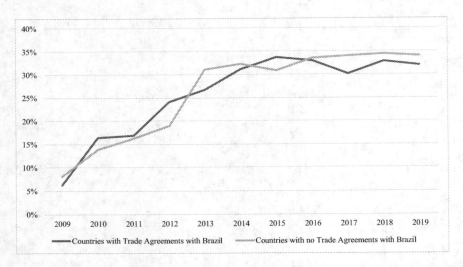

Figure 5.33 Share of close and not close trading partners' exports to Brazil impacted by Brazil's protectionism.

Source: Author's creation based on Global Trade Alert, www.globaltradealert.org/

Considering now the number of measures implemented (and not the share of trade affected), Figure 5.34 shows that Brazil has consistently enacted more protectionist measures against countries with which it has no trade agreements than toward close trading partners (e.g., with an FTA in force). Even more consistent is the case that those protectionist measures that have most affected Brazil are from countries with which it has no trade agreements (Figure 5.35). This evidence for Brazil supports the results presented in Table 4.3, where we can see from a large-N analysis that the existence of a PTA between *A* and *B* is negatively correlated with protectionist dynamics.

Focusing now on the level of transparency in trade measures, Figure 5.36 shows that the share of protectionist nontransparent instruments used by Brazil toward close trading partners is much higher (74%, on average, between 2009 and 2019) than toward countries with which it has no trade agreements (56%). This is in line with research proposition B (H4), which states that we would expect to see more nontransparent protectionist dynamics between close trading partners (e.g., through PTAs). I quote from an interview I had with an International Trade and Public Policies expert:

> Mercosur is a good example for your argument. Although the countries do not apply tariffs among them (with some exceptions), there are numerous non-tariff and other barriers (like, for example, extremely complex rules of origin, and different sanitary and phytosanitary requirements that make agricultural trade within the bloc very difficult). I agree with your statement

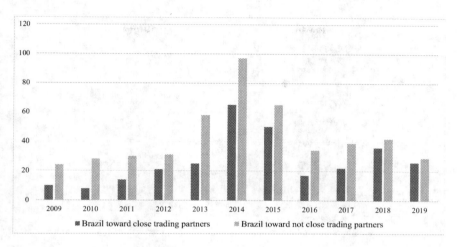

Figure 5.34 Brazil's number of protectionist measures implemented toward close and not close trading partners.

Source: Author's creation based on Global Trade Alert, www.globaltradealert.org/

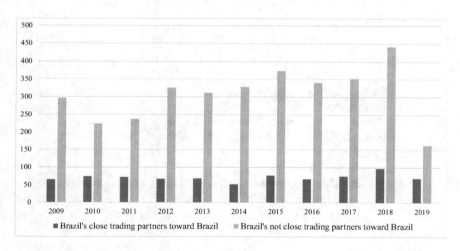

Figure 5.35 Number of protectionist measures toward Brazil by close and not close trading partners.

Source: Author's creation based on Global Trade Alert, www.globaltradealert.org/

that governments are influenced by interest groups that advocate for more protectionism and import substitution. But I would not say that, in the case of existing trade agreements, this happens in a less transparent and perceptible way. Non-tariff barriers in Brazil are usually not directed toward

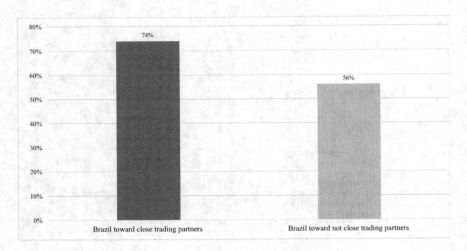

Figure 5.36 Share of protectionist interventions that use nontransparent measures by Brazil (Mercosur) toward close and not close trading partners (average 2009–19).

Source: Author's creation based on Global Trade Alert, www.globaltradealert.org/

specific countries. At the same time, it is usually more difficult for the Brazilian government to justify such barriers within Mercosur.[53]

At the same time, Brazil has been consistently more affected by non-tariff barriers from not close trading partners (Figure 5.37). This is probably because Brazil (and Mercosur as a bloc) is a global player and many countries implement barriers against it. In an interview I had with a former Brazilian government secretary, they said:

If we look at all the countries to which Brazil exports, we can see that Brazil suffers a lot from non-tariff protectionism, such as health barriers, especially with meat. It is with these types of measures that Brazil has had the most problems. If you look at the cases that Brazil has brought to the WTO, you can see that many are cases of antidumping and some cases of subsidies, as was the case with Canada on the matter of Embraer, or the case against the United States on the subject of cotton. For Brazilian exports, the vast majority of cases are derived from subsidy measures that were used by importing countries of our products. If we take the case of Brazilian exports to Europe, there are many sanitary barriers and also very high tariffs. What I can say is that, in the case of Brazil, the 2008 crisis did not greatly effect Brazilian exports, but rather followed the practices that already existed.[54]

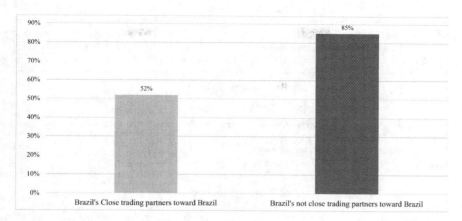

Figure 5.37 Share of protectionist interventions that use nontransparent measures toward Brazil (Mercosur) by close and not close trading partners (average 2009–19).

Source: Author's creation based on Global Trade Alert, www.globaltradealert.org/

Table 5.15 concentrates on sectoral dynamics. As we can see, for the case of Brazil, there is an important "within-sector" retaliation in motor vehicles, trailers & semi-trailers, and fabricated metal products, which are highly industrialized sectors. This is not in line with H7, which predicts that we would not expect to find much within-sector retaliation in sectors with high levels of industrialization. This can be explained by the fact that Brazil (and Mercosur in general) is producing outside of GVCs. I discussed these sectoral dynamics with an employee of the Foudaçao Getulio Vargas, Rio de Janeiro:

> Much like the dynamic in most Western economies, threatened sectors lobby for protection or retaliation before the government. A whole governmental apparatus exists—again not much different from those existing in many countries—for channeling such demands. These usually end up in a conciliatory agreement or with a standard WTO panel. Other actions may involve specifically designed non-tariff barriers, usually imposed by regulatory or supervisory agencies, that may cause effective damage to those which started the measure. Finally, with political support, taxation may also be used for certain retaliations.[55]

Figure 5.38 illustrates the proportion of employment that each sector represents out of the total number of employed persons in Brazil. Then, in Figure 5.39, I divide the share of employment into the three main sectors of the economy (industry, services, and agriculture). As we can see, employment in industry was the most affected by far. When I link these figures with the

Table 5.15 Most affected sectors in and by Brazil (2009–19)

Most affected sectors in Brazil (by main trading partners' protectionism)	Most affected sectors by Brazil's protectionism (toward main trading partners)
Close Trading Partners	
Sugar & molasses	Electric motors, generators & transformers
Motor vehicles, trailers & semi-trailers	Basic organic chemicals
Products of iron or steel	Motor vehicles, trailers & semi-trailers
Pumps, compressors, pneumatic & engines	Electrical energy
Other general-purpose machinery & parts	Other fabricated metal products
Not Close Trading Partners	
Products of iron or steel	Basic organic chemicals
Basic iron & steel	Machinery for mining & construction
Other fabricated metal products	Electric motors, generators & transformers
Motor vehicles, trailers & semi-trailers	Other fabricated metal products
Aircraft & spacecraft	Motor vehicles, trailers & semi-trailers

Source: Author's creation based on Global Trade Alert, www.globaltradealert.org/

proportion of employed persons in each sector to the total number of workers in Brazil (Figure 5.38), we can reach an approximate number of employed people who are exposed to protectionism in Brazil. More specifically, we can see that between 2009 and 2019, an average of 19.2 million people worked in the industrial sector, which was exposed to approximately 10,800 protectionist measures from the rest of the world, while 4.7 million worked in the service sector, which was exposed to 950 measures, and 29.6 million people worked in the agricultural sector, which was exposed to 800 measures. In sum, 80% of the protectionist measures that affected Brazil were in the industrial sector, which represents, on average, less than 35% of employed persons in Brazil.

5.6.4.2 *Political economy insights based on the case of Mercosur*

Many questions arise surrounding the political economic impact of protectionism in Argentina's and Brazil's respective developmental trajectories. First, the lost opportunities for trade-led development in these two cases is shocking. The data show that these two countries are not only highly protectionist, but they have not even cultivated a GVC with each other as part of Mercosur. Moreover, Brazil—a main player in the G20 and the world's ninth-largest economy in 2020—has forsaken GVC integration with other trade partner regions in favor of protectionism. The third decade of the twenty-first century is very late in the game for this rampant protectionism and lack of trade

Protectionism and trade policy responses in Latin America 139

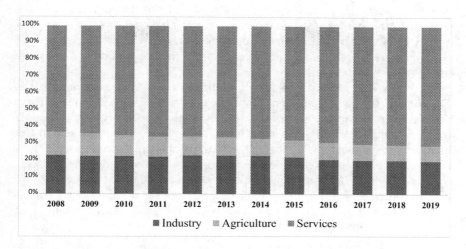

Figure 5.38 Brazil's employment in industry, agriculture, and services (% of total employment).

Source: Author's creation based on Global Trade Alert, www.globaltradealert.org/

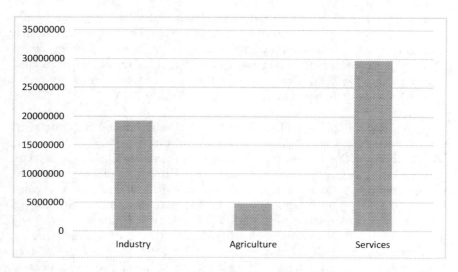

Figure 5.39 Number of total measures affecting Brazil by main economic sectors (2009–19).

Source: Author's creation combining data from International Labour Organization, ILOSTAT database and Global Trade Alert.

interconnectivity for both countries. It also shows how far away these countries are from having a strategic regional integration model that can drive productive economic growth. Both countries have been in a severe recession since 2015 and now face further economic stress from the immeasurable impacts of the COVID-19 pandemic.

Mercosur is an example of an economic integration project gone wrong. The combination of deep integration with high levels of murky protectionism, even between members, has not served these member countries well. Indeed, their participation in GVCs should be exceedingly higher, as we saw in the Mexican case. It seems clear that both Argentina and Brazil need to seek PTAs beyond Mercosur, but to do so necessitates that the bloc modernize and that each country simultaneously undertake serious domestic reforms. Let us start with the latter.

Brazil, for example, has implemented several trade-related reform initiatives aimed at buttressing growth (WTO, 2017a, p. xx):

> including in trade facilitation, anti-dumping, production and trade incentives (e.g., SME support), state-owned enterprises, energy, manufacturing, transport infrastructure, and more are under consideration. Monetary policy interventions were calibrated to contain inflation, which remained at the upper limit of the tolerance range established by the Central Bank of Brazil (BCB) during most of the period under review. The easing of inflationary pressures since 2016 has enabled the BCB to progressively cut its policy rate from a peak of 14.15%, which should help rekindle growth. The BCB has not sought to influence the exchange rate, limiting its currency market interventions to containing excessive short-term volatility. During 2013–15, the real depreciated by around 20% in real effective terms, moving towards levels more consistent with fundamentals, but appreciated by around 6% in 2016.

Beyond these reforms, unilateral trade liberalization in Brazil as one of its main domestic reforms could create a more favorable context for domestic industrial production (Oliveira et al., 2018). As for Argentina, O'Farrell et al. (2018, p. 69) state that there were at least three main reform mechanisms in the last decade: compensation ("to potential losers from liberalization"), transformation ("to support firms and workers to transit from a 'restructuring process' as a consequence of trade liberalization to dynamic firms"), and concertation ("of jobs, though which government took a gradual stance in the liberalization of cell phones and the special promotion regime"). However, there was "low incidence in minimizing resistance to liberalization from potential losers or gaining support from potential winners. The reasons for that are multifold and specific to each of them."

For both countries, it is key to take their relations with China into account as an explanation for some current trade policy dynamics. Wise (2020, p. 169) talks about a "Southern Cone Style of Developmentalism" with China:

The onset of the China boom in 2003 saw both countries with newly elected leftist executives, Lula in Brazil and Nestor Kirchner in Argentina. Although the political economy literature is laced with references to this period as "post-neoliberal," there are important nuances between the market reforms embraced by the two countries in the 1990s. These differences, in turn, shaped the varying content and emphases of the developmentalist programs that both administrations rolled out in the early 2000s.

However, there are distinct differences in the economic strategies employed by Brazil and Argentina during the China boom (Wise, 2020, p. 177):

In Brazil, Lula's new developmentalism had a strong institutional base in BNDES, and the effort to promote company innovation and an outward orientation was transparent and explicit. The macro prudent economic policy framework worked at cross-purposes and ultimately hampered the quest to promote value-added exports with greater technological intensity. In Argentina, the strategy was based on the Kirchners' coalition of the urban unemployed and underemployed, blue-collar workers, and the powerful ABCD trading companies, which have passed soybean export taxes on to weakly organized domestic producers. Given the discretionary nature of this spending, developmentalism was whatever the Kirchners said it was. If there was an industrial policy, it was difficult to discern. As for China, Argentina had naively expected south–south solidarity and a lender-of-last-resort relationship that never gelled; with Brazil, China has been an active trade and investment partner since the onset of the China boom. Both countries have had trade conflicts with China, although the China–Argentina relationship has been more acrimonious.

Regarding Mercosur as a bloc, as I have written elsewhere, it is first relevant to say that it is more than just a commercial agreement (Albertoni, 2019, p. 9). This is demonstrated by its normative framework, which reflects a complex shared history of its members with broader ambitions of forming a seamless CU (similar to the EU), the defense of democracy, and broader policy coordination. The challenge facing the organization, which is not limited to Mercosur but is plaguing many of the region's multilateral bodies, is to use this framework as an opportunity for driving development rather than as an obstacle to genuinely free trade among its members and to becoming a formidable market. We also need to be realistic. A 37-year-old institution is not easily dismantled or reformed, but to stay relevant Mercosur must evolve with the times. The bloc's leaders need to identify and attempt to implement a clear, predictable plan of action to promote the export sectors of member countries and maintain the confidence of international investors. Incremental changes without considering the ramifications will accomplish nothing. Mercosur members need to look to the United Kingdom's ongoing Brexit debacle for an example of how not to proceed. To avoid a Brexit effect during Mercosur reform, the foreign ministers of Argentina, Brazil, Paraguay, and Uruguay must cooperate to maintain transparency among member countries and for the world at large.

Given some of Mercosur´s restrictions mentioned above, the best initial move would be to allow freedom of action for individual members states to negotiate trade agreements bilaterally without losing the advantages already provided by the bloc. This reform would allow small subgroups within Mercosur to negotiate at faster speeds than the bloc as a whole. But here the small economies (Uruguay and Paraguay) must tread carefully. For them, reform efforts could easily turn current bloc partners into competitors (Albertoni, 2019, p. 9).

So the solution is yes to modernization, but the question that arises here is how. I suggest four key steps for reform of this regional bloc (Albertoni, 2019, p. 9):

1. The first step in the modernization process should be the signing of an agreement in which the members ratify the consolidation and deepening of the existing free trade area. This would lend certainty to all the economic actors of the member countries that the regional benefits of Mercosur will not be in doubt. This consolidation must be on paper, and with a commitment by member states to address all of the exceptions that have been used up until now to limit market access.
2. Once this crucial first step has been accomplished, members will need to amend the bloc's founding language and processes to allow greater flexibility for the CU and its members to negotiate international agreements with other countries or blocs. In conducting individual trade policy, members will be transitioning to a PTA rather than a CU (I discuss this transition in the following point). In recent years, bloc-wide negotiations have been plagued by delays in the process between the signing of agreements and their ratification. It has become typical for agreements to be signed by governments, only for parliaments to spend years debating their ratification. If Mercosur is going to modernize, this tedious process needs to come to an end.
3. It is important to consider "flexible clauses," such as the text of the renegotiated Comprehensive and Progressive Agreement for Trans-Pacific Partnership (CPTPP, formerly TPP). The revised agreement, signed by 11 countries, established that the CPTPP would come into force "60 days after the date on which at least six or at least 50 per cent of the number of signatories to this Agreement, whichever is smaller, have notified the Depositary in writing of the completion of their applicable legal procedures."[56] A similar mechanism for Mercosur reform would require that the agreement be ratified by two member countries (one of which must be either Uruguay or Paraguay, to protect smaller members).
4. In terms of bilateral negotiations and negotiations between subgroups, each country should be free to negotiate bilaterally with countries outside of Mercosur. For this to be possible within a balanced and transparent framework, Chapter 32 of the new trade agreement between the United States,

Mexico, and Canada (USMCA) serves as a useful guideline. The chapter establishes that if one of the three partners wishes to start a commercial agreement with a country outside the bloc, it must notify the other two USMCA members three months before beginning negotiations.

The main point is that, to achieve proper modernization, Mercosur should concentrate on mechanisms under a process of transparency rather than binding consultation or veto. To avoid indirect harm to the bloc's domestic economies, it is essential for all member countries to know whether another member is planning on undertaking bilateral negotiations with a non-Mercosur country.

A final aspect regarding Mercosur modernization, which links this analysis with the Mexico case study, is for the member countries to consider working more closely with the Pacific Alliance countries (Chile, Colombia, Mexico, and Peru). As previous studies suggest, "there are enough reasons to conclude that the Pacific Alliance (PA) and Mercosur could attempt convergence in the future" (Albertoni & Rebolledo, 2018, p. 108). Of relevance here is that there are numerous plurilateral agreements currently in the pipeline around the world. Hence, the convergence of two blocs such as Mercosur and the PA makes sense from an economic perspective. For example, convergence could provide the region with stronger negotiating power with the rest of the world, and it could foster integration into global supply-chain trade. Baldwin et al. (2014, p. 12) note that, while

> traditional trade means selling into one nation goods that were made in another nation [...] Supply-chain trade arises when high-tech firms combine their know-how with low-wage labor in developing nations; supply-chain is thus mostly about making things internationally, although international selling is also important.

The proposal toward convergence between the two blocs was announced by Chile in June 2014 during the summit meeting of the PA presidents in Mexico. At that meeting, Chile also conceded that in the event of a possible convergence between the two blocs, a "two speed" approach should not be disregarded. The main conclusion here is that, considering the divergent patterns of integration with Latin America, the regional leaders need to rethink trade, economic, and political ties in ways that would enable this region to become a more active and dynamic player in the global economy. Given the relevance of PA and Mercosur for the region, convergence between these initiatives could help considerably in achieving this aim.

5.7 Conclusions and country case summary

As demonstrated in previous chapters, one of the most demanding issues challenging the global economy is the rapid proliferation of opaque or murky trade protectionism. Latin America is no exception to these global trends. Indeed, it is still one of the most protectionist regions in the world. Much has been written about how different nations have been affected by and responded to protectionism (Amadeo, 2019; Baldwin & Evenett, 2020; Evenett & Fritz, 2018) and, more generally, about the political economy of protectionism (Fajgelbaum et al., 2019). However, this literature pertains almost exclusively to developed countries. We know little about how developing countries have been affected by and responded to protectionist trends since the GFC. This chapter has sought to expand our knowledge of the political economy of protectionism between 2009 and 2019 by exploring these dynamics in three key Latin American emerging economies. I conclude here with some political economy insights based on the main results presented above.

Before I dig into each case, recall that (as shown in detail in previous sections of this chapter) Latin America has recently experienced a policy reversal in the liberalization process. A slew of studies on this topic have cautioned that "the pace towards open markets has not been steady" (IDB, 2018, p. 1), although most countries in this region have at least some type of trade agreement with one or more countries. My results show that interconnectivity through regional trade agreements does not seem to be a decisive factor in deterring protectionism and nontransparent protectionism in particular. Some 47% of the measures implemented within the region have been "murky instruments," while the share of "murky instruments" deployed by Latin American countries toward the G20 countries is 33% (see Figure 5.8). Additionally, during my fieldwork interview in Latin America, trade policymakers confirmed that PTAs do not deter less transparent trade measures.

Another perspective on Latin American trade protectionism concerns whether there is a pattern between the destinations of intermediate goods exported by region and the types of measures implemented. As shown, since 2008, Asia and the United States have consistently been the leading destination of Latin American intermediate goods (possible GVC possible linkages). Interestingly, the regions where Latin America is exporting more intermediate goods are also those with which it has implemented murkier instruments (see Figure 5.9 and Table 5.6). This not only confirms one of the main research propositions of this book (countries with high trade interdependence will retaliate more with less transparent measures), but it also shows how far away is Latin America from being integrated into more extraregional GVCs.

In terms of the impact of protectionism on sectors and potential retaliatory dynamics, the results show that the sectors most affected in Latin America by protectionism from the RoW are also those most affected by Latin America's protectionism toward RoW exports. Still, in general terms, Latin America has been less protectionist toward RoW than RoW has been toward Latin America. For example, while the maximum number of measures by sector affected in Latin America is around 70—such as products of iron or steel in 2019—the maximum number of protectionist measures deployed by Latin American toward RoW in terms of sector was 26—for such products as cereals in 2019.

At the same time, there are some potential "within-sector" retaliatory dynamics in sectors that normally have high involvement in industrialized global value chains—goods such as motor vehicles, trailers, semi-trailers, and products of iron or steel. This is in not line with Hypothesis 7, which states that the higher the level of industrialization of the sector, the lower the within-sector retaliation. Again, this within-sector retaliation in Mercosur has been a big obstacle to productive growth in Argentina and Brazil.

In the case of Mexico, we can see that it has been very responsive to protectionist measures (see Figure 5.11). Overall, this confirms H1, which states that when a country is adversely affected by a protectionist measure adopted by another country, it will systematically respond to that country by adopting protectionist measures in return. Also, Mexico's share of exports has been consistently more impacted by those countries with which Mexico has no FTA. On average, between 2009 and 2019, 14% of Mexico's exports have been affected by close trading partners (e.g., the United States), and 21% by those countries with which it has no trade agreement. When we consider close trading partners through potential GVC ties (e.g., the United States, Canada, China, Colombia, Brazil, as shown in Table 5.9), this reflects a contrasting scenario. Indeed, between 2009 and 2019, on average, 36% of Mexico's exports were affected by close trading partners and 21% by those countries with which it has no trade agreements. This suggests that GVCs do not seem to restrain protectionism as do PTAs. In the same way, the case of Mexico confirms H2 on the negative relationship between protectionist dynamics and PTAs. Moreover, it does not confirm H3 (GVCs are negatively correlated with protectionist responses), in line with the quantitative results presented above.

My results also show that, since 2011, Mexico has consistently implemented more protectionist measures against countries with which it has no trade agreements than toward close trading partners (e.g., with an FTA in force). We can also see that the same occurred with those measures that affected Mexico. The only exception is in 2019, when Mexico found itself wedged between the US–China trade war. Mexico's exports to China between 2018 and 2019 decreased in value by 4% (UN COMTRADE, 2019). Moreover, President Trump threatened to impose an extraordinary escalating tariff on Mexico if it did not address the problem of undocumented migration flows from Central America.[57] Although much of this bilateral tension was at the rhetorical level, there were many nontransparent measures implemented by the United States toward Mexico.[58]

Focusing on the level of transparency of trade measures, the share of nontransparent protectionist interventions used by Mexico toward close trading partners is much higher (on average, 47% between 2009 and 2019) than for countries with which it has no trade agreements (32%, on average, between 2009 and 2019). The share of nontransparent protectionist interventions in measures toward Mexico by close trading partners (82%) is also higher than countries with which it has trade agreements (80%). This is in line with research proposition *B* (H4), which states that we would expect to see more nontransparent protectionist dynamics between close trading partners (e.g., through PTAs).

When we concentrate on sectoral dynamics, we can see that there are more cross-sectoral retaliatory dynamics for the case of Mexico rather than from within sectors. This can be explained by the fact that most of the sectors affected are embedded in GVCs, such as fabricated metal products, basic iron and steel, and products of iron or steel. Hence, a retaliatory dynamic from within sectors would severely impact the domestic consumption of Mexico's key products.

With regard to Brazil and Argentina, we can see interesting protectionist dynamics from a political economy perspective. Let us start with Argentina. This country was very responsive to protectionist measures until 2015. Since 2016, the first year of Macri's presidency, the impact of protectionism toward Argentine exports remained the same, but its protectionist responses decreased. Overall, this partially confirms H1. Second, we can see that, until 2014, Argentina's share of exports had been consistently more impacted by protectionism from "not close" trading partners. However, since 2014, Argentina has been impacted by protectionism from close and not close trading partners alike. This can be explained by increasing protectionism in Brazil, the key destination of Argentine exports. On average, between 2009 and 2019, 50% of Argentina's exports have been affected by close trading partners, and 47% by those countries with which it has no trade agreements. In the case of Argentina, its only PTA is Mercosur, and the data clearly show that rather than PTAs reducing the protectionist impact, Mercosur has increased it.

This evidence for Argentina does not support my hypothesis that the existence of a PTA between A and B is negatively correlated with protectionist dynamics. As mentioned above, from a policy perspective, this result suggests that Argentina needs to negotiate more strategic trade agreements with countries that it exports to, such as Chile and the United States. In other words, the country must pursue PTAs with those countries with which trade complementarities exist (Albertoni et al., 2020). When considering the current number of measures implemented (and not the share of trade affected), Argentina has consistently implemented more protectionist measures against countries with which it has no trade agreements than toward its Mercosur trading partners. Further, Argentina has been consistently more affected by protectionist measures from countries with which it has no trade agreements.

As for the level of transparency, we can see that the share of murky protectionist instruments used by Argentina toward close trading partners is much higher (33%, on average, between 2009 and 2019) than with countries with which it has no trade agreements (24%). This is in line with H4, which states that we would expect to see more nontransparent protectionist dynamics between close trading partners (e.g., through PTAs).

When we concentrate on sectoral dynamics, we can see that there exists an important within-sector retaliatory dynamic between Argentina and Brazil in motor vehicles, trailers & semi-trailers, all in the industrialized sector. This contradicts H7, which predicts that we would not expect to find much within-sector retaliation in those sectors with high levels of industrialization. This can be explained by Argentina's very low access to GVCs, not to mention high protection between Brazil and Argentina within the same PTA.

Regarding Brazil, my results demonstrate that it has been very responsive to protectionist measures overall since 2012, which marked the first year of Dilma Rousseff's (Worker's Party) presidency. Since then, the level of protectionism toward Brazilian exports has remained the same, but Brazil's protectionist responses have increased (see Figure 5.31). Moreover, we can see that Brazil has been impacted (and responded) almost in the same way by protectionism from close and not close trading partners. This can be explained by the increasing protectionism of key trading partners such as China, the United States, and its own Mercosur partners (see Figures 5.32 and 5.33). Considering the number of measures implemented (and not the share of trade affected), we can see that Brazil has steadily enacted more protectionist measures against countries with which it has no trade agreements than toward its Mercosur partners (e.g., with an PTA in force). Even more consistent is my finding that Brazil has been repeatedly more affected by countries with no trade agreement (see Figures 5.34 and 5.35). This is in line with proposition A (H2), which states that we would expect that PTAs are negatively correlated with protectionist responses.

Regarding the levels of transparency of measures, we can see that the share of protectionist interventions that use nontransparent instruments, employed by Brazil toward close trading partners is much higher (74%, on average, between 2009 and 2019) than with countries with which it has no trade agreements (56%). This is in line with research proposition B (H4), which states that we would expect to see more nontransparent protectionist dynamics between close trading partners (e.g., through PTAs). At the same time, Brazil has been consistently more affected by non-tariff barriers used by not close trading partners. This is most likely because Brazil (and Mercosur as a bloc) is a global player that has retained highly protectionist policies and, hence, many countries implement barriers against it in return.

Finally, regarding sectoral dynamics, we can see that for the case of Brazil there are important "within-sector" retaliatory dynamics in motor vehicles, trailers & semi-trailers, and fabricated metal products, which are highly industrialized sectors, something that is not in line with H7, which predicts that we would not expect to find much within-sector retaliation in those sectors with high levels of industrialization. This can be explained precisely by the fact that Brazil (and Mercosur in general) does not participate in significant GVCs (Table 5.15 shows a summary of the results obtained in each case for each research proposition). In this respect, Brazil has been its own worst enemy. Rather than playing the role of industrial anchor and innovator within Mercosur, it has thwarted GVC development with the bloc by coddling its own motor vehicle sector—not to mention Mercosur's prospects for deeper industrialization overall.

Notes

1 Part of this chapter was written with Carol Wise—the author is grateful for her permission to use the material. This chapter is extended version of a chapter, "Trade Protectionism and Integration in Latin America. The Cases of Brazil and Mexico," coauthored with Carol Wise, in Manfred Elsig, Andrew Lugg, and Rodrigo Polanco, *What Does the Future Hold for Trade Policy*? (forthcoming). Cambridge University Press. Earlier versions of this chapter were presented at USC's Comparative Politics Group, where I received excellent comments and suggestions. I especially want to thank Bryn Rosenfeld, Gerardo Munck, and Saori Katada for their suggestions. My colleague and friend Victoria Chonn Ching also gave me very helpful comments on earlier versions of this chapter. Additionally, this chapter was presented at the Institute for Qualitative and Multi-Method Research, where I received many comments and suggestions that positively impacted my work.
2 Zandi et al. (2018) estimate the impact of the "Trump trade war" for the years 2018–20. Interestingly, under the scenario of 25% tariffs on all Sino–US trade and other "qualitative" actions taken by China against American firms operating there, their results show that protectionism reduces GDP growth from second quarter 2018 to second quarter 2020 in Argentina, Brazil, and Mexico in very different ways: in Argentina by more than 0.6%, in Brazil 0.3% to 0.6%, and in Mexico less than 0.3%. For more information, see Evenett & Fritz (2018).
3 As part of its follow-up process concerning the US–Sino trade conflict, Chile has created three sectoral committees (agriculture, agroindustry, and fisheries and aquaculture). See: DIRECON (2018) "Riesgos y oportunidades de la guerra comercial." Departamento de estudios, www.subrei.gob.cl/wp-content/uploads/2018/07/riesgos_y_oportunidades_gc_final.pdf.
4 Global Trade Alert (GTA), www.globaltradealert.org/.
5 The G20 comprises Argentina, Australia, Brazil, Canada, China, France, Germany, India, Indonesia, Italy, Japan, the Republic of Korea, Mexico, Russia, Saudi Arabia, South Africa, Turkey, the United Kingdom, the United States, and the EU. It is "the premier forum for international economic cooperation." Available at: *What Is the G20?* https://g20.org/en/about/Pages/whatis.aspx. This is different from the developing nations' G20 group at the WTO, which is a coalition of developing countries formed in 2003 during the Doha Round Negotiations.
6 OAS-SICE, *Treaty Establishing a Common Market Between the Argentine, Brazil, Paraguay and Uruguay*, www.sice.oas.org/trade/mrcsr/treatyasun_e.asp.
7 G20, *What is the G20?* https://g20.org/en/about/pages/whatis.aspx.
8 In the three cases, considering the share of the world's exports to Argentina affected by its import restrictions.
9 Closer to zero means a better performance. For more information, visit *The Observatory of Economic Complexity*, https://oec.world/.
10 WTO, *Trade in Value-Added and Global Value Chains: Statistical Profiles*, www.wto.org/english/res_e/statis_e/miwi_e/countryprofiles_e.htm.
11 These WTO profiles on value added and GVCs rely on the OECD trade in value added database (TIVA) stemming from a joint OECD-WTO TIVA initiative. The TIVA online database can be accessed at: http://oe.cd/tiva. TIVA indicators "cover goods and services and are available for a set of 64 economies and 36 industries from the international standard industrial classification, (ISIC revision 4). Hence,

the number of profiles available as well as the main partners and industries shown in the tables reflect the current coverage of the TIVA database" (OECD-WTO TIVA).
12 WTO, *Trade in Value-Added and Global Value Chains: Statistical Profiles*, www.wto. org/english/res_e/statis_e/miwi_e/countryprofiles_e.htm.
13 WTO, *Trade in Value-Added and Global Value Chains: Statistical Profiles*, www.wto. org/english/res_e/statis_e/miwi_e/countryprofiles_e.htm.
14 WTO, *Trade in Value-Added and Global Value Chains: Statistical Profiles*, www.wto. org/english/res_e/statis_e/miwi_e/countryprofiles_e.htm.
15 This interview design was reviewed and approved by the University of Southern California Institutional Review Board (IRB) (ID: UP-20-00392).
16 I would especially like to thank the contacts related to strategic trade policy in Latin America provided by Prof. Carol Wise, which enabled me to reach high-level experts and policymakers.
17 The interviewees were expected to speak Spanish, Portuguese, or English.
18 For more information on good practices of qualitative data management, see: *Qualitative Data Repository*, https://qdr.syr.edu/guidance/managing.
19 Author's interview with a former Chilean government minister, November 2019.
20 Author's interview with an researcher of the Catholic University of Chile, June 2020.
21 For an extended analysis of Latin America regional integration, see Albertoni & Rebolledo (2018).
22 Author's interview with a former Colombian government vice minister, April 2020.
23 Author's interview with a former Mexican government undersecretary, January 2020.
24 Author's interview with an economist and former Peruvian government minister, April 2020.
25 For an in-depth analysis of participation in GVC in Latin America, see Cadestin et al. (2016) and Hernández et al. (2014).
26 For an extensive analysis of Mexico's trade policy with Latin America, see Pastor & Wise (1994) and De Mateo Veiga (2003).
27 OAS Foreign Trade Information System, *Mexico's Trade Agreement*, www.sice.oas. org/ctyindex/MEX/MEXAgreements_e.asp.
28 ITC calculations based on UN COMTRADE, www.trademap.org/.
29 Author's interview with a Mexican trade policy expert, April 2020.
30 Author's interview with an employee of COPARMEX, the Mexican Employers' Association, November 2019.
31 Author's interview with an employee of COPARMEX.
32 Author's interview with an employee of COPARMEX.
33 For more information about this bilateral tension between the United States and Mexico, see Pérez Arguello & Albertoni, "Tariffs on Mexico? That Could Result in Trump's Nightmare," *New York Times*, June 20, 2019, www.nytimes.com/2019/06/ 20/opinion/tariffs-on-mexico-would-mean-more-immigrants.html.
34 Examples are: Reclassification of surfboard transport systems resulting in the imposition of a tariff (implemented in November 2019), www.cbp.gov/document/ bulletins/customs-bulletin-weekly-vol-53-september-25-2019-no-34; $10 million in Agricultural Trade Promotion Program support to the US Meat Export Federation (implemented in July 2019), www.fas.usda.gov/atp-funding-allocations. For other measures implemented by the United States toward Mexico in 2019, see www.globa ltradealert.org/country/222/affected-jurisdictions_132/period-from_20190101/per iod-to_20191231.

35 However, recent studies have shown that Mexico's participation in GVCs has failed to capture enough value added, in part due to its low production interconnectivity with China (Chiquiar & Tobal, 2019).
36 Tenaris, www.tenaris.com/en.
37 Author's interview with an employee of Tenaris Mexico, November 2019. Section 232 authorizes the president to "impose imports restrictions on products, imported into the United States in such quantities or under such circumstances as to threaten to impair the national security." (See https://ustr.gov/about-us/policy-offices/press-off ice/press-releases/2020/august/statement-presidential-proclamation.) Under Section 301 of the Trade Act of 1974, the USTR can initiate "an investigation to determine whether China's acts, policies, and practices related to technology transfer, intellectual property, and innovation are unreasonable or discriminatory, and burden or restrict U.S. commerce" (See https://ustr.gov/issue-areas/enforcement/section-301-investigations/tariff-actions.)
38 Author's interview with an employee of the University of Chile, April 2020.
39 Author's interview with a former Mexican government undersecretary, January 2020.
40 "First, China does not export revolution; second, it does not export famine and poverty; and third, it does not mess around with you. So, what else is there to say?" See Xi Jinping, *Wall Street Journal*, October 19, 2010, www.wsj.com/articles/SB10001424052702304410504575559623101416204.
41 This subsection on Mercosur draws on Albertoni & Rebolledo (2018, pp. 104–05).
42 See Treaty of Asuncion: www.sice.oas.org/trade/MRCSR/treatyasun_e.asp, accessed February 2016.
43 Treaty of Asuncion, www.sice.oas.org/trade/MRCSR/treatyasun_e.asp, accessed February 2016.
44 In Brazil, 17% of total exports go to countries that have a trade agreement with Mercosur, and in Argentina 29% (ITC calculations based on UN COMTRADE, www.trademap.org/).
45 See Saxton (2003) for a detailed description of Argentina's economic crisis and causes.
46 See O'Farrell et al. (2018) for an analysis of the political economy of trade policy in Argentina under Macri's administration (2015–18).
47 Interestingly, between 2008 and 2009, around 85% of trade policies implemented by countries consisted of protectionist measures. However, only a third of these policies consisted of tariffs, while the remainder were nontraditional protection measures (Kosacoff et al., 2008, p. 36).
48 Author's interview with a former Argentinean government secretary, October 2019.
49 Author's interview with a former Argentinean government minister, November 2019.
50 On this debate about signing PTAs with countries where there are strong trade complementarities, see Albertoni et al. (2020).
51 Author's interview with an Argentinean economist, employee of the Center iDeAS/UNSAM, October 2019.
52 Author's interview with an Argentinean economist.
53 Author's interview with an international trade and public policies expert, May 2020.
54 Author's interview with a former Brazilian government secretary, June 2020.
55 Author's interview with an employee of the Foudaçao Getulio Vargas, Rio de Janeiro, January 2020.

56 *Comprehensive and Progressive Agreement for Trans-Pacific Partnership*, www.international.gc.ca/trade-commerce/trade-agreements-accords-commerciaux/agr-acc/cptpp-ptpgp/text-texte/cptpp-ptpgp.aspx?lang=eng.
57 For more information about this bilateral tension between the United States and Mexico, see Pérez Arguello & Albertoni, "Tariffs on Mexico? That Could Result in Trump's Nightmare," *New York Times*, June 20, 2019, www.nytimes.com/2019/06/20/opinion/tariffs-on-mexico-would-mean-more-immigrants.html.
58 Examples are: Reclassification of surfboard transport systems resulting in the imposition of a tariff (implemented in November 2019), www.cbp.gov/document/bulletins/customs-bulletin-weekly-vol-53-september-25-2019-no-34; $10 million in Agricultural Trade Promotion Program support to the US Meat Export Federation (implemented in July 2019), www.fas.usda.gov/atp-funding-allocations. For other measures implemented by the United States toward Mexico in 2019, see www.globaltradealert.org/country/222/affected-jurisdictions_132/period-from_20190101/period-to_20191231.

6 Conclusions and final thoughts*

6.1 This book's main contribution and why it is relevant to the field

This book is neither about free trade nor protectionism. It is about the point where the two may converge. One distinctive aspect of rising protectionism over the last decade is that it is occurring against a backdrop of increased global interconnectivity. As I have argued throughout, countries around the world have become more integrated through PTAs and GVCs, even though they are erecting trade barriers *within* these same trade venues. What explains these contradictory trajectories? Earlier work on the political economy of trade protectionism offers compelling arguments about the circumstances under which governments decide to protect their economies (Milner, 1999), and the recent literature tells us how PTAs and GVCs promote trade interdependences and openness. However, the question of how these two trajectories—openness and protectionism—may simultaneously interact has been largely ignored. Thus, my overriding research question concerns why and how increased global trade interconnectivity has also become a channel for new forms of trade protectionism. These counterintuitive dynamics constitute the newest wave in the literature on trade interdependence. The literature on trade policy has heretofore concentrated on one side of the coin with respect to the effects of an interconnected global economy: the more political and economic linkages countries build among themselves, the less tension they will generate across borders (Baldwin, 2012; Gawande et al., 2015; Jensen et al., 2015; Lamy, 2013). From a trade policy perspective, this causal claim has held steady for many decades.

Under Bretton Woods, the world saw sustained trade liberalization for half a century. However, since the completion of the Uruguay Round in 1994 and the incorporation of the GATT into a newly created WTO in 1995, the world has experienced a rapid proliferation of PTAs, which have radically changed the internal logic of the global trading system. PTAs, for instance, have transformed the ways in which countries trade among themselves (Egger et al., 2011) and how they implement liberalizing policies with closer trading partners (Cieślik & Hagemejer, 2011). In a similar way, GVCs have overhauled the ways in which countries and their large multinational corporations produce

DOI: 10.4324/9781003340393-6

internationally. The ways these institutional trade and production mechanisms have also become channels for the spread of protectionism are subtle and enshrouded in high levels of economic uncertainty. This book is motivated precisely by this contradiction. I hypothesize that protectionist trends over the last decade reveal a possible downside to the proliferation of PTAs and GVCs, as these have become the institutional locus for less observable, NTMs. In other words, economic interdependence in the context of high economic uncertainty can devolve into a spiral of protectionism because "many governments simultaneously face pressure to reflate national economies and defend national commercial interests" (Evenett, 2019, p. 26).

The broader research agenda on post-GFC trade policies is still limited due to a short time line of just one decade, as well as the emergence of new types and forms of trade protectionism that are difficult to measure. Nevertheless, these phenomena have been under-researched. This book contributes to this research agenda and the broader theoretical debate on trade policy substitution between NTMs and tariffs (Beverelli et al., 2019; Niu et al., 2018). The data limitations mentioned in earlier chapters have given rise to a pattern of "omitted variable bias" in regression studies, which is "particularly important when analyzing the impact of commercial policy, as governments can substitute between transparent and murkier forms of protectionism" (Evenett 2019, p. 13). What we do know is that the more tariffs are lowered via bindings created by WTO rules, the more countries are coming to rely on NTMs. This raises a bigger challenge regarding the relationship between trade policy and transparency. It is precisely these opaque NTMs and their effects that this book has sought to specify and quantify. As mentioned at the outset, the combined effects of the GFC, the US–China trade war, and COVID-19 have rendered the international political economy a virtual social science laboratory in which the variables are still at play (Baker et al., 2020; Albertoni & Wise, 2020; Pinna & Lodi, 2021). Taking these extenuating circumstances into account, this book leverages the empirical findings in the literature since the GFC and gleans new insights to better understand the sheer volume and nature of twenty-first-century protectionism.

Figure 6.1 maps out my theory and the main research questions of this book. Based on empirical evidence, three key dynamics are considered: (1) a highly an uncertain global economy; (2) given this uncertain context, governments face more domestic pressure to protect their products and markets; and (3) this current uncertainty is nested in an interconnected global economy that has no precedent (e.g., PTAs and GVCs). Figure 6.2 offers a summary of my argument, hypotheses, methods, and results.

6.2 Implications for international political economy theory and practice

Interestingly, since the launching of the GATT treaty in 1947, the global economy has experienced four major recessions, in 1975, 1982, 1991, and 2009. However, as Kose et al. (2020, p. 3) note, "the 2009 GFC global recession, set

154 Conclusions and final thoughts

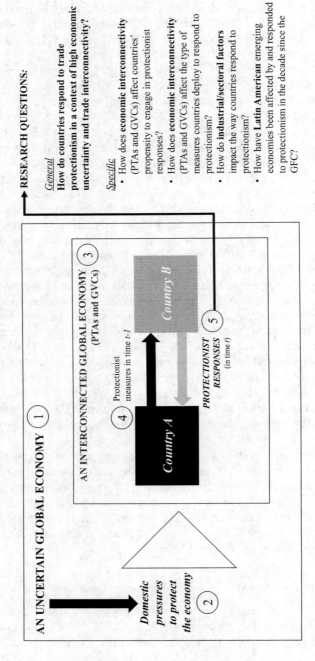

Figure 6.1 A logical diagram summarizing theory and main research questions.
Source: Author's creation.

Conclusions and final thoughts 155

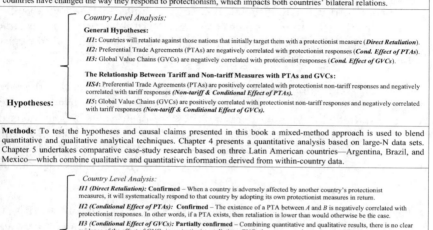

Figure 6.2 Summary of theory background, argument, hypotheses, methods, and results.

Source: Author's creation.

off by the global financial crisis, was by far the deepest and most synchronized of the four recessions."[1] Despite the failure to create an international trade organization in 1948, the GATT sufficed as the multilateral trade forum in 1995 when the WTO was founded. Ironically, it was at this same time that countries formally started to negotiate trade agreements among themselves. For example, by 1972, just 12 regional trade agreements had been notified to the GATT, and by the end of the 1990s, the number of PTAs had increased to 81.[2] Since then, the number of PTAs has grown consistently, a trend defined in the literature as a "New Wave of Regionalism" (Mansfield & Milner, 1999, p. 589).

In sum, the 2009 recession was the first to occur after countries had created a solid network of trade agreements and GVCs, which had become a main locus of production.[3] The Great Recession triggered high levels of economic uncertainty and motivated governments to seek out PTAs to hedge against further risks in a more interconnected world. From a trade policy perspective, the different debates about the real consequences of the 2009 recession are still underway. As Reinhart and Rogoff (2009, p. 15) claim, it was a different kind of recession because

> the essence of the this-time-is-different syndrome is simple. It is rooted in the firmly held belief that financial crises are things that happen to other people in other countries at other times; crises do not happen to us, here and now. We are doing things better, we are smarter, we have learned from past mistakes. The old rules of valuation no longer apply.

Following Reinhart and Rogoff (2009), we would also expect that the ways in which countries were affected by and responded to protectionism and recession also shifted. Could it be that countries are protecting their markets in "smarter ways" because they may "have learned from past mistakes?" During my fieldwork interviews, I probed the possible effect of PTAs on trade policy and commercial flows. I quote a researcher of the University of Chile, on this subject:

> The effects of free trade agreements [...] are more legal rather than instruments of real economic connection. Sometimes I think free trade agreements have been overvalued in terms of what they generate. When one asks students about those channels that connect us commercially, free trade agreements is always an answer, when in reality this is not always the case. Just look at Mexico, which has free trade agreements and only remains connected to the United States. I do not know if free trade agreements have been overestimated. So, I'm not really sure if today the world is more connected through PTAs or not.[4]

At the same time, different studies challenge the widespread perception among analysts and practitioners that traditional trade barriers have become irrelevant. For instance, Goldberg and Pavcnik (2016, p. 1) provocatively ask in one of their studies, "does trade policy still matter?" They note that over the last two decades, international trade research has shifted its focus from trade policy to other forms of trade friction. They also challenge this idea by examining a large body of evidence and conclude that:

> The perception that trade policy is no longer relevant arises to a large extent from the inability to precisely measure the various forms of non-tariff barriers that have replaced tariffs as the primary tools of trade policy. Better measurement is thus an essential prerequisite of policy-relevant research in the future. Despite measurement challenges and scant evidence on the impact of actual policy changes, existing evidence when properly interpreted points to large effects of trade policy on economically relevant

outcomes, especially when trade policy interacts with other developments, e.g., technological change.

As I have shown in previous chapters, trade policy is still very relevant, but we need to consider and measure new factors such as murky trade policies that impact trade relations between countries. In doing so, this book seeks to better understand the past, but also provide a road map of sorts for the kinds of commercial policy reforms that will be essential for the successful revival of world markets following the pandemic downturn.

This book has been concluded during a period of intense flux. In terms of theory expansion, the main contribution of this research is my analysis of how three main variables have interacted with ongoing trade policy dynamics since the GFC. By this, I refer to the political economy "trilemma" between trade protectionism, trade interconnectivity (e.g., PTAs and GVCs), and uncertainty (mostly generated by economic crises). More specifically, I have explored how rising trade interconnectivity via PTAs and GVCs can also generate an unexpected increase in nontransparent protectionism, given the context of exceedingly high economic uncertainty. In such times, countries protect themselves from trade partners with which they have strong commercial ties through less observable, non-tariff protectionist measures. These patterns have important implications for the relationship between PTAs and GVCs, as well as for political economy and policy trends overall.

I do not dispute the robustness of existing research indicating a correlation between PTAs, GVCs, and trade openness measured by tariff levels and, to some extent, by the more traditional non-tariff barriers such as antidumping measures. Rather, what is demonstrated in this book is that trade interconnectivity, generated by PTAs and GVCs in the context of high economic uncertainty, induces governments to substitute transparent trade barriers with less transparent ones. These results are in line with the "optimal obfuscation" that Kono (2006, p. 369) talks about in a seminal work in which he finds that "democracy leads to lower tariffs, higher core NTBs, and even higher quality NTBs [...] democracy promotes 'optimal obfuscation' that allows politicians to protect their markets while maintaining a veneer of liberalization." Keeping Kono's framework in mind, I suggest that PTAs and GVCs also promote the "optimal obfuscation" that he discusses.

More generally, my research contributes to the fields of international political economy, development studies, and trade policy. Another main point of my research has been to measure how the proliferation of protectionist policies since the 2008–09 GFC has affected key economic sectors. Relying on a mixed-methods approach, I undertook a quantitative analysis of the spread of trade protectionism based on a large sample of countries. For the qualitative part of this book research, case studies were compiled based on three Latin American emerging economies—Argentina, Brazil, and Mexico.

To elaborate on this last point, Yi (2009) argues that a "massive reorientation of trade flows towards multiple-step supply chains" has played an important role in spurring protectionist dynamics (p. 2). Bems et al. (2009, p. 4) are even more specific:

> Vertical specialization transmission mechanism is subtle, with several ways in which it could help generate a large and widespread collapse in trade [...] There could be re-nationalization of international production chains (triggered perhaps by an increase in protectionism). Second, growing vertical specialization implies that more cross-border transactions occur between separate stages of the production process. If the elasticity of substitution across stages is very low, then shocks to production in one country could be transmitted forcefully to other stages undertaken elsewhere. Third, if demand shocks are concentrated on goods that are vertically specialized, then trade is highly sensitive to changes in demand.[5]

At the same time, Bems et al. (2009, p. 2) assert that "while all these channels seem plausible and many analysts have asserted that they have played an important role in the trade collapse, there has been, to date, little evidence supporting the notion."[6] Gawande et al. (2015), using trade policy data for seven large emerging market countries (Argentina, Brazil, China, India, Mexico, South Africa, and Turkey), find that participation in GVCs is "a powerful economic factor determining trade policy responses" (p. 102). In the same vein, Blanchard et al. (2016) show that GVCs have increased the share of firms that rely on international supply and lobby for international trade openness. In the interview I conducted with a research economist affiliated with the WTO, about the potential negative side of GVCs, they said:

> Not all effects of trade agreements and GVCs work in favor of an ever-freer trade regime. As trade agreements have increasingly become deeper, they touch upon a wider array of subjects, including sensitive subjects like food or health regulations. This has caused a strong backlash in some countries against trade agreements from CETA to TTIP or TPP. Similarly, the offshoring of jobs that is associated with GVCs could have weakened the political sway of trading firms as they have reduced their domestic workforce.[7]

On the effect that PTAs can have with regard to trade policy, the literature on the political economy of PTAs has been concentrated mostly on why countries negotiate and sign PTAs (Baccini & Dür, 2012; R. Baldwin, 1993; Chase, 2003; Manger, 2009). More recently, the focus has been on the effect PTAs have on signatory countries in terms of trade flows (Baier & Bergstrand, 2007) and other areas of political concern, such as their ability to reduce bilateral conflict between PTA members (Hafner-Burton, 2005; Mansfield et al., 2008; Mansfield & Reinhardt, 2008). Some more recent studies report contradictory

Conclusions and final thoughts 159

findings. For instance, Kono (2007), in investigating the effect of PTAs in 30 countries from 1988 to 1998, found that they have

> important but contradictory conditional effects: they promote multilateral liberalization when members' intra- and extra-FTA comparative advantages are similar but impede such liberalization when these comparative advantages are different. FTAs can thus, depending on the circumstances, either help or hinder broader trade liberalization.
>
> (p. 165)

Nevertheless, most of the studies on this topic have concentrated more on the positive aspects of PTAs (Limão, 2016). PTAs can cause various levels of integration, including "deep" integration (Young, 2017).

It is relevant to analyze within-sector dynamics because these may play a role in a state's protectionist dynamics and improve our understanding of how the composition of trade influences protectionist retaliation. As Peterson and Thies (2015, p. 177) state, "higher proportions of bilateral intra-industry trade within bilateral relationships may promote the formation of preferential trade agreements, foster increasing political affinity, and reduce states propensity to engage in military conflict." As the World Bank's 2020 *Global Economic Perspective* states (p. 81):

> COVID-19 has sharply worsened economic conditions in Latin America and the Caribbean (LAC). The regional economy is projected to contract by 7.2 percent in 2020, a much steeper decline than during the global financial crisis, reflecting the impact of the measures necessary to slow the spread of the pandemic, significant deterioration in financing conditions and commodity prices, and spillovers from a global recession. As mitigation measures are scaled back and financing, commodity price, and external demand conditions become more supportive, regional growth is projected to recover to 2.8 percent in 2021. However, the near-term outlook is subject to significant downside risks. These include a resurgence of last year's wave of social unrest, increasingly adverse market reactions to rising public debt, weaker-than-expected commodity prices, and persistent pandemic-related uncertainty slowing the recovery of the services sector.

In sum, the contribution of this academic work is threefold: first, it fills a gap in our knowledge about the rise of post-GFC protectionism in developing countries. Second, it identifies a new murky protectionism in the form of opaque and pernicious non-tariff barriers, a topic that has been under-researched and demands attention. Third, I have built a series of datasets that better enable us to measure the damage done to sectors, producers, workers, and consumers since the rapid escalation of non-tariff barriers over the past decade. A central element of this project is that it bridges academics and trade policymakers and contributes to the search for commercial policy reforms that will be essential for the successful revival of world markets post-COVID-19.

6.3 Implications for policy

Regarding policy prescriptions, a key finding here is that a reliable set of trade agreements can be a buffer against straight tariff protectionism but not much use in combating non-tariff protectionism. Moreover, the number of PTAs a given country negotiates is less important than the type of trade agreements that are signed. Based on the positive effects of trade interdependence highlighted by previous studies, many countries have sought to strengthen their trade ties with new foreign partners. However, my research suggests that trade interconnectivity can be "double-edged": it limits tariff protectionism overall but can also prompt nontransparent protectionism at the same time. In other words, PTAs without clear enforcement mechanisms can actually be a negative long-term tool to improve bilateral trade. Evidence of this is that some original PTAs are now being renegotiated in a process called modernization. Most of these renegotiations include chapters related to non-tariff measures. Examples of this are the recent modernization of such PTAs as the EU–Chile, EU–Mexico, EU–Canada, China–Chile, Canada–Ukraine, and European Free Trade Area (EFTA) with Turkey and Canada.[8] Many of these agreements that are—or were—in the process of modernization, concentrate on topics that go well beyond tariff issues and concentrate on "murkier" regulations that were not fully considered in "first-generation" PTAs (Lechner, 2016).

Politically, this book suggests that PTAs and GVCs are neither promoters of protectionism nor protectionist deterrents. That is, although PTAs and GVCs seem to have important effects in limiting tariff protectionism, they can be strong channels for nontransparent protectionism (e.g., consumption subsidy, loan guarantee, import ban and licensing requirement, among others presented in Table 1.4). From a policy perspective, trade interconnectivity via PTAs and GVCs can lure policymakers into lowering their guards as tariffs are reduced drastically and in a transparent manner. However, non-tariff barriers can discretely increase. This means two things from a policy point of view. First, apart from rules to limit traditional NTMs, which are included in many agreements, trade negotiators must also seek ways to address other types of murky measures. Second, policymakers must be proactive in the enforcement of these updated rules. New PTAs, in short, have to be as creative as the sponsoring governments have been in implementing new types of NTMs. In an era of "murky" protectionism, we need "bright" rules. A former Chilean government minister elaborated on this point during our interview:

> It is very difficult to find a specific chapter that talks about NTMs in a PTA. What we do find is specific articles that talk about specific types of measures such as sanitary and phytosanitary measures, and technical barriers to trade, which are examples of NTMs.[9] However, in all cases these chapters

tend to be very general, in which countries commit to transparency in the implementation of these norms. From my experience, what PTAs do with regard to NTMs, is to discipline their implementation but not necessarily to remove them for the simple reason that enforcement here is very difficult. Once a trade agreement is signed, I would say that 80 percent of the conflicts are related to non-tariff measures. And the main problem is that we rarely find specific and clear chapters on how NTM restrictions will be enforced. I think the problem is not the PTA itself but how countries use these less transparent norms within a PTA. In sum, all this discussion is a good example that PTAs are neither heaven nor hell; they are just one instrument that by itself doesn't do too much if there is no commitment to transparency by trading partners.[10]

Countries normally rely on the WTO general framework text for NTMs when they negotiate bilateral PTAs. Using text analysis techniques, recent studies show that the presence of WTO text in PTAs is substantial: "at least one hundred PTAs take 80 percent or more of their contents directly from a single, existing treaty [the WTO]—with many copying and pasting 95 percent or more" (Allee & Elsig, 2019, p. 603). When specifically talking about NTMs (e.g., SPS, TBT), the percentage of text in PTAs that is copied and pasted from WTO agreements reaches 60%. At the same time, in the context of the WTO, the handling of NTMs is still an open debate. For instance, in July 2019, the WTO Goods Council meeting suggested the importance of enhanced transparency and of strengthening notification requirements under WTO agreements.[11] In sum, the current structure of PTAs' rules with regard to NTMs is still not clearly defined at the multilateral level (Allee & Elsig, 2019, p. 603). Many institutions have reiterated concerns about the challenge of nontransparent protectionism. This is clear from a recent European Commission (2019, p. 9) report:

Analysis of non-tariff barriers and their impact remains challenging. The main reason is that non-tariff barriers are characterized by different degrees of restriction. Other than outright bans, most trade-restrictive measures do not fully eliminate trade but reduce it. Moreover, restrictions regarding the same products or services may overlap. As a result, additional barriers may not necessarily mean additional impact, nor does the removal of one barrier imply automatic improvement in market access.

Finally, the world community faces important unknowns related to the economic fallout of the COVID-19 pandemic. As of January 2021, there was an emerging consensus that the virus is still far from being under control, although the vaccine is now being distributed around the world.[12] Here, commitments and resources have been uneven, and US infection rates continue to surge. This delay on the part of the world's largest economy will surely prolong the pandemic and wreak further havoc on global markets. What will the international political economy look like once the pandemic is finally under control? The fact that there is no answer to these questions has wrought a level of uncertainty and insecurity on par with the Great Depression, which lasted a full decade (Albertoni & Wise, 2020).

6.4 Insights for further research

This book constitutes a first step in a research agenda has plenty of room to expand. Future studies can build on the results presented here to gain further understanding of the risk of trade protectionism in an interconnected and uncertain global economy. For example, the main quantitative focus of this book is on dyadic dynamics rather than triadic ones. Although this study goes one step forward by considering bilateral data rather than monadic—one state as the unit of analysis—we still need a clearer picture of current global trade dynamics. In essence, a network analysis in which many factors and countries interact at the same time would tell us more. My large-N bilateral analysis sheds light on retaliatory responses between country A and B, but not country C. A state's position in an international trading network also affects its retaliatory dynamics. That is, given the high levels of trade interconnectivity within the global economy, it is likely that dyadic mechanisms may give way to more triadic dynamics.

The application of network theory to the study of international trade is becoming more relevant in the literature (Chaney, 2011). According to this systemic view of trade protectionism, countries are categorized not just by how much they apply protectionist trade policies but also "against" whom. Recent literature suggests that the field of international relations can benefit from the incorporation of network analysis into methodological approaches (Lupu & Traag, 2013).[13] For example, relational event approaches (Butts & Marcum, 2017), in which the systemic effect can be better specified, could capture the whole system and perhaps render a better explanation than one based on the sum of its parts.

Another limitation of this book relates to data restrictions, including the short period of analysis, that is, the 2008–09 GFC to 2019. In a context of economic crisis—and post-crisis—governments tend to implement more protectionist measures than they normally would so as to redirect demand toward domestically produced goods. Although this study goes until 2019, other studies have shown that the recovery of global trade after the GFC has been weak compared with the marked acceleration in global trade in the previous two decades prior to the GFC (Wozniak & Galar, 2018). It is thus possible that much of the retaliation captured here is more explicit to the GFC but not to other less turbulent economic contexts. As such, it cannot be claimed that the findings of this study are generalizable to other periods of economic history.

Regarding the county case analyses, further research could be expanded to other regions such as Africa and Asia as a way to validate my domestic level of analysis. A possible new causal explanation for why governments may be willing to retaliate against a country that previously targeted them, may originate in the exporting sector of the affected country. Before lobbying for retaliation, ex-ante, the exporting sector may pressure the government to initiate a diplomatic conversation to persuade the trading partner to remove a protectionist measure. If "trade diplomacy" does not work, the exporting sector could then put pressure on the government to retaliate. The effect of media coverage on the implementation of a protectionist measure by a trading partner could also be relevant in further studies.[14]

Further studies should build on this research at the country level and explore different casual mechanisms as to why countries are embracing new forms of protectionism. For instance, a reason why countries may or may not be willing to escalate trade protectionist dynamics, especially in developing economies in Asia and Latin America, can be found in lessons learned from past protectionist experiences during the 1970s and 1980s. There could, in other words, be a "path dependence" mechanism at work in the way countries decide to respond to protectionism. Indeed, as Wise et al. (2015) document, emerging economies in both Latin America and East Asia showed remarkable resilience and restraint from protectionism when faced with the GFC in 2008–09. As they describe it,

> one of the more surprising features of the 2008–09 global financial crisis was the comparative ease with which emerging economies in Asia and Latin America rebounded. That rebound was a radical departure from the effects of previous crises on these regions, be it the decade-long recession wreaked on Latin America by the 1982 debt shocks or the financial crisis that dramatically slowed Asian economies in the late 1990s.
>
> (p. 1)

In general, at the country level further studies could identify those emerging economy cases in which the exporting sector—which is traditionally part of the lobby for trade openness—is pushing for trade protection. This approach may help in specifying trade preferences at the firm level. Until now, there has been little evidence of exporters lobbying for protection. This type of exporter protection lobby may be transitory and does not necessarily mean that exporters have changed their overall trade preferences. However, it does show that in the context of a trade conflict, exporters may be willing to set aside their traditional trade preferences in order to solve the conflict and return the trade relationship to the status quo. Exporters could lobby for protection, for instance, if a "trade war" happens between the United States, China, and the EU. This could invoke retaliation responses that result in a never-ending spiral of protectionism with little incentive or intention to negotiate a resolution to the conflict.

On a final note, this study offers a cautionary tale about trade protectionism in an era of high interconnectivity and economic uncertainty. From a policy perspective, it shows how relevant it is to direct our attention toward the

164 *Conclusions and final thoughts*

increased need for trade transparency, something that multilateral institutions have acknowledged without promoting it consistently in ongoing policy debates. The escalation of trade protectionism during and after a COVID-19 economic recession may be the (unfortunate) catalyst for pushing this topic higher up on the multilateral policy agenda.

Notes

* Some sections of this chapter have been used in Albertoni, N. (2023). The risk of murky trade protectionism in an interconnected and uncertain global economy, *Estudios Internacionales*, 55(205).
1 For a deep understanding of how the 2009 GFC and subsequent "Great Recession" was different to previous ones, see Reinhart & Rogoff (2009). Also see *Harvard Behavioral Finance & Financial Stability*, www.hbs.edu/behavioral-finance-and-financial-stability/data/Pages/global.aspx.
2 WTO, *Regional Trade Agreements*, www.wto.org/english/tratop_e/region_e/region_e.htm.
3 The IMF defines a global recession as "a decline in annual per-capita real World GDP (PPP weighted), backed up by a decline or worsening for one or more of the following macroeconomic indicators: Industrial production, trade, capital flows, oil consumption, unemployment rate, per-capita investment, and per-capita consumption" (See Bob Davis, "What's a Global Recession?" *Wall Street Journal*, April 22, 2009. https://blogs.wsj.com/economics/2009/04/22/whats-a-global-recession/.
4 Author's interview with an employee of the University of Chile, April 2020.
5 Bems et al. (2009), "The Collapse of Global Trade: Update on the Role of Vertical Linkages," *VoxEU CERP Policy Portal* (November 27, 2009). https://voxeu.org/article/collapse-global-trade-update-role-vertical-linkages.
6 Bems et al. (2009), "The Collapse of Global Trade."
7 Author's interview with a research economist with the WTO, February 7, 2020. The Comprehensive Economic and Trade Agreement (CETA) is a free-trade agreement between Canada and the EU concluded in 2014. The Transatlantic Trade and Investment Partnership (TTIP) was a trade agreement proposed between the EU and the United States, in 2010. Trans-Pacific Partnership Agreement (TPP) was a proposed trade agreement between 12 countries, signed on February 4, 2016. In January 2017, the elected US president, Donald Trump, withdrew the US signature from the TPP, and the remaining countries created a new one called Comprehensive and Progressive Agreement for Trans-Pacific Partnership (CPTPP), which entered into force on December 30, 2018.
8 For more information on these modernization trade agreements, see: www.sice.oas.org/news_e.asp.
9 Examples of this in recent agreements are Chapters 9 and 11 in the USMCA; and Chapters 5 and 6 in the Mercosur and EU trade agreement. See *Agreement between the United States of America, the United Mexican States, and Canada 12/13/19 Text*, https://ustr.gov/trade-agreements/free-trade-agreements/united-states-mexico-canada-agreement/agreement-between; and Mercosur and EU agreement: https://publications.iadb.org/pt/acordo-mercosul-uniao-europeia-impactos-normativosregulatorios-no-mercosul.
10 Author's interview with a former Chilean government minister, November 2019.

11 WTO (2019), *WTO Members Consider Transparency Reforms at Goods Council Meeting,* www.wto.org/english/news_e/news19_e/good_10jul19_e.htm.
12 *Coronavirus Trend: The Pandemic Is Far from Over,* Deutsche Welle, January 29, 2021, www.dw.com/en/coronavirus-global-pandemic-trend/a-53954594.
13 For a critical review of the literature that has recently applied network theory to the study of international trade, see Fagiolo (2017) and Chaney (2016).
14 For more information about the public diplomacy of interactional trade, see Albertoni (2018).

References

Abbott, F. M. (2009). Cross-retaliation in TRIPS: Options for developing countries. ICTSD Issue Paper, No. 8. www.files.ethz.ch/isn/102241/2009-06_cross-retaliation-in-trips.pdf

Ahir, H., Bloom, N., & Furceri, D. (2018). The World Uncertainty index. [Unpublished manuscript.] https://nbloom.people.stanford.edu/research

Ahir, H., Bloom, N., & Furceri, D. (2020). 60 years of uncertainty. *Finance & Development, 57*(1), 58–60.

Aizenman, J., & Jinjarak, Y. (2010). The role of fiscal policy in response to the financial crisis. United Nations' Development Policy and Analysis Division. http://csf.rrojasdatabank.info/wesp2011paper_aizenman.pdf

Aizenman, J., & Marion, N. P. (1996). *Volatility and the investment response*. NBER Working Paper Series, No. 5841 (November). https://papers.ssrn.com/sol3/papers.cfm?abstract_id=225627

Albertoni, N. (2016, May 2). Los 25 años del Mercosur. *El País* (Spain). https://elpais.com/internacional/2016/05/02/america/1462201971_247462.html

Albertoni, N. (2018). The new dynamics of the international trading system. *Global Policy, 9*(1), 156–158.

Albertoni, N. (2019a, January 1). *Can Mercosur be updated and reformed or is it a relic of the past?* Global Americans. https://theglobalamericans.org/2019/01/can-mercosur-be-updated-and-reformed-or-is-it-a-relic-of-the-past/

Albertoni, N. (2019b). *Uruguay como solución. Su inserción internacional cuando lo importante se transforma en urgente*. Penguin Random House.

Albertoni, N. (2021). A historical overview of the 21st-century protectionism. *Latin American Journal of Trade Policy, 4*(10), 5–23.

Albertoni, N. (2023, forthcoming). The risk of murky trade protectionism in an interconnected and uncertain global economy, *Estudios Internacionales*.

Albertoni, N., & Rebolledo, A. (2018). Trade, economic and political integration in Latin America: The cases of the Southern Common Market (Mercosur) and the Pacific Alliance. In P. Sauvé et al. (Eds.), *The Pacific Alliance in a world of preferential trade agreements* (pp. 99–112). Springer.

Albertoni, N., & Wise, C. (Forthcoming). Trade Protectionism and Integration in Latin America. The Cases of Brazil and Mexico. In M. Elsig, A. Lugg, & R. Polanco (Eds.), *What Does the Future Hold for Trade Policy*? Cambridge University Press.

Albertoni, N., Iturralde, A., & Correa, R. (2020). *Índice de Vulnerabilidad Comercial*. Centro de Estudios para el Desarrollo. Centro de Estudios para el Desarrollo.

References

Alexander, K. W., & Soukup, B. J. (2010). Obama's first trade war: The US–Mexico cross-border trucking dispute and the implications of strategic cross-sector retaliation on US compliance under NAFTA. *Berkeley Journal of International Law, 28*(2), 313–342.

Allee, T. (2012). The role of the United States: A multilevel explanation for decreased support over time. In A. Narlikar et al. (Eds.), *The Oxford handbook on the World Trade Organization* (pp. 235–253). Oxford University Press.

Allee, T., & Elsig, M. (2019). Are the contents of international treaties copied and pasted? Evidence from preferential trade agreements. *International Studies Quarterly, 63*(3), 603–613.

Altig, D., Baker, S., Barrero, J., Bloom, N., Bunn, P., Chen, S., Davis, S., Leather, J., Meyer, B., Mihaylov, E., Mizen, P., Parker, N., Renault, T., Smietanka, P., & Thwaites, G. (2020, July 24). *Economic uncertainty in the wake of the COVID-19 pandemic*. VoxEU.org. https://voxeu.org/article/economic-uncertainty-wake-covid-19-pandemic

Amadeo, K. (2019, May 2). *Why trade wars are bad and nobody wins*. The Balance www.thebalance.com/trade-wars-definition-how-it-affects-you-4159973

Autor, D., Dorn, D., & Hanson, G. (2016). The China shock: Learning from labor-market adjustment to large changes in trade. *Annual Review of Economics, 8*(1), 205–240.

Baccini, L., & Dür, A. (2012). The new regionalism and policy interdependence. *British Journal of Political Science, 42*(1), 57–79.

Baccini, L., & Urpelainen, J. (2014). International institutions and domestic politics: Can preferential trading agreements help leaders promote economic reform? *Journal of Politics, 76*(1), 195–214.

Baier, S. L., & Bergstrand, J. H. (2007). Do free trade agreements actually increase members' international trade? *Journal of International Economics, 71*(1), 72–95.

Baker, S., Bloom, N., Davis, S., & Terry, S. (2020, April 13). *COVID-induced economic uncertainty and its consequences*. VoxEU.org. https://voxeu.org/article/covid-induced-economic-uncertainty-and-its-consequences

Baldwin, R. (1993, January 18). *A domino theory of regionalism*. NBER Working Paper Series, No. 4465. www.nber.org/papers/w4465.

Baldwin, R. (2009, April 7). *The greater trade collapse of 2020*. VoxEU.org. https://voxeu.org/article/greater-trade-collapse-2020

Baldwin, R. (2009, November 27). *The great trade collapse: What caused it and what does it mean?* VoxEU.org. https://voxeu.org/article/great-trade-collapse-what-caused-it-and-what-does-it-mean

Baldwin, R. (2012). *WTO 2.0: Global governance of supply-chain trade*. Centre for Economic Policy Research, Policy Insight No. 64. VoxEU.org. https://voxeu.org/article/greater-trade-collapse-2020

Baldwin, R. E. (1970). *Non-tariff distortions of international trade*. Brookings Institution.

Baldwin, R. E. (1988). *Trade policy in a changing world economy*. University of Chicago Press.

Baldwin, R., & Evenett, S. (2009). *The collapse of global trade, murky protectionism, and the crisis: Recommendations for the G20*. Centre for Economic Policy Research (CEPR).

Baldwin, R., & Evenett, S. (2020). *COVID-19 and trade policy: Why turning inward won't work*. Centre for Economic Policy Research (CEPR).

References

Baldwin, R., Kawai, M., & Wignaraja, G. (2014). *A world trade organization for the 21st century: The Asian perspective*. Edward Elgar.

Barbieri, K. (1996). Economic interdependence: A path to peace or a source of interstate conflict? *Journal of Peace Research, 33*(1), 29–49.

Bellégo, C., & Pape, L.-D. (2019). Dealing with logs and zeros in regression models. *Political Methods: Quantitative Methods EJournal, 1*(2), 1–16.

Bems, R., Johnson, R., & Yi, K. (2009, November 27). *The collapse of global trade: Update on the role of vertical linkages*. VOX CEPR Policy Portal. VoxEU.org. https://voxeu.org/article/collapse-global-trade-update-role-vertical-linkages

Bems, R., Johnson, R., & Yi, K. (2013). The great trade collapse. *Annual Review of Economics, 5*(1), 375–400.

Beverelli, C., Boffa, M., & Keck, A. (2014). *Trade policy substitution: Theory and evidence from Specific Trade Concerns*. WTO Staff Working Papers ERSD-2014-18. Ideas.repec.org. https://ideas.repec.org/p/zbw/wtowps/ersd201418.html

Beverelli, C., Boffa, M., & Keck, A. (2019). Trade policy substitution: Theory and evidence. *Review of World Economics, 155*(4), 755–783.

Beverelli, C., Stolzenburg, V., Koopman, R. B., & Neumueller, S. (2019). Domestic value chains as stepping stones to global value chain integration. *World Economy, 42*(5), 1467–1494.

Beyers, J., & Kerremans, B. (2007). The press coverage of trade issues: A comparative analysis of public agenda-setting and trade politics. *Journal of European Public Policy, 14*(2), 269–292.

Bhagwati, J. (1991). *The world trading system at risk*. Princeton University Press.

Bhagwati, J. (2003). *Free trade today*. Princeton University Press.

Bhagwati, J., Krishna, P., & Panagariya, A. (2016). *The world trade system: Trends and challenges*. MIT Press.

Blanchard, E., Bown, C., & Johnson, R. (2016). *Global supply chains and trade policy*. NBER Working Paper No 21883. https://doi.org/10.3386/w21883

Boffa, M., & Olarreaga, M. (2012). Protectionism during the crisis: Tit-for-tat or chicken-games? *Economics Letters, 117*(3), 746–749.

Bonomo, D. (2014, March 1). *Hitting where it hurts: Retaliation requests in the WTO*. CEPR Policy Paper. VoxEU.org. https://voxeu.org/article/retaliation-wto

Bordo, M. D., Eichengreen, B., & Irwin, D. A. (1999). *Is globalization today really different than globalization a hundred years ago?* National Bureau of Economic Research.

Bown, C., & Kolb, M. (2019). Trump's trade war timeline: An up-to-date guide. *PIIE*, 2–15.

Bussière, M., Pérez-Barreiro, E., Straub, R., & Taglioni, D. (2011). Protectionist responses to the crisis: Global trends and implications. *World Economy, 34*(5), 826–852.

Butts, C., & Marcum, C. (2017). A relational event approach to modeling behavioral dynamics. In A. Pilny & M. Scott (Eds.), *Group processes: Data-driven computational approaches* (pp. 51–92). Springer.

Cadestin, C., Gourdon, J., & Kowalski, P. (2016). *Participation in global value chains in Latin America: Implications for trade and trade-related policy*. OECD Trade Policy Papers, No. 192. OECD Publishing. https://doi.org/10.1787/5jlpq80ts8f2-en

Canto, V. A. (1983). U.S. trade policy: History and evidence. *Cato Journal, 3*(3), 679–703.

Casey-Sawicki, K. (2018). *Seattle WTO protests of 1999*. Encyclopedia Britannica.

Chaney, T. (2011). *The network structure of international trade*. NBER Working Paper 16753. www.nber.org/papers/w16753

Chase, K. A. (2003). Economic interests and regional trading arrangements: The case of NAFTA. *International Organization, 57*(1), 137–174.

Chiquiar, D., & Tobal, M. (2019). *Global value chains in Mexico: A historical perspective*. Working Papers 2019-06 Banco de México. Ideas.recep.org. https://ideas.repec.org/p/bdm/wpaper/2019-06.html

Chisik, R., & Fan, C. (2020. *Cross-retaliation and international dispute settlement*. Working Papers 078. Ryerson University, Department of Economics. Ideas.recep.org. https://ideas.repec.org/p/rye/wpaper/wp078.html

Chong, T. T. L., & Li, X. (2019). Understanding the China–US trade war: Causes, economic impact, and the worst-case scenario. *Economic and Political Studies, 7*(2), 185–202.

Cieślik, A., & Hagemejer, J. (2011). The effectiveness of preferential trade liberalization in Central and Eastern Europe. *International Trade Journal, 25*(5), 516–538.

Collier, D., Brady, H. E., & Seawright, J. (2004). Sources of leverage in causal inference: Toward an alternative view of methodology. In H. E. Brady & D. Collier (Eds.), *Rethinking social inquiry: Diverse tools, shared standards* (pp. 229–266). Rowman & Littlefield.

Conconi, P., Facchini, G., & Zanardi, M. (2014). Policymakers' horizon and trade reforms: The protectionist effect of elections. *Journal of International Economics, 94*(1), 102–118.

Copeland, D. C. (1996). Economic interdependence and war: A theory of trade expectations. *International Security, 20*(4), 5–41.

Córdova Bojórquez, G., Meardon, S., Nava Aguirre, K. M., & Schaffler-González, F. (2018). *The political economy of Mexico–U.S. trade policy*. [Unpublished]. IDB. Working Paper.

Crowley, M. A. (2019). *Trade war: The clash of economic systems threatening global prosperity*. CEPR Press.

De Backer, K., & Miroudot, S. (2014). Mapping global value chains. *OECD Trade Policy Papers, 15*(1), 1–24.

De Mateo Veiga, F. (2003). La política comercial de México con América Latina. In R. F. De Castro (Ed.), *En la frontera del imperio*. Planeta.

Dedrick, J., Kraemer, K., & Linden, G. (2010). Who profits from innovation in global value chains? A study of the iPod and notebook PCs. *Industrial and Corporate Change, 19*(1), 81–116.

Directorate of International Economic Relations (DIRECON). (2018). *Riesgos y Oportunidades de la Guerra Comercial*. Departamento de Estudios. www.subrei.gob.cl/

Dür, A., Baccini, L., & Elsig, M. (2014). The design of international trade agreements: Introducing a new dataset. *Review of International Organizations, 9*(3), 353–375.

Egger, P., Larch, M., Staub, K. E., & Winkelmann, R. (2011). The trade effects of endogenous preferential trade agreements. *American Economic Journal of Economic Policy, 3*(3), 113–143.

Elsig, M., Lugg, A., & Polanco, R. (Forthcoming). *What does the future hold for trade policy?* Cambridge University Press.

Escaith, H., Lindenberg, N., & Miroudot, S. (2010). *Global value chains and the crisis: Reshaping international trade elasticity?* World Bank. https://openknowledge.worldbank.org/handle/10986/2509

Estevadeordal, A., Suominen, K., Harris, J., & Shearer, M. (2009). *Bridging regional trade agreements in the Americas*. IDB.

European Commission. (2002). Mercosur—European Community Regional Strategy Paper 2002–2006,E.C. www.sice.oas.org/tpd/mer_eu/Studies/Regionalpaper_e.pdf

European Commission. (2019). *Report from the Commission to the European Parliament and the Council on Trade and Investment Barriers*. https://eur-lex.europa.eu/legal-content/EN/TXT/HTML/?uri=CELEX:52020DC0236&rid=1

Evenett, S. (2019). Protectionism, state discrimination, and international business since the onset of the Global Financial Crisis. *Journal of International Business Policy, 2*(1), 1–28.

Evenett, S., & Fritz, J. (2017). *Will awe Trump rules?* 21st Global Trade Alert Report. London: CEPR Press. www.globaltradealert.org

Evenett, S., & Fritz, J. (2018). *Brazen unilateralism: The US–China tariff war in perspective*. Global Trade Alert Report 23. CEPR Press. www.globaltradealert.org

Evenett, S., & Fritz, J. (2020). The Global Trade Alert database handbook. [Manuscript]. www.globaltradealert.org

Evenett, S., Fritz, J., Gerasimenko, D., Nowakowska, M., & Wermelinger, M. (2011). *The resort to protectionism during the great recession: Which factors mattered?* Working Paper. University of St Gallen. www.alexandria.unisg.ch/publications/89753

Fajgelbaum, P., Goldberg, P., Kennedy, P., & Khandelwal, A. (2019). *The return to protectionism*. Working Paper No. 25638. National Bureau of Economic Research. https://doi.org/10.3386/w25638

Farrell, H., & Newman, A. L. (2019). Weaponized interdependence: How global economic networks shape state coercion. *International Security, 44*(1), 42–79.

Felbermayr, G., Teti, F., & Yalcin, E. (2019). Rules of origin and the profitability of trade deflection. *Journal of International Economics, 121*(1), 103–248.

Felter, C., Renwick, D., & Chatzky, A. (2019, July 10). *Mercosur: South America's fractious trade bloc*. Council on Foreign Relations. www.cfr.org/backgrounder/mercosur-south-americas-fractious-trade-bloc

Franko, P. (2018). *The puzzle of Latin American economic development*. Rowman & Littlefield.

Frieden, J. (2000). The method of analysis of modern political economy. In J. A. Frieden, M. Pastor, & M. Tomz (Eds.), *Modern political economy and Latin America: Theory and policy* (pp. 35–37). Westview Press.

Garciadiego, J., & Hernández, B. (1994). *El TLC día a día: Crónica de una negociación*. Miguel Angel Porrúa Editorial.

Garred, J. (2018). The persistence of trade policy in China after WTO accession. *Journal of International Economics, 114*(1), 130–142.

Garred, J. (2019, July 9). *The persistence of trade policy beyond import tariffs*. VoxEU. Org. https://voxeu.org/article/persistence-trade-policy-beyond-import-tariffs

Garrett, G. (2000). Capital mobility, exchange rates and fiscal policy in the global economy. *Review of International Political Economy, 7*(1), 154–171.

Gaulier, G., Sztulman, A., & Ünal, D. (2019). Are global value chains receding? The jury is still out. key findings from the analysis of deflated world trade in parts and components. *International Economics, 161*(1), 219–236.

Gawande, K., Hoekman, B., & Cui, Y. (2011, November 10). *Determinants of trade-policy responses to the 2008 financial crisis*. VOX CEPR Policy Portal. VoxEU. org. https://voxeu.org/article/determinants-trade-policy-responses-2008-financial-crisis

Gawande, K., Hoekman, B., & Cui, Y. (2015). Global supply chains and trade policy responses to the 2008cCrisis. *World Bank Economic Review, 29*(1), 102–128.

Georgiadis, G., & Gräb, J. (2016). Growth, real exchange rates and trade protectionism since the financial crisis. *Review of International Economics, 24*(5), 1050–1080.

Gereffi, G. (2014). Global value chains in a post-Washington Consensus world. *Review of International Political Economy, 21*(1), 9–37.

Gereffi, G. (2018). *Global value chains and development: Redefining the contours of 21st century capitalism*. Cambridge University Press.

Gerring, J., & Cojocaru, L. (2016). Selecting cases for intensive analysis: A diversity of goals and methods. *Sociological Methods & Research, 45*(3), 392–423.

Ghodsi, M., & Stehrer, R. (2016). *Non-tariff measures trickling through global value chains*. Productivity, non-tariff measures and openness (PRONTO) working paper. Vienna Institute for International Economic Studies.

Gleditsch, K. S., & Ward, M. D. (1999). Interstate system membership: A revised list of the independent states since 1816. *International Interactions, 25*(4), 393–413.

Goldberg, P. K., & Pavcnik, N. (2016). The effects of trade policy. In K. Bagwell & R. W. Staiger (Eds.), *Handbook of commercial policy* (Vol. 1, pp. 161–206). North-Holland.

Gould, D. M., & Woodbridge, G. L. (1998). The political economy of retaliation, liberalization and trade wars. *European Journal of Political Economy, 14*(1), 115–137.

Gowa, J., & Mansfield, E. (2004). Alliances, imperfect markets, and major power trade. *International Organization, 58*(4), 775–805.

Graham, B., & Tucker, J. (2017). The International Political Economy data resource. *Review of International Organizations, 12*(1), 1–13.

Grant, W., & Kelly, D. (2005). *The politics of international trade in the twenty-first century*. Palgrave Macmillan.

Grossman, G., & Helpman, E. (1994). Protection for sale. *American Economic Review, 84*(4), 833–850.

Grundke, R., & Moser, C. (2019). Hidden protectionism? Evidence from non-tariff barriers to trade in the United States. *Journal of International Economics, 117*, 143–157.

Hafner-Burton, E. M. (2005). Trading human rights: How preferential trade agreements influence government repression. *International Organization, 59*(3), 593–629.

Henn, C., & McDonald, B. (2014). Crisis protectionism: The observed trade impact. *IMF Economic Review, 62*(1), 77–118.

Hernández, R., Martínez Piva, J. M., & Mulder, N. (2014). *Global value chains and world trade: Prospects and challenges for Latin America*. ECLAC.

Hites, A., Bloom, N., & Furceri, D. (2019, September 9). New index tracks trade uncertainty across the globe. *IMF Blog*. https://blogs.imf.org/2019/09/09/new-index-tracks-trade-uncertainty-across-the-globe/

Hofmann, C., Osnago, A., & Ruta, M. (2019). The content of preferential trade agreements. *World Trade Review, 18*(3), 365–398.

Hollyer, J., Rosendorff, P., & Vreeland, J. (2014). Measuring transparency. *Political Analysis, 22*(4), 413–434.

Hopewell, K. (2016). *Breaking the WTO: How emerging powers disrupted the neoliberal project*. Stanford University Press.

Hummels, D., Ishii, J., & Yi, K.-M. (2001). The nature and growth of vertical specialization in world trade. *Journal of International Economics, 54*(1), 75–96.

Ianchovichina, E., & Martin, W. (2004). Impacts of China's accession to the World Trade Organization. *World Bank Economic Review, 18*(1), 3–27.

Inter-American Development Bank (IDB) (2018). The political economy of trade policy in Latin America and the Caribbean. Research Department, Integration and Trade Sector RG-K1198. Iadb.org. https://research-proposals.iadb.org/system/files/RES/documents/EZSHARE-1728116555-3751.pdf

International Monetary Fund (IMF). (2016). *World economic outlook. Subdued demand: Symptoms and remedies.* IMF. www.imf.org/en/Publications/WEO/Issues/2016/12/31/Subdued-Demand-Symptoms-and-Remedies

Irwin, D. (1998). *Against the tide: An intellectual history of free trade.* Princeton University Press.

Irwin, D. (2016, June 13). The truth about trade: What critics get wrong about the global economy. *Foreign Affairs.* www.foreignaffairs.com/articles/2016-06-13/truth-about-trade

Irwin, D. (2017, April 17). The false promise of protectionism. *Foreign Affairs.* www.foreignaffairs.com/articles/united-states/2017-04-17/false-promise-protectionism

Jensen, J., Quinn, D. P., & Weymouth, S. (2015). The influence of firm global supply chains and foreign currency undervaluations on US trade disputes. *International Organization, 69*(4), 913–947.

Joller, Y., & Kniahin, D. (2020, July 8). Global chain reaction: Unprecedented trade measures to tackle COVID-19. *ITC Blog.* www.intracen.org/covid19/Blog/Global-chain-reaction-Unprecedented-trade-measures-to-tackle-COVID-19/

Jones, K. (2015). *Reconstructing the World Trade Organization for the 21st century: An institutional approach.* Oxford University Press.

Kee, H. L., Neagu, C., & Nicita, A. (2013). Is protectionism on the rise? Assessing national trade policies during the Crisis of 2008. *Review of Economics and Statistics, 95*(1), 342–346.

Kim, I. S. (2017). Political cleavages within industry: Firm-level lobbying for trade liberalization. *American Political Science Review, 111*(1), 1–20.

Kim, I. S., & Osgood, I. (2019). Firms in trade and trade politics. *Annual Review of Political Science, 22*, 399–417.

King, G., Keohane, R. O., & Verba, S. (1994). *Design social inquiry: Scientific inference in qualitative research.* Princeton University Press.

Kolb, M. (2019, February 4). What is globalization? And how has the global economy shaped the United States? *Peterson Institute for International Economics.* www.piie.com/microsites/globalization/what-is-globalization

Kono, D. (2006). Optimal obfuscation: Democracy and trade policy transparency. *American Political Science Review, 100*(3), 369–384.

Kono, D. (2007). When do trade blocs block trade? *International Studies Quarterly, 51*(1), 165–181.

Kosacoff, B., López, A., & Pedrazzoli, M. (2008, January). Trade, investment and fragmentation of the global market: Is Latin America lagging behind? *CEPAL Studies and Perspectives.* www.cepal.org/en/publications/4867-trade-investment-and-fragmentation-global-market-latin-america-lagging-behind

Kose, M. A., Sugawara, N., & Terrones, M. E. (2020, February 10). Global recessions. CAMA Working Paper No. 10/2020, http://dx.doi.org/10.2139/ssrn.3535972

Lake, D. (2009). Open economy politics: A critical review. *Review of International Organizations, 4*(3), 219–244.

Lamy, P. (2013, December 18). Global value chains, interdependence, and the future of trade. VOX CEPR Policy Portal. VoxEU.org. https://voxeu.org/article/global-value-chains-interdependence-and-future-trade

References

Lardy, N. R. (2001, May 9). Issues in China's WTO accession. *Brookings Institute.* www.brookings.edu/testimonies/issues-in-chinas-wto-accession/

Lechner, L. (2016). The domestic battle over the design of non-trade issues in preferential trade agreements. *Review of International Political Economy, 23*(5), 840–871.

Lee, J., & Swagel, P. (1997). Trade barriers and trade flows across countries and industries. *Review of Economics and Statistics, 79*(3), 372–382.

Levy, P. (2018, February 4). Was letting China into the WTO a mistake? *Foreign Affairs.* www.foreignaffairs.com/articles/china/2018-04-02/was-letting-china-wto-mistake

Lijphart, A. (1971). Comparative politics and the comparative method. *American Political Science Review, 65*(3), 682–693.

Limão, N. (2016). Preferential trade agreements. In K. Bagwell & R. W. Staiger (Eds.), *Handbook of commercial policy* (Vol. 1, pp. 279–367). North-Holland.

Lüthje, T. (2001). Intra industry trade in intermediate goods. *International Advances in Economic Research, 7*(4), 393–408.

Manger, M. (2009). *Investing in protection: The politics of preferential trade agreements between North and South.* Cambridge University Press.

Mansfield, E., & Milner, H. (1999). The new wave of regionalism. *International Organization, 53*(3), 589–627.

Mansfield, E., & Reinhardt, E. (2008). International institutions and the volatility of international trade. *International Organization, 62*(4), 621–652.

Mansfield, E., Milner, H., & Jon, P. (2008). Democracy, veto players and the depth of regional integration. *World Economy, 31*(1), 67–96.

Manzetti, L. (1993). The political economy of Mercosur. *Journal of Interamerican Studies and World Affairs, 35*(4), 101–141.

Mesquita Moreira, M. (2018, May). *Connecting the dots: A road map for a better integration of Latin America and the Caribbean.* Inter-American Development Bank. https://doi.org/10.18235/0001132

Milner, H. (1999). The political economy of international trade. *Annual Review of Political Science, 2*(1), 91–114.

Milner, H., & Kubota, K. (2005). Why the move to free trade? Democracy and trade policy in the developing countries. *International Organization, 59*(1), 107–143.

Miyagiwa, K., Song, H., & Vandenbussche, H. (2016). Size matters! Who is bashing whom in trade war? *International Review of Economics & Finance, 45*(1), 33–45.

Monge-González, R., & Rivera, L. (2018, March). *The political economy of trade openness in Costa Rica.* IDB Working Paper. https://publications.iadb.org/publications/english/document/Productive-Development-Policies-in-Costa-Rica-Market-Failures-Government-Failures-and-Policy-Outcomes.pdf

Moreira, M., Stein, E., Li, K., Merchán, F., Martincus, C., Blyde, J., Trachtenberg, D., Cornick, J., Frieden, J., & Chatruc, M. R. (2019). *Trading promises for results: What global integration can do for Latin America and the Caribbean.* Inter-American Development Bank.

Mukherjee, B. (2016). *Democracy and trade policy in developing countries.* University of Chicago Press.

Niu, Z., Liu, C., Gunessee, S., & Milner, C. (2018). Non-tariff and overall protection: Evidence across countries and over time. *Review of World Economics, 154*(4), 675–703.

Noland, M. (2019). *Protectionism under Trump: The China shock, intolerance, and the "First White President."* PIIE. Peterson Institute for International Economics Working Paper (19-10).

References

Noland, M. (2020). Protectionism under Trump: The China shock, deplorables, and the first white president. *Asian Economic Policy Review, 15*(1), 31–50.

Nugent, J. B., & Hakimian, H. (2003). *Trade policy and economic integration in the Middle East and North Africa*. Routledge.

O'Farrell, J., Obaya, M., & Marín, A. (2018). *The political economy of trade policy in Argentina under Macri's administration (2015–2018)*. [Unpublished]. CENIT.

Oliveira, I., da Motta Veiga, P., Polónia Rios, S., & Ribeiro, F. (2018). *The political economy of trade policy in Brazil*. Working Paper. CINDES/IPEA. www.ipea.gov.br/portal/index.php?option=com_content&view=article&id=35017&Itemid=432

Olson, M. (1965). *Logic of collective action: Public goods and the theory of groups*. Harvard University Press.

Organization for Economic Cooperation and Development (OECD). (2005, November). *Measuring globalisation: OECD Handbook on Economic Globalisation Indicators*. www.oecd.org/sti/ind/oecdhandbookoneconomicglobalisationindicators.htm

Pastor, M., & Wise, C. (1994). The origins and sustainability of Mexico's free trade policy. *International Organization, 48*(3), 459–489.

Peluffo, A. (2020). China US trade war: Will it impact on Latin American countries? *Serie Documentos de Trabajo—FCEA, 8*(20).

Pérez Arguello, M., & Albertoni, N. (2019, June 20). Tariffs on Mexico? That could result in Trump's nightmare. *New York Times*. www.nytimes.com/2019/06/20/opinion/tariffs-on-mexico-would-mean-more-immigrants.html

Peterson, T., & Thies, C. (2015). Intra-industry trade and policy outcomes. In L. L. Martin (Ed.), *The Oxford handbook of the political economy of international trade* (pp. 177–195). Oxford University Press. www.oxfordhandbooks.com.libproxy1.usc.edu/view/10.1093/oxfordhb/9780199981755.001.0001/oxfordhb-9780199981755-e-17

Pierce, J., & Schott, P. (2016). The surprisingly swift decline of US manufacturing employment. *American Economic Review, 106*(7), 1632–1662.

Pinna, A., & Lodi, L. (2021). Trade and global value chains at the time of Covid-19. *International Spectator, 1*(1), 1–19.

Pita, N. (2017). *Is populism against trade? Argentina's trade policy in the context of Latin American populism*. [Unpublished senior thesis]. University of South Carolina. https://scholarcommons.sc.edu/senior_theses/2017

Puyana, A. (2018). Trump politics towards Mexico. Renegotiating NAFTA while invocating the Monroe Doctrine. *Real-World Economics Review, 85*(1), 123–141.

Ray, E. (1991). Protection of manufactures in the United States. In D. Greenaway (Ed.), *Global protectionism: Is the U.S. playing on a level field?* (pp. 12–36). Macmillan.

Ray, E., & Marvel, H. (1984). The pattern of protection in the industrialized world. *Review of Economics and Statistics, 66*(3), 452–458.

Reich, A. (2017, November). *The effectiveness of the WTO dispute settlement system: A statistical analysis*. EUI Working Paper. Department of Law. https://cadmus.eui.eu/bitstream/handle/1814/47045/LAW_2017_11.pdf?sequence=1

Reinhart, C., & Rogoff, K. (2009). This time it's different: Eight centuries of financial folly. In *This time it's different: Eight centuries of financial folly* (pp. 3–20). Princeton University Press.

Reisen, H., & Stemmer, M. (2018, April 17). Shifting wealth: The three acts of the "China shock." Shifting Wealth. http://shiftingwealth.blogspot.com/2018/04/the-three-acts-of-china-shock.html

Riguzzi, P., & de los Ríos, P. (2012). *Las relaciones México-Estados Unidos 1756–2010*. Universidad Nacional Autónoma de México.

References

Rodríguez-Piñero, I. (2020). Modernization of the trade pillar of the EU–Mexico Global agreement. *EPRS. European Parliamentary Research Service, Members' Research Service.* www.europarl.europa.eu/RegData/etudes/BRIE/2017/608680/EPRS_BRI(2017)608680_EN.pdf

Rodrik, D. (1995). Political economy of trade policy. In R. Jones, P. Kenen, G. Grossman, and K. Rogoff (Eds.), *Handbook of international economics* (Vol. 3, pp. 1457–1494). North-Holland.

Rodrik, D. (2009, October 12). *The myth of rising protectionism*. Project Syndicate Blog. www.project-syndicate.org/commentary/the-myth-of-rising-protectionism?barrier=accesspaylog

Roosevelt, M. (2016, November). *Disparate distribution of exporting vs import-competing firms and their implications for trade policy openness*. Working Paper. Presented at the Annual meeting of the International Political Economy Society. https://ncgg.princeton.edu/new_ipes/2016/papers/F945_rm3.pdf

Ruta, M. (2017). *Preferential trade agreements and global value chains: Theory, evidence, and open questions*. World Bank. Working Paper S8190. http://documents.worldbank.org/curated/en/991871505132824059/Preferential-trade-agreements-and-global-value-chains-theory-evidence-and-open-questions

Salinas De Gortari, C. (2002). *Mexico: The policy and politics of modernization*. Plaza y Janes.

Saxton, J. (2003, June). Argentina's economic crisis: Causes and cures. *Testimony before the Joint Economic Committee of the United States Congress* www.house.gov/jec/imf/06-13-03.pdf

Seawright, J. (2016). Better multimethod design: The promise of integrative multimethod research. *Security Studies, 25*(1), 42–49.

Seawright, J., & Gerring, J. (2008). Case selection techniques in case study research: A menu of qualitative and quantitative options. *Political Research Quarterly, 61*(2), 294–308.

Sykes, A. O. (2000). Regulatory competition or regulatory harmonization? A silly question? *Journal of International Economic Law, 3*(2), 257–264.

Tanaka, K. (2009). Trade collapse and international supply chains: Japanese evidence. In R. Baldwin & S. Evenett (Eds.), *The great trade collapse: Causes, consequences and prospects* (pp. 199–206). CEPR Press.

The Economist Intelligence Unit. (2020). *Will Latin America take advantage of supply chain shifts?* www.eiu.com/n/campaigns/will-latin-america-take-advantage-of-supply-chain-shifts/

The Economist. (2009, April 30). Low expectations exceeded. www.economist.com/united-states/2009/04/30/low-expectations-exceeded

The Economist. (2019, January 24). Globalisation has faltered: It is now being reshaped. www.economist.com/briefing/2019/01/24/globalisation-has-faltered

The Global Trade Alert (GTA). (2019). www.globaltradealert.org

Thoms, A. (2019, November 1). *Why trade wars have no winners*. World Economic Forum. www.weforum.org/agenda/2019/11/who-benefits-from-a-trade-war/

Tussie, D. (2009). Latin America: Contrasting motivations for regional projects. *Review of International Studies, 35*(1), 169–188.

UN Comtrade Database. (2019). https://comtrade.un.org

UNCTAD. (2010). *International trade after the economic crisis: Challenges and new opportunities*. United Nations Press.

References

Urata, S., & Okabe, M. (2010). The impacts of free trade agreements on trade flows: An application of the Gravity Model approach. *Free Trade Agreements in the Asia Pacific, 11*(1), 195–240.

Varian, H. (2007, June 28). An iPod has global value: Ask the (many) countries that make it. *New York Times.* www.nytimes.com/2007/06/28/business/worldbusiness/28scene.html

Vickers, B. (2012). The role of the BRICS in the WTO: System-supporters or change agents in multilateral trade. In A. Narlikar, M. Daunton, & R. Stern (Eds.), *The Oxford handbook on the World Trade Organization* (pp. 254–273). Oxford University Press.

Waltz, K. (2000). Structural realism after the Cold War. *International Security, 25*(1), 5–41.

Wilkinson, R. (2006). *Multilateralism and the World Trade Organisation: The architecture and extension of international trade regulation.* Routledge.

Williamson, J. (1990). What Washington means by policy reform. In J. Williamson (Ed.), *Latin American adjustment: How much has happened* (pp. 353–420). Institute for International Economics.

Wise, C. (2020). *Dragonomics: How Latin America is maximizing (or missing out on) China's international development strategy.* Yale University Press.

Wise, C., & Quiliconi, C. (2007). China's surge in Latin American markets: Policy challenges and responses. *Politics & Policy, 3*(3), 410–438.

Wise, C., Elliott Armijo, L., & Katada, S. (2015). *Unexpected outcomes. How emerging economies survived the Global Financial Crisis.* Brookings Institution Press.

World Bank. (2020a). *World Development Report 2020: Trading for development in the age of global value chains.* World Bank.

World Bank. (2020b). *Global economic prospects.* A World Bank Group Flagship Report. http://pubdocs.worldbank.org/en/267761588788282656/Global-Economic-Prospects-June-2020-Highlights-Chapter-1.pdf

World Economic Forum (WEF). (2019). Global Future Council on International Trade and Investment. *World Economic Forum.* www.weforum.org/communities/gfc-on-trade-and-investment

World Trade Organization (WTO). (2016a). *World Trade statistical review 2016.* www.wto.org/english/res_e/statis_e/wts2016_e/wts2016_e.pdf

World Trade Organization (WTO). (2016b, July 4). *Report to the TPRB from the Director-General on trade-related developments.* www.wto.org/english/news_e/news16_e/trdev_22jul16_e.htm

World Trade Organization (WTO). (2017, November 9). *Report on G20 trade measures.* www.wto.org/english/news_e/news17_e/g20_wto_report_november17_e.pdf

World Trade Organization (WTO). (2017a). *World trade statistical review 2017.* www.wto.org/english/res_e/statis_e/wts2017_e/wts17_toc_e.htm

World Trade Organization (WTO). (2017b). *Trade policy review Brazil.* WTO Secretariat WT/TPR/S/358. www.wto.org/english/tratop_e/tpr_e/tp458_e.htm

World Trade Organization (WTO). (2017c). *Trade policy review Mexico.* WTO Secretariat WT/TPR/S/352. www.wto.org/english/tratop_e/tpr_e/tp452_e.htm

World Trade Organization (WTO). (2020). Trade set to plunge as COVID-19 pandemic upends global economy. *WTO Secretariat 20–2749.* www.wto.org/english/news_e/pres20_e/pr855_e.pdf

Wozniak, P., & Galar, M. (2018, January). *Understanding the weakness in global trade.* European Commission, Economic Brief 033. https://ec.europa.eu/info/sites/info/files/economy-finance/eb033_en_0.pdf

Yi, K.-M. (2009). The collapse of global trade: The role of vertical specialisation. In R. Baldwin & Evenett, S. (Eds.), *The collapse of global trade, murky protectionism, and the Crisis: Recommendations for the G20* (pp. 45–48). CEPR Press.

Young, A. R. (2017). The politics of deep integration. *Cambridge Review of International Affairs, 30*(5–6), 453–463.

Yu, Z. (2000). A model of substitution of non-tariff barriers for tariffs. *Canadian Journal of Economics, 33*(4), 1069–1090.

Zabludovsky, J., & Pasquel, L. (2010). The case of Mexico. In A. Capling & P. Low (Eds.), *Governments, non-state actors and trade policy making* (pp. 89–124). Cambridge University Press.

Zandi, M., Kamins, A., & Cohn, J. (2018). Trump trade war. *Moody's Analytics*. www.economy.com/getlocal?q=d3a731c7-0018-450d-90f5-20e2efa8c6e0&app=eccafile

Appendix
Detailed analysis of the data sources used in this book

This research is based on several data sources that were retrieved from public repositories. The four main datasets used for this project are: 1) the Global Trade Alert (GTA), which provides information on those government-led trade interventions undertaken since 2008, which are most likely to affect foreign trade;[1] 2) BACI–CEPII trade data, which disaggregates data on bilateral trade flows for more than 5,000 products and 200 countries;[2] 3) the International Political Economy Data Resource (IPE),[3] which compiles data from different IPE data sources into a single dataset (Graham & Tucker, 2017); and 4) data from the Harmonized System (HS) classification of products, which classifies "traded goods on a common basis for customs purposes."[4]

Global Trade Alert (GTA)

Since its inception in 2009, the GTA has tracked state-to-state interventions by year, that may influence foreign trade, including "state interventions affecting trade in goods and services, foreign investment and labor force migration."[5] It was formed to help alleviate concerns that "the global financial crisis would lead governments to adopt widespread 1930s-style beggar-thy-neighbor policies" (Evenett & Fritz, 2020, p. 1). Since it was launched, many studies have relied on the GTA database (examples are Evenett et al., 2011; Evenett et al., 2011; Boffa & Olarreaga, 2012; Henn & McDonald, 2014; Georgiadis & Gräb, 2016; Evenett, 2019). Although the GTA is relatively new, covering the past 12 years, this project has been praised for its extensive scope. For instance, in 2016, the IMF noted in its World Economic Outlook that GTA "has the most comprehensive coverage of all types of trade-discriminatory and trade-liberalizing measures, although it begins only in 2008" (IMF, 2016, p. 76). As explained by Evenett and Fritz (2020, p. 1), the authors of this dataset:

> Each GTA database entry documents a government statement […] which included a credible announcement of a meaningful and unilateral change in the relative treatment of foreign versus domestic commercial interests

Table A.1 Name and description of GTA variables

Name of the variable	Description
Implementing country	The country that implements the trade policy
Affected country	The country that is affected by the trade policy
Implementing date	The day the policy was implemented
Intervention type	The type of intervention implemented (e.g., Import tariff, subsidy, etc.)
Affected sectors	The three-digit sector (or group of sectors) most affected by the measure
Affected product	The six-digit product (or group of products) affected by the measure

Source: Author's creation.

[...] includes various forms of government action from national legislation to the contract terms of individual state agencies. All documented changes reflect unilateral government action and thus exclude changes coordinated within bilateral trade agreements or the multilateral trading system. The foreign commercial interests considered by the GTA are trade in goods and services, investment as well as labor force migration.

For the purposes of this project, it is relevant to note that the GTA records both trade protectionist and liberalization measures. It thus measures both sides of the trade policy mechanism. This means that the GTA has its own built-in control variable. This enables me to test the real weight of both protectionist and liberalizing measures when we consider them as explanatory variables. Table A.1 shows those variables included in the GTA database, which will be used for this book.

For each entry, the GTA provides the official document issued by the acting institution within a given country. As described in the GTA's codebook (Evenett & Fritz, 2020, p. 1):

For cases where an official statement cannot be located, press clippings from multiple original sources are analyzed for their consistency. All database entries undergo a two-stage review process before publication. The monitoring period starts in November 2008, when the G20 heads of state pledged to refrain from protectionist action in the aftermath of the Global Financial Crisis. The GTA database only includes relative treatment changes announced since this pledge. The database is updated continuously as new information arrives.

Before each database submission, the GTA team checks that the following criteria have been met: first, a possible measure is identified and investigated. Then, a report is compiled and reviewed separately by two senior members of the GTA research team. An entry is included in the dataset when these two review checks have been satisfied. Once the data is published, third parties also check for errors.

In recent years, the GTA has incorporated new strategies to increase the efficiency of its data collection and coverage. For example, as Evenett (2019, p. 10) highlights:

> The GTA team has built up a library of websites of government agencies, ministries, and gazettes (official journals) and of international organizations that are consulted on a regular basis. Whenever possible, official sources are used to document an entry, and this has been accomplished with over 93% of entries in the GTA database. However, the GTA team scours newspapers, reports by industry associations and law firms for leads of government policy intervention. Once a lead is identified, a team member investigates it and the goal is to find an official source to support any write-up. Increasingly, website scraping tools are being used to identify potential changes in government policy. Automation offers the potential to cover even more government websites and expand the GTA's coverage.

In 2018, the GTA included in its data the percentage of goods traded bilaterally that have been affected by policy interventions implemented between 2009 and 2018. This newly included data offers an enormous opportunity to analyze not only the number of measures implemented, but also the extent to which protectionist measures affect trade flows. Hence, at the empirical level, one of the main contributions of this new data included by the GTA is to concentrate not only on the number of measures implemented by countries, but also on how these measures affected the share of exports and imports; the latter is still an open question in debates related to current trade disputes.[6]

Here is a real example of data collection, step by step (Global Trade Alert, www.globaltradealert.org):

1. On August 17, 2018, the government of Mexico temporarily increased the import duty on certain steel products.
2. The document was published by the Secretariat of Economy (DOF: 17/08/2018) on its web page: http://dof.gob.mx/nota_detalle.php?codigo=5535213&fecha=17/08/2018.
3. The official document states that it is implemented on November 30, 2018. The affected country will be the United States, and the sectors affected will be those with the following HS codes: 7207.12.01, 7207.12.99, 7224.90.02, 7216.32.04, 7216.33.02, 7216.33.01.
4. Based on the official document, the GTA coders report the following information: implementing country, affected country, implementing date, intervention type, affected sector, and affected product.

BACI-CEPII trade data

The quantitative analysis of this book draws mainly on BACI-CEPII trade data. This dataset contains estimates of the composition of trade between countries. In particular, for each country pair (exporter A, importer B), it has an entry of a product (HS 2012 code) with the estimate of how much that product accounts for exports from A to B.[7]

The version of BACI-CEPII that I am using is HS 2012.[8] Following the GTA dataset structure, I use three years of data (2005, 2006, 2007) and take the annual averages, which allows me to avoid endogeneity issues. In some cases, there is only information about one or two years, so when computing the annual averages, we use less than three years.[9] Hence, the main variable that I consider from the BACI-CEPII trade data is the percentage (*pcent* suffix in the dataset) that estimates the proportion of exports from A to B of a given product in the total exports from A to B. Then, by combining that percentage by product from BACI-CEPII with the data provided by the GTA, or the product affected by each protectionist measure implemented from A to B, I can obtain the percentage of trade between A and B that is affected by each protectionist measure. In sum, for this research, I will use two types of variables to measure protectionism. One is the number of protectionist measures one country implemented against another. The second measurement I will consider, which has not been used extensively within the literature, is the share of trade that is affected by these protectionist measures. Given the specificity of this data, the time frame of some factors will vary (i.e., for some measures I have data until 2018, while I have data up to 2019 for number of measures implemented).

The IPE Data Resource

The IPE Data Resource is a standardized dataset that compiles variables from 89 IPE data sources into a single dataset. Its main goal is "increasing efficiency and reducing the risk of data management errors" (Graham & Tucker, 2017, p. 149). The IPE Data Resource attempts to draw all data from its original source (i.e., downloading the data directly from the scholar or the institution that produced the data). For both country-year and dyad-year, the unit of analysis in the dataset is Gleditsch-Ward number (*gwno*) and year (Gleditsch & Ward, 1999). Alternative country identifiers, that is, Correlates of War (COW) codes and International Financial Statistics (IFS) codes, are provided for convenience, but the Gleditsch-Ward numbers are the basis upon which component datasets are merged together. For the purpose of this book, from the IPE Data Resource, I consider the relative economic difference bilaterally (*B's GDPpc / A's GDPpc*),[10] bilateral investment treaty between A and B, common official language, and *Geographic Data CEPII*: population weighted distance (typically used in a gravity model).[11]

Data sources for other variables of interest: PTAs and GVCs

Measuring preferential trade agreements (PTAs)

The main dataset used in this book to measure PTAs derives from Baccini and Urpelainen (2014). It compiles bilateral data on PTAs from 1948 to 2018 for 203 countries. As Ruta (2017, p. 175) states, the "GVC has changed international trade, with trade in parts and components increasing almost six times between 1990 and 2015, faster than the 4.5 times for other forms of trade." PTAs have not only expanded in number, but they are also diversifying in content, beginning from the negotiation of 50 PTAs in the 1990s to 303 as of January 2020.[12]

Following the World Bank's definition, Dür et al. (2014) provide a more general description of international trade agreements as "all the agreements that have the potential to liberalize trade" (p. 1).[13] I will use this definition in this chapter, as it is the one most used in the literature (Hofmann et al., 2019; Ruta, 2017). Hence, when I refer to a PTA, this includes FTAs, CUs, or partial FTAs, which can take bilateral (e.g., two countries), plurilateral (e.g., many countries), plurilateral with a third country (e.g., EU–Australia Trade Agreement), or region–region (e.g., EU–Mercosur Trade Agreement) forms.

Measuring global value chains (GVCs)

To measure GVCs, I combine the Global Trade Alert data, the Classification by Broad Economic Categories (BEC), and BACI-CEPII trade data. As mentioned, BACI-CEPII in particular collects data on trade flows (by product) for each country pair (A, B) (exporter, importer). The data is collected using the HS 2012 classification and with an estimate of how much a given product accounts for exporter A to importer B of the total exports from A to B. Once I have the bilateral data (country A, country B, year, and percentage in total flows of each product), I merge this information with the BEC. The BEC is the data normally used to measure the share of trade in intermediate goods (a proxy of GVC). The BEC provides "a means for international trade statistics to be analyzed by broad economic categories such as food, industrial supplies, capital equipment, consumer durables and consumer non-durables."[14]

Notes

1 For more details about the Global Trade Alert (GTA), visit: www.globaltradeal ert.org/.
2 For more details about BACI–CEPII trade data, visit: www.cepii.fr/CEPII/en/bdd_ modele/bdd_modele.asp.
3 For more details about the IPE Data Resource, visit: https://doi.org/10.7910/DVN/ X093TV.

Appendix 183

4 For more details about the Harmonized System (HS), visit: https://unstats.un.org/unsd/tradekb/Knowledgebase/Harmonized-Commodity-Description-and-Coding-Systems-HS.

5 Global Trade Alert, www.globaltradealert.org/.

6 My development of this new dataset is part of a joint project with George Gerald Vega, from the USC Center for Applied Network Analysis (CANA).

7 The raw data is publicly available at www.cepii.fr.

8 The Harmonized System (HS) is an international nomenclature for the classification of products. It allows participating countries to classify traded goods on a common basis for customs purposes. At the international level, the HS for classifying goods is a six-digit code system. It is comprised of approximately 5,300 article/product descriptions that appear as headings and subheadings, arranged in 99 chapters, grouped in 21 sections. The six digits can be broken down into three parts. The first two digits (HS-2) identify the chapter in which the goods are classified, for example, 09 = Coffee, Tea, Maté and Spices. The next two digits (HS-4) identify groupings within that chapter, for example, 09.02 = Tea, whether or not flavored. The next two digits (HS-6) are even more specific, e.g., 09.02.10 Green tea (not fermented). Up to the HS 6-digit level, all countries classify products in the same way (a few exceptions exist where some countries apply old versions of the HS). For this project, I use HS2012. For more details about the Harmonized System (HS), visit: https://unstats.un.org/unsd/tradekb/Knowledgebase/Harmonized-Commodity-Description-and-Coding-Systems-HS.

9 Because of this, I created a new variable (with _by_3) in which, instead of taking the average with whatever number of observations we observe, I simple divide the total export flow (sum through the 2005–2007 range) by three.

10 The International Political Economy Data Resource (IPE), which compiles data from 89 IPE data sources into a single dataset (Graham & Tucker, 2017); visit https://doi.org/10.7910/DVN/X093TV.

11 See Mayer & Zignago (2011), Notes on CEPII's Distances Measures: The GeoDist Database. *CEPII Working Paper 2011–25*, www.cepii.fr/CEPII/en/bdd_modele/presentation.asp?id=6.

12 WTO, *Regional Trade Agreements*, www.wto.org/english/tratop_e/region_e/region_e.htm.

13 For other studies on why the term "PTA" is preferred to the term "RTA," see, for instance, Hofmann et al. (2019) and Ruta (2017).

14 UNSTATS, *Classification by Broad Economic Categories (Rev.4)*, https://unstats.un.org/unsd/tradekb/knowledgebase/50089/classification-by-broad-economic-categories-rev4.

Index

Andean Community of Nations (CAN) 91–92
APEC *see* Asia Pacific Economic Cooperation
Argentina: employment sectors 127–128; and European Union (EU) 117–118; exports *see* Argentina exports; global value chains (GVCs) 119; gross domestic product (GDP) 76, 78; protectionism and trade policy responses 116–127, 146–147; and rest of world (RoW) 23, 47, 120; sectoral dynamics 126; trade figures 76, 78; trade protectionism economics 119–127; trading partners 121–125; Washington Consensus (WC) 116
Argentina exports: goods 119–120; protectionist measures 120
Argentina trade policy, and Mercosur (Mercado Común del Sur) 114–116, 146–147
Asia Pacific Economic Cooperation (APEC) 100; *see also* East Asia Pacific
Association of Southeast Asian Nations (ASEAN) 96
Asunción, Treaty of 115
Australia, and European Union (EU) 182

BACI-CEPII trade data 181
BCB *see* Central Bank of Brazil
BEC *see* Broad Economic Categories
bilateral investment treaties (BITs) 60, 181; exports affected by 62–63
Brazil: employment sectors 137–139, 144; exports *see* Brazil exports; foreign direct investment (FDI) 128; free trade agreements (FTA) 134; global value chains (GVCs) 138; gross domestic product (GDP) 76, 78, 128; Latin America trading partner 89–90; protectionism and trade policy responses 127–143, 146–147; and rest of world (RoW) 132; sectoral dynamics 137–138; trade figures 76, 78; trade protectionism economics 130–138; trading partners 130, 133–137, 147; Washington Consensus (WC) 128; World Trade Organization (WTO) 136–137
Brazil exports: goods 131–132; protectionist measures 130, 132, 147
Brazil, Russia, India, China, and South (BRICS) 33
Brazil trade policy, and Mercosur (Mercado Común del Sur) 114–116, 138–143, 146–147
Broad Economic Categories (BEC) 17, 28; international trade 62, 71, 79, 182–183
Buenos Aires Act, common market (CM) 115

CACM *see* Central American Common Market
CAN *see* Andean Community of Nations
CANA *see* Center for Applied Network Analysis
Canada: and European Union (EU) 158, 164; Latin America trading partner 89–90
capital goods 17; Brazil 130–131
Caribbean, trade policy dynamics 8–10
Caribbean Community and Common Market (CARICOM) 91–93
Center for Applied Network Analysis (CANA) 28, 183

Central American Common Market (CACM) 91–92
Central Bank of Brazil (BCB) 140
Central Product Classification (CPC) 8
CETA *see* Comprehensive Economic and Trade Agreement
Chile, free trade agreements (FTA) 74, 100
China: and European Union (EU) 39, 163; foreign direct investment (FDI) 114; global financial crisis (GFC) 35; Latin America trading partner 89–90; most favored nations (MFN) 34, 42; non-tariff measures (NTM) 35; and rest of world (RoW) 34; tariff rates from 35; technical barriers to trade (TBT) 35; United States tensions 36–40; World Trade Organization (WTO) 30, 33–36, 110
CM *see* common market
CMC *see* Consejo del Mercado Común
common colonizer, exports affected by 62–63
Common Market, Caribbean Community *see* Caribbean Community and Common Market
Common Market, Central American *see* Central American Common Market
common market (CM) 16; Buenos Aires Act 115; Latin America 91–93, 115, 148; *see also* Mercosur
Common Market, Southern Cone *see* Mercosur
common official language, exports affected by 62–63
Comprehensive Economic and Trade Agreement (CETA) 158, 164
Comprehensive and Progressive Agreement for Trans-Pacific Partnership (CPTPP) 100, 142, 164
Consejo del Mercado Común (CMC) 56, 116
consumer goods, Brazil 130–131
consumption goods 17
control variables, protectionism and trade policy responses 62
correlates of war (COW) 181
COVID-19 pandemic: gross domestic product (GDP) 54; International Monetary Fund (IMF) 55; protectionism 53–55; World Trade Organization (WTO) 54
CPC *see* Central Product Classification

CPTPP *see* Comprehensive and Progressive Agreement for Trans-Pacific Partnership
CU *see* customs unions
customs unions (CU) 16; most favored nations (MFN) 15; trade integration 16, 52, 56; World Trade Organization (WTO) 16; *see also* Andean Community of Nations; Mercosur

data, protectionism and trade policy responses 60–62
Dominican Republic–Central America FTA 92

East Asia Pacific 8–10; *see also* Asia Pacific Economic Cooperation
Economist Intelligence Unit (EIU) 29
EFTA *see* European Free Trade Agreement
EIU *see* Economist Intelligence Unit
emerging market and developing economies (EMDEs) 54
emerging markets 54, 158
employment sectors: Argentina 127–128; Brazil 137–139, 144; Mexico 110–111
European Free Trade Agreement (EFTA) 100, 160
European Union (EU) 8–10; and Argentina 117–118; and ASEAN 96; and Australia 182; and Canada 158, 164; and China 39, 163; free movement 16; G20 countries 23, 55, 148; General Agreement on Trade and Tariffs (GATT) 31–33; and Mercosur 61, 116–118, 164, 182; and Mexico 113–114; and North American Free Trade Agreement (NAFTA) 100; preferential trade agreements (PTAs) 15, 52, 61, 80, 160 *see also* individual agreements; protectionist measures 47, 49; Sino–American trade conflict 24, 74; tariff rates 35; trade policy dynamics 8–10; trade protectionism 8; and United States 164
exports: bilateral investment treaties (BITs) 62–63; common colonizer 62–63; common official language 62–63; liberalizing measures 62–63; population weighted distance 62–63; quotas 12–13; relative economic distance 62–63; tariff quotas 12–13; taxes 12–13; *see also* exports

186 Index

Argentina; exports Brazil; exports Latin America; exports Mexico
exports Argentina: goods 119–120; protectionist measures 120
exports Brazil 130–131; goods 131–132; protectionist measures 130, 132, 147
exports Latin America: goods and services 89; intermediate goods 96–97; trends 87–88
exports Mexico: global value chains (GVCs) 104, 106; goods 103, 106; protectionist measures 104–106, 145

foreign direct investment (FDI) 8, 12; Brazil 128; China 114; Mexico 112; Washington Consensus (WC) 86
free movement, European Union (EU) 16
free trade agreements (FTA) 16, 101, 159; Brazil 134; Chile 74, 100; Latin America 75, 91–92, 100; Mexico 76, 100, 102, 104, 112, 145; most favored nations (MFN) 15; *see also* Comprehensive Economic and Trade Agreement (CETA); Dominican Republic–Central America FTA; North American Free Trade Agreement (NAFTA); Pacific Alliance (PA)

G20 countries: European Union (EU) 23, 55, 148; Latin America trade policy 95–96; preferential trade agreements (PTAs) 79–80; protectionism, less developed countries (LDC) 6–7; and rest of world (RoW) 48
GDP *see* gross domestic product
General Agreement on Trade and Tariffs (GATT) 15, 30–32, 152–153, 155; European Union (EU) 31–33; Mexico 86, 99–100
Generalized System of Preferences (GSP) 15
global economy, uncertainty 153–154
global financial crisis (GFC) 1–6; China 35; global value chains (GVCs) 52; Mexico 112; protectionism 12, 19, 33, 38; protectionist policy instruments 47, 50; trade barriers 36–37; trade policies 22–24
global recession, International Monetary Fund (IMF) 164

Global Trade Alert (GTA) 11–12, 178–180; International Monetary Fund (IMF) 178; trade policy interventions 45, 60–62; trade policy measures 71; variables 179
global value chains (GVCs) 3–4, 51–53, 56–57, 60; Argentina 119; Brazil 138; global financial crisis (GFC) 52; Latin America 144–145; Mercosur 147; Mexico 104, 106; and non-tariff measures (NTM) 65, 67; North American Free Trade Agreement (NAFTA) 53; Participation Index 79–81, 103–104; preferential trade agreements (PTAS) 182; regressors 62–63; and tariffs 65–68; trade policy measurement 16–18, 64, 70, 96, 182
goods 17; Brazil 130–131; capital 130–131; consumer 130–131; intermediate 17, 81–82, 98; Latin America 98
gross domestic product (GDP) 26, 28, 39, 57; Argentina 76, 78; Brazil 76, 78, 128; COVID-19 pandemic 54; Latin America 71, 76, 89; Mercosur 75; Mexico 76, 78, 112–113; United States-China trade war 39, 148; world recession 164
gross world product (GWP) 23, 44, 76
GSP *see* Generalized System of Preferences
GTA *see* global trade alert
GVC *see* global value chain
GWP *see* gross world product

harmonized system (HS) data 28, 60

IDB *see* Inter-American Development Bank
IFS *see* International Financial Statistics
IIT *see* intra-industry trade
IMF *see* International Monetary Fund
import-substitution-industrialization (ISI): Latin America 85–86, 93; Mexico 99, 111
imports: Latin America trends 87–88; monitoring 12–13; tariff quotas 12–13; tariffs 12–13
intellectual property (IP) 13, 31–32, 34, 39, 57, 150
Inter-American Development Bank (IDB) 94

Index 187

intermediate goods 17; Brazil 130–131; Latin America 98; trade in 81–82
International Financial Statistics (IFS) 181
International Monetary Fund (IMF) 11; COVID-19 pandemic 55; global recession 164; Global Trade Alert 178; Latin America 86; Washington Consensus (WC) 86
international political economics (IPE) 19, 24
International Political Economy (IPE) Data Resource 60, 62, 181–182
international trade, Broad Economic Categories (BEC) 62, 71, 79, 182–183
International Trade Organization (ITO) 30–31, 155
interventions, and transparency 12–13
intra-industry trade (IIT) 27–28, 71–72, 159
IP *see* intellectual property
IPE *see* international political economics; International Political Economy
ISI *see* import-substitution-industrialization
ITO *see* International Trade Organization

LAC *see* Latin America and the Caribbean
LAFTA *see* Latin American Free Trade Association
LAIA *see* Latin American Integration Association
large-N analysis 6; trade protectionism 22–23
Latin America: common market (CM) 91–93, 115, 148; exports *see* Latin America exports; free trade agreements (FTA) 75, 91–92, 100; global value chains (GVCs) 144–145; gross domestic product (GDP) 71, 76, 89; import trends 87–88; import-substitution-industrialization (ISI) 85–86, 93; intermediate goods 98; International Monetary Fund (IMF) 86; non-tariff measures (NTM) 96; North American Free Trade Agreement (NAFTA) 92; preferential trade agreements (PTAs) 79–80; protectionism *see* Latin America protectionism; regional agreements 91–94; regional integration 91–94; and rest of world (RoW) 75, 94, 144; sanitary and phytosanitary (SPS) measures 96, 114; technical barriers to trade (TBT) 96; trade policy *see* Latin America trade policy; trade protectionism 94–98; trading partners 89–90; Trans-Pacific Partnership (TPP) 96; *see also* individual countries
Latin America and the Caribbean (LAC) 91, 159
Latin America exports: goods and services 89; intermediate goods 96–97; trends 87–88
Latin America protectionism: measures 75, 81; responses 94
Latin America trade policy: actors 83–85; cases 74–83, 98–99; dynamics 8–10; evolution 85–94; measures for G20 95–96; measures in Latin America 95–96; responses 73–74, 98–99
Latin American Free Trade Association (LAFTA) 92–93
Latin American Integration Association (LAIA) 92–93
less developed countries (LDC), G20 protectionism 6–7
liberalizing measures 1–2; exports affected by 62–63

MAST *see* multi-agency support team
Mercosur (Mercado Común del Sur) 75; and Argentina trade policy 114–116, 146–147; and Brazil trade policy 114–116, 138–143, 146–147; and European Union (EU) 61, 116–118, 164, 182; global value chains (GVCs) 147; gross domestic product 75; sanitary and phytosanitary (SPS) measures 134; trade agreements 116–117
Mexico: employment sectors 110–111; and European Union (EU) 113–114; exports *see* Mexico exports; foreign direct investment (FDI) 112; free trade agreements (FTA) 76, 100, 102, 104, 112, 145; global financial crisis (GFC) 112; gross domestic product (GDP) 76, 78, 112–113; import-substitution-industrialization (ISI) 99, 111; non-tariff measures (NTM) 102; North American Free Trade Agreement (NAFTA) 11, 76, 99–100,

104, 111–114, 125; and Pacific Alliance (PA) 100; protectionism *see* Mexico protectionism; and rest of world (RoW) 105; sectoral dynamics 108–109; technical barriers to trade (TBT) 114; trade agreements 100–101; trade figures 76, 78; trade policy *see* Mexico trade policy; Washington Consensus (WC) 111–112
Mexico exports: global value chains (GVCs) 104, 106; goods 103, 106; protectionist measures 104–106, 145
Mexico protectionism 99–114; impacts of 104–111; insights from 111–114, 145–146
Mexico trade policy: actors 99–104; evolution 99–104; trading partners 107–109
Middle East, trade policy dynamics 8–10
most favored nations (MFN): China 34, 42; customs unions (CU) 15; free trade agreements (FTA) 15
multi-agency support team (MAST) 11–12

NAFTA *see* North American Free Trade Agreement
non-automatic licensing (NAL) 7, 9, 48–50, 56, 96, 118–119
non-tariff measures (NTM) 2, 7, 11, 42; China 35; and global value chains (GVCs) 65, 67; Latin America 96; Mexico 102; and preferential trade agreements (PTAs) 59, 65–67, 69, 161; *see also* non-automatic licensing
North Africa, trade policy dynamics 8–10
North America, trade policy dynamics 8–10
North American Free Trade Agreement (NAFTA) 29; and European Union (EU) 100; free trade agreements (FTAs) 15; global value chains (GVCs) 53; Latin America 92; Mexico 11, 76, 99–100, 104, 111–114, 125
NTM *see* non-tariff measures

Organization for Economic Cooperation and Development (OECD): China 110; Mexico 100; *see also* Trade in Value Added (TIVA) database

Pacific Alliance (PA) 93, 96, 104, 143; and Mexico 100

Participation Index, global value chains (GVCs) 79–81, 103–104
population weighted distance, exports affected by 62–63
preferential trade agreements (PTAs) 14, 16, 20, 51–52; European Union (EU) 15, 52, 61, 80, 160; G20 countries 79–80; global value chains (GVCs) 182; Latin America 79–80; and non-tariff measures (NTM) 59, 65–67, 69, 161; regressors 62–63; and tariffs 65–69; trade policy measurement 14–16, 182; World Trade Organization (WTO) 15, 52, 61–62
protectionism: COVID-19 pandemic 53–55; effect on employment Argentina 127–128; Brazil 137–139, 144; Mexico 110–111; global financial crisis (GFC) 12, 19, 33, 38; publication numbers 24–25
protectionism responses, Latin America 94
protectionism and trade policy responses 58–59; in Argentina 116–127, 146–147 trading partners 121–125; in Brazil 127–143, 146–147 trading partners 130, 133–137, 147; control variables 62; data 60–62; dependent variables 61; in Latin America 73–74 cases 74–83, 98–99 trade policy actors 83–85; in Mexico 99–114; effect on employment 110–111; impacts of 104–111; insights from 111–114, 145–146; trade policy actors 99–104; trade policy evolution 99–104; trading partners 107–109; models 59–60; regressors 61–62; state-level analysis 62–71
protectionist measures 1–2; Argentina, exports 120; Brazil, exports 130, 132, 147; European Union (EU) 47, 49; G20 countries 47–48, 76–77; Latin America 75, 81; Mexico, exports 104–106, 145; retaliation 14; trade share 62–64; and world imports 46–47
protectionist policy instruments: and global financial crisis (GFC) 47, 50; targeted countries 51
PTA *see* preferential trade agreement

quotas 12–13

regional dynamics 6
regressors: global value chains (GVCs) 62–63; preferential trade agreement

Index 189

(PTA) 62–63; protectionism and trade policy responses 61–63
relative economic distance, exports affected by 62–63
rest of world (RoW) 8, 10; and Argentina 23, 47, 120; and Brazil 132; and China 34; and G20 countries 48; and Latin America 75, 94, 144; and Mexico 105
retaliation, protectionist measures 14

safeguards 12–13
sanitary and phytosanitary (SPS) measures 13, 36, 47–48, 50, 160–161; Latin America 96, 114; Mercosur 134
sectoral dynamics: Argentina 126; Brazil 137–138; Mexico 108–109
Sino–American trade conflict, European Union (EU) 24, 74
small-n analysis, trade protectionism 23–24
Southern Common Market *see* Mercosur
SPS *see* sanitary and phytosanitary
state-level analysis, protectionism and trade policy responses 62–71
state-level dynamics 6; trade protectionism 18–21
state-level trade policy dynamics, twenty-first-century protectionism 44–47
sub-Saharan Africa, trade policy dynamics 8–10
subsidies 12–13

targeted countries, protectionist policy instruments 51
tariff rates: European Union (EU) 35; from China 35; weighted mean 87, 99
tariffs 12–13; and global value chains (GVCs) 65–68; and preferential trade agreements (PTAs) 65–69; trade policy measurement 11–12; World Trade Organization (WTO) 22, 49
taxes, export 12–13
technical barriers to trade (TBT) 12–13, 47, 50, 160–161; China 35; global financial crisis (GFC) 36; Latin America 96; Mexico 114
TIVA *see* trade in value added
TPP *see* Trans-Pacific Partnership
trade: after global financial crisis 36; Broad Economic Categories (BEC) 62, 71, 79, 182–183

trade agreements: Mercosur (Mercado Común del Sur) 116–117; Mexico 100–101
Trade Analysis Information System (TRAINS) 56
trade barriers, global financial crisis (GFC) 36–37
trade figures: Argentina 76, 78; Brazil 76, 78; Mexico 76, 78
trade integration, customs unions (CU) 16, 52, 56
trade policy: global financial crisis (GFC) 22–24; meaning of 8–11; publication numbers 24–25
trade policy actors, Mexico 99–104
trade policy dynamics: Caribbean 8–10; European Union (EU) 8–10; Latin America 8–10; Middle East 8–10; North Africa 8–10; North America 8–10; sub-Saharan Africa 8–10
trade policy evolution, Latin America 85–94
trade policy interventions 45; Global Trade Alert (GTA) 45, 60–62
trade policy measurement 8–18; global value chains (GVCs) 16–18, 64, 70, 96, 182; non-tariffs 11–12; preferential trade agreements (PTAs) 14–16, 182; tariffs 11–12; trade policy responses 12–14; trade protectionism 11–12
trade policy measures: Global Trade Alert (GTA) 71; Latin America toward G20 95–96; within Latin America 95–96
trade policy responses: in Latin America, Argentina 116–127, 146–147; trade policy measurement 12–14
trade protection 1–8
trade protectionism 1–26; Argentina, economics of 119–127; Brazil, economics of 130–138; case studies 23–24; European Union (EU) 8; large-N analysis 22–23; Latin America 94–98; small-n analysis 23–24; state-level dynamics 18–21; trade policy measurement 11–12; twenty-first-century 30–41
trade share, protectionist measures 62–64
trade and sustainable development (TSD) 114
Trade in Value Added (TIVA) database 54, 79, 148–149; *see also* Organization

for Economic Cooperation and Development (OECD)
trading partners: Argentina, protectionism and trade policy responses 121–125; Brazil, protectionism and trade policy responses 130, 133–137, 147; Latin America 89–90; Mexico, protectionism and trade policy responses 107–109
TRAINS *see* Trade Analysis Information System
Trans-Pacific Partnership (TPP) 142, 158, 164; Latin America 96; *see also* European Union
Transatlantic Trade and Investment Partnership (TTIP) 158, 164
transparency, and interventions 12–13
TSD *see* trade and sustainable development
TTIP *see* Transatlantic Trade and Investment Partnership
twenty-first-century protectionism 30–41; measures 44, 47–51; sectors 44–5; state-level trade policy dynamics 44–47

uncertainty, global economy 153–154
United Nations Conference on Trade and Development (UNCTAD) 11, 29
United States: and European Union (EU) 164; Latin America trading partner 89–90; tensions with China 36–40

United States-China trade war, gross domestic product (GDP) 39, 148

value added tax (VAT) 35, 113
VAT *see* value added tax

Washington Consensus (WC): Argentina 116; Brazil 128; foreign direct investment (FDI) 86; International Monetary Fund (IMF) 86; Mexico 111–112
weighted mean tariff rate 87, 99
World Economic Forum (WEF) 39
world imports: and protectionism measures 46–47; and world policy restrictions 45–46
world policy restrictions, and world imports 45–46
world recession, gross domestic product (GDP) 164
World Trade Organization (WTO) 1, 5, 31–32; Brazil 136–137; China 30, 33–36, 110; COVID-19 pandemic 54; customs unions (CUs) 16; murky protectionism 12; preferential trade agreements (PTAs) 15, 52, 61–62; rules 87, 102, 153; tariffs 22, 49
world trade system, since World War II 30–33
World Trade Uncertainty (WTU) index 24, 29
World War II (WWII) 30–31
WTO *see* World Trade Organization

Printed in the United States
by Baker & Taylor Publisher Services